In the last ten years, general equilibrium modelling has become a significant area of applied economic research. Its focus is to develop techniques to facilitate economy wide quantitative assessment of allocative and distributional impacts on policy changes. *UK Tax Policy and Applied General Equilibrium Analysis* presents the first book length treatment of the development and application of an applied general equilibrium model of the Walrasian type, constructed to analyse UK taxation and subsidy policy.

The material splits naturally into two parts. Part I provides an account of the formal structures of general equilibrium models, with and without taxation and describes the procedures used for empirical implementation. This allows actual policies to be realistically analysed. These procedures depend upon the policies that the model is designed to address and for this reason an early chapter is devoted to a description of UK tax and subsidy policies.

Part II presents and interprets the results of a series of model experiments. These include the distorting effects of taxes on household consumption, industry production and factory use. A variety of further model extensions are also described, motivated by consideration of more specific tax policy issues. These include the interaction of taxes on savings and inflation, and the effects of taxes on the appropriate level at which public goods should be provided.

As a whole, *UK Tax Policy and Applied General Equilibrium Analysis* offers the reader two things. First, it gives a detailed account of the development of an applied general equilibrium model of the UK. Second, it provides results of model experiments which have been designed to inform the policy debate, not only in the UK but also in other countries. I should thus be of interest to both researchers and students undertaking research in the applied general equilibrium area, and to policymakers concerned with tax reform.

UK tax policy and applied general equilibrium analysis

UK tax policy
and
applied general equilibrium analysis

JOHN PIGGOTT
Australian National University

JOHN WHALLEY
University of Western Ontario

The right of the
University of Cambridge
to print and sell
all manner of books
was granted by
Henry VIII in 1534
The University has printed
and published continuously
since 1584

CAMBRIDGE UNIVERSITY PRESS

Cambridge

London   New York   New Rochelle

Melbourne   Sydney

CAMBRIDGE UNIVERSITY PRESS
Cambridge, New York, Melbourne, Madrid, Cape Town, Singapore, São Paulo, Delhi

Cambridge University Press
The Edinburgh Building, Cambridge CB2 8RU, UK

Published in the United States of America by Cambridge University Press, New York

www.cambridge.org
Information on this title: www.cambridge.org/9780521104593

First published 1985
This digitally printed version 2009

A catalogue record for this publication is available from the British Library

Library of Congress Cataloguing in Publication data
Piggott, John (John R.)
UK tax policy and applied general equilibrium analysis.
Bibliography: p.
1. Taxation—Great Britain—Mathematical models.
2. Equilibrium(Economics) I. Whalley, John.
II. Title.
HJ2619.P5 1985   336.2'00724   85-10969

ISBN 978-0-521-30148-0 hardback
ISBN 978-0-521-10459-3 paperback

To our wives, Dorry and Maggie

PREFACE

This manuscript was originally prepared in camera ready copy in 1981, at which point the original publisher withdrew due to concerns over the small market for such a specialized research monograph. Since this date there have been many developments both within the field of applied general equilibrium analysis, and in UK tax policies.

Recent developments in applied general equilibrium are reflected in two conference volumes [Scarf and Shoven (1983) and Piggott and Whalley (forthcoming)]. A recent survey paper by Shoven and Whalley (1984) provides an up to date summary. On the tax front, developments in the UK have continued with the usual round of budget and other changes.

We decided not to revise our manuscript to reflect all of these developments. Not only does this involve a large volume of work, but we were concerned not to interrupt the flow of the present draft with a series of inserts. Even without any revisions we believe that our book makes a significant contribution to the applied general equilibrium literature by focussing applied modelling heavily towards results, and their ultimate policy applicability. While some of the model structure has been extended in subsequent work (particulary in dynamic sequenced models used to analyze taxation and savings issues), there are features of our model which are still not present in other modelling efforts. Among these are the incorporation of public goods as a model variant, and household detail on the demand side.

While the numbers may be a little dated, the approach to tax policy outlined and its ultimate policy applicability seem to be generating increasing interest. Our hope is that, even in its present slightly dated form, this book will help in the process of assimilating these developments.

ACKNOWLEDGEMENTS

This book has its origins in a model of the UK economy and tax system used in a Ph.D. thesis written by the second author at Yale in the early 1970's (Whalley, 1973). Since then a large number of adaptations and extensions have been made. The original model was of limited dimensionality, with few of the present features, and used data which in places were highly stylized.

During this period of time, help, encouragement, and support have been received from many quarters. The second author would like to acknowledge the excellent thesis supervision he received at Yale from William Brainard and Herbert Scarf, and the help and encouragement of John Shoven. John Shoven's support has been instrumental in this work from the beginning and still continues.

While at LSE (1973-1976) where the present model form developed, a research grant from the Social Science Research Council provided vitally needed support and enabled John Piggott to join the project. At this time, a number of United Kingdom government departments and statistical agencies, too numerous to list here but referred to in the text, dealt with our requests for data and information kindly, courteously, and expeditiously. LSE provided the significant amounts of computer time that model execution required at this stage.

At Western Ontario (1976 to the present), a research grant from the Social Sciences and Humanities Research Council, Ottawa, has enabled work to continue on the model, and for the present volume to be brought to fruition. The University has also generously provided additional computer support.

As our work and drafting has developed, many comments have been received from colleagues, students, and seminar participants too numerous to individually list, but we would nonetheless like to thank them all. We would also like to acknowledge the fine research assistance of France

ACKNOWLEDGEMENTS

St. Hilaire, Jon Fuller, Bob Hamilton and Bernard Yeung.
Various drafts have been typed by patient secretaries at the
Universities of Western Ontario and Adelaide, and at the
Australian National University. Mrs. Jan Anthony expertly
prepared the final drafts and camera ready manuscript.

In two previous papers, Piggott and Whalley (1977),
Piggott and Whalley (1981), we have discussed the structure
of the model we use together with some of the results presented in the present volume. One point for readers to keep
in mind is a difference in emphasis on summary statistics
used to evaluate income distribution impacts of tax changes
between Piggott and Whalley (1981) and the present volume.
This is discussed more fully in the text.

INTRODUCTION AND SUMMARY OF STUDY

1. Introduction

In the UK, as in other countries, there has been substantial
discussion in recent years of tax reform. Many of the problems and difficulties encountered by the UK economy have, at
times, been attributed to the structure of the tax system,
and over the years both politicians and academic economists
have produced a number of alternative proposals for tax
reform. The Report of the Royal Commission on Taxation
(1966), and more recently the Meade Report (1978), are evidence of this continuing interest. In spite of pressure for
change, however, quantitative analysis of the effects which
taxes and subsidies produce (especially those on resource
allocation) remains surprisingly sparse, both in the UK and
elsewhere.

In this study we use a conceptual approach, widely
explored in theoretical literature in public finance, to
analyze the impacts of the UK tax/subsidy system on the
allocation of resources and the distribution of income using
1973 data. We explore general equilibrium efficiency and
incidence effects of taxes and subsidies, emphasizing a
numerical, empirically oriented version of this well-known
approach. In Part I of the study we describe the structure
of the model we use. Part II reports our empirical results.

The approach used is to build a general equilibrium model
using explicit demand and production functions. In the model
all markets clear in equilibrium. Demands equal supplies for
both goods and factors, and no industry does any better than
break even in terms of profitability. Equilibrium conditions
hold both in the data which we use for the benchmark
solution for the model, and in the counterfactual equilibria
which we simulate for alternative policy regimes. We assume
full employment of all factors, an absence of any monetary
non-neutralities and complete information, all of the
assumptions characteristic of classical general equilibrium
analysis. The use of the model is based on the belief that
the essence of the behaviour of the economic system is

captured through a sequence of market interactions which are distorted through government intervention. Though highly stylized and excluding many features of actual economies, this approach is widely used in the analytical literature in public finance. On that basis it provides the framework for our analysis, even though we abstract from many important phenomena (such as unemployment).

The model incorporates production functions for UK industries and demand patterns for households and incorporates the distorting effects of the major taxes and subsidies which operate. We work with a basic variant model into which we incorporate a number of extensions as model alternatives. Counterfactual equilibria generated by alternative policies to those which charaterize the assumed base year of 1973 are compared to a base period equilibrium. We emphasize welfare and distributional comparisons between equilibria, and summarize the implications of our results for tax/subsidy policy in the UK.[1]

2. The Basic Structure of General Equilibrium Tax Models

The central idea underlying general equilibrium analysis of tax policy is that in order to evaluate the effects of changing a major tax, important economy-wide effects must be taken into account. Taxes distort the allocation of resources in the marketplace by causing resources to be used where productivity is lower than elsewhere and commodities to be offered to consumers at tax distorted prices adversely affecting consumer choice.

The basic analytics of general equilibrium tax models can be illustrated with the aid of diagrams depicting a two-factor, two-product, perfectly competitive economy, with fixed aggregate factor supplies, and, for convenience, consumers with identical, homothetic preference functions. In the absence of externalities and government interventions, such an economy will, in equilibrium, satisfy all the marginal conditions required for a Pareto optimal allocation. With distorting taxes this will no longer be true.

Figure I.1 depicts the simple case of a consumption tax on product X in a two-commodity economy. We consider a single consumer who selects from alternative combinations of the two goods X and Y represented by the economy's production possibilities frontier. The revenues from the tax are returned in lump sum form to the single consumer. Productive efficiency is not affected since the economy remains on the production possibility frontier AB, but the product mix is altered by the tax. The tax produces a distortion between the marginal rate of transformation (MRT) (the net of tax price ratio facing producers) and the marginal rate of substitution (MRS) (the gross of tax price ratio facing consumers). In an equilibrium in the presence of the tax (point F), consumers adjust their purchases so that their marginal rate of substitution equals the gross of tax commodity price ratio. The consumer price ratio exceeds the ratio of prices received by producers since these are net of taxes. The distorted equilibrium at point F corresponds to a lower indifference curve than that associated with the undistorted equilibrium at point E. Because MRS ' MRT the allocation of resources corresponding to point F cannot be Pareto optimal.

A consumer tax which induces a move along the production possibility frontier from E to F may also have other effects beyond those represented in the diagram. One issue frequently analyzed is the incidence of such a tax. In the two-sector framework, this usually involves functional incidence analysis; the impact on the income return to the two factors, capital and labour. The functional incidence of the tax in Figure 1 will depend upon the relative factor intensities of the two industries and cannot be analyzed simply by the same diagram. A proposition from the literature on the Harberger model (see Mieszkowski [1969]) is that the factor which is relatively intensively used in the taxed industry will bear some of the burden of the tax; whether it will fully bear the tax burden, however, depends on the parameters of demand and production functions.

The two sector framework represented in Figure I.1 is not confined to analyzing tax distortions of choices by consum-

FIGURE I-1

Simple Analysis of a Distorting

Consumer Tax on Good X

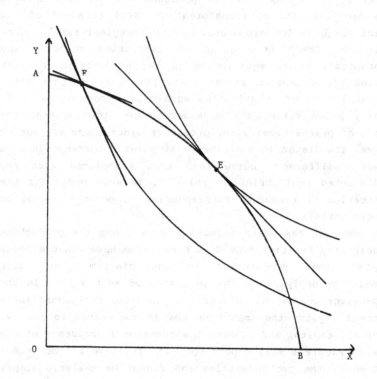

ers among commodities, as one ordinarily thinks of them. Any household decision distorted through the tax system can be fitted into this framework. Distortions of household choices between labour and leisure, and between present and future consumption can be analyzed analogously.

A similar framework can also be used to analyze tax distortions of production decisions. Figure I.2 contains an Edgeworth box diagram showing the effects of a tax distortion on the production side of the economy induced by a tax on the use of one factor in one industry. We consider a tax on the use of capital in industry X. Because of the tax, the marginal rate of substitution between factors will differ between industries. In Figure I.2, A is a point on the contract curve where the marginal rates of substitution between factors are equalized, while B is a point where, because of the tax on capital use in X, the marginal rates of substitution differ across industries. In this case the economy will not operate on its production possibility frontier in the presence of the tax, and Pareto optimality is not attained. Either labour or capital can bear the burden of the tax, depending on the factor intensities and substitution possibilities in the two industries.

3. Quantitative Assessment of General Equilibrium Tax Effects

In our modelling, we attempt to go beyond the diagrammatic framework outlined above by using a numerical higher dimensional approach. The need to quantify, however imperfectly, we see as an integral element of the process through which policy decisions are made.

There are two active strands of research activity which address this problem of quantification of general equilibrium impacts of taxes. The first begins with the pioneering efforts of Harberger (1959, 1962, 1966, 1974); the second is the algorithmic approach which builds on the work of Scarf (1973). To place our study in the context of these developments we briefly review each.

FIGURE I-2

Simple Analysis of a Factor Tax Distortion

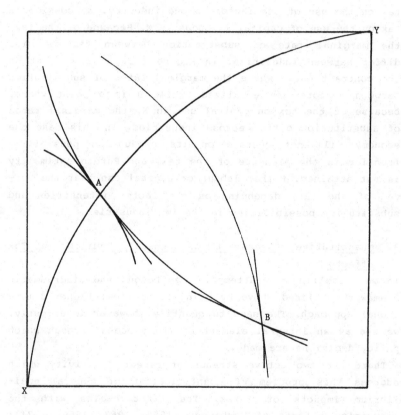

a. The Harberger General Equilibrium Tax Model

In the general equilibrium tax literature, Harberger's contributions (1959, 1962, 1966, 1974) have been of landmark
proportions. Earlier contributors such as Rolph (1952) and
Musgrave (1959) had pointed out both the general equilibrium
nature of tax incidence, and the need for a general equilibrium approach. But it was Harberger who provided public
finance with the explicit general equilibrium model that met
this need. While our formulation goes further than Harberger
in many ways, the dependence of our work on these developments will be obvious to anyone familiar with the literature.

The Harberger model is based on standard neo-classical
assumptions. He assumes fixed aggregate factor supplies;
perfect factor mobility between industries; two factors and
two products; perfect competition in factor and product
markets; a closed economy (no foreign trade); linear homogeneous production functions; and a one-distortion economy.[2]

This model, with particular values of elasticities of
substitution in production and demand, is able to generate
estimates of the incidence and efficiency effects of particular taxes. The model is represented by a reduced form of
three equations, and changes in tax rates are evaluated
through the model. Strictly speaking, only infinitesimally
small changes in taxes and their comparative static impacts
upon other variables can be considered, and for discrete
changes the analysis provides only approximate results.
Perhaps the most famous numerical finding from this model is
that the US corporate tax is borne by all capital owners,
whether or not their capital is used in incorporated enterprises.

Harberger also develops a procedure for estimating the
size of the welfare cost of a distortionary factor tax. In
the case of capital taxation distortions, he considers the
economy to be represented by two sectors, "heavily taxed"
and "lightly taxed". These are labelled sectors X and Y in
Figure I.3. Each sector uses capital in production, and
marginal revenue product schedules are assumed to be linear

FIGURE I-3

Harberger's Two-Sector Analysis of Efficiency Impacts

of Distortionary Capital Taxation

Sector X
(Heavily taxed)

Sector Y
(Lightly taxed)

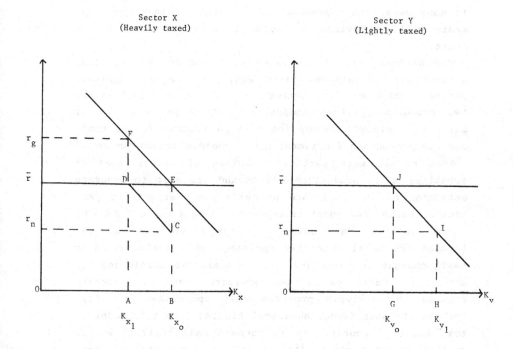

(a local approximation). The economy has a fixed capital
endowment. In the absence of any taxes, market forces will
ensure that capital is allocated between the two sectors
such that the rate of return $\bar{r}$ in each is equalised, and the
capital endowment is fully employed. If, instead, a tax on
capital income in sector X operates, the gross rate of
return r_g in that sector must be such that the net rate of
return r_n is equalized across the sectors, and capital is
again fully employed. The difference between r_g and r_n is
the tax on each unit of capital utilized in sector X.

In Figure I.3, the tax and no tax situations are charac-
terized by the capital allocations K_{x_1}, K_{y_1}, and K_{x_0} and K_{y_0}
respectively. The area ABEF represents the loss in output in
sector X when K_x decreases from K_{x_0} to K_{x_1} as the tax is
imposed. GHIJ represents the increase in output of sector Y.
Full employment guarantees that $K_{x_0} - K_{x_1} = K_{y_1} - K_{y_0}$. The
area FECD (= ABEF-GHIJ) represents the efficiency cost of
the tax, L, and is given by:

$$L = \frac{1}{2} T \Delta K_x$$

where T represents the tax distortion $r_g - r_n$, and ΔK_x is
the change in capital use in sector X from the removal of
the tax. Harberger finds a solution for ΔK_x by solving a
system of three reduced form equations describing the local
behaviour of the two sector general equilibrium model. This
form of calculation has been generalized by Harberger (1964)
into an extension of the famous welfare loss formula due to
Hotelling (1938). In spite of the simplicity of the procedure, a number of difficulties are immediately apparent,
not the least of which is the reliance on local approximations when the large changes often associated with tax
distortions are being analyzed. In addition, it is unclear
how the Harberger procedure can be applied where several
distortions simultaneously operate and change together. The
approach used in this monograph extends the Harberger literature in both of these directions.

b. The Algorithmic Approach

In a series of papers beginning in 1972, Shoven and Whalley have presented an alternative approach to general equilibrium analysis of taxation which does not rely on local approximations nor limit analysis to single distortions. Their work builds on an algorithm due to Scarf (1967, 1973) which makes possible the computation of general economic equilibria using fixed point techniques. In applying these methods to general equilibrium with taxes Shoven and Whalley (1973) present both a computational procedure and an existence proof. In subsequent papers, Shoven and Whalley (1974, 1977) have extended the approach to capture international trade distortions and equal yield tax alternatives. In essence, these techniques permit full general equilibria associated with alternative tax regimes to be computed and compared. Policy regimes may involve the simultaneous operation of many different taxes and subsidies. Since 'true' general equilibria are computed, localization approximations are not required, and large changes may be analyzed with somewhat more confidence than under Harberger procedures.

The empirical implementation of this approach in the present study embodies a higher dimensional version of traditional two sector general equilibrium models. This yields a number of advantages over earlier attempts to deal with incidence and efficiency questions associated with tax policy.

Firstly, considerable disaggregation of commodities and consuming groups is possible. This allows incidence analysis to focus on the size distribution of personal income, rather than solely on factor incomes. It also permits a more general representation of tax distortions, which treats alternative agents, factors and commodities differently. Taxes and subsidies can be introduced on all transactions, so that multiple tax instruments can be represented and changed simultaneously.

Secondly, the extension of this approach to include equal yield alternatives makes possible differential incidence calculations. These are easier to interpret than the incidence experiments associated with the Harberger approach, or

the incidence assumptions used in much of the partial equilibrium literature.

Thirdly, there is much more flexibility in the tax changes
that may be considered. Taxes may be changed by discrete
amounts, and a number of tax instruments simultaneously
altered. This allows complex tax reform proposals to be
assessed. It also opens the way to an analysis of the economic effects of the overall tax system which escapes some
of the methodological difficulties confronting statistical
tax burden calculations which have been stressed in the
literature.[3]

We use this approach in the analysis that follows. Part I
presents the methods we have used in our analysis of the UK
tax/subsidy system. In Part II we present and interpret
results from a series of computations with the model, and
consider a number of model extensions.

4. Summary of Results
We present a brief summary of what seem to us some of the
more interesting implications of our computations at this
point to provide the reader with an overview which we
amplify later. Most of our calculations concentrate on welfare analyses using 1973 data. To obtain estimates of
aggregate welfare cost of tax/subsidy policy changes, we
take the sum of Hicksian compensating and equivalent variations across households. The more striking implications can
be summarized as follows:

(1) Our basic variant model suggests that the static
annual welfare loss from the distortions in the tax/subsidy
system may be in the region of 6% to 9% of NDP per year.
This is a flow loss which recurs each year and is larger
than most extrapolations of single tax distortion loss estimates which have been made at various times for whole tax
systems.

(2) We find that the distortions from local authority
housing subsidies are one of the major tax/subsidy distortions in the economy. In addition we estimate distortionary losses from excise taxes and capital income taxation
as significant. These three distortions account for approxi-

mately 80% of the total distorting costs of the tax/subsidy system. Depending upon how it is modelled, we also find that the interesting effects of inflation and the tax system (in the absence of indexation in the tax system) yield another significant source of distorting loss. Distorting losses from excise taxes need careful qualification and are subject to special ambiguities of interpretation which we discuss in the text. Also data and modelling issues arise with the treatment of housing subsidies and capital income taxes which further qualify results.

(3) Two widely analyzed distortions we find not to be as major in terms of their distortionary losses as the three areas identified above when extensions to our basic model variant are used. The welfare losses from the tax distortion of labour supply and of savings we estimate to be quite modest in their impacts - perhaps less than $\frac{1}{2}$ % of NDP per year. As with our other findings, qualifications are needed in interpreting these estimates, and these are also discussed in the text.

(4) Our central estimate of the welfare loss from the whole tax/subsidy system is about £250 per household in 1973 prices. In 1980 prices this is approximately £650 per household. An alternative way of presenting this calculation is that the tax/subsidy system extracts approximately 30% of NDP in terms of net revenues, but in the process 'destroys' $\frac{1}{4}$ of revenue raised through the welfare loss which it inflicts on the economy. This is an average welfare loss, and though we have not computed it, the marginal social welfare cost of an extra £1 collected through the tax system will significantly exceed the average 25% figure.

(5) We find that the distorting effects of components of the tax system can both compound and offset, although in most instances tax distortions operate largely independently of each other. A prominent distortionary offset occurs with rates (the UK property tax) and the corporate tax.

(6) The income redistribution impact of the tax/subsidy system measured in terms of the Gini coefficient, appears in aggregate to be relatively mild, although the Gini co-efficient is widely regarded as an index which is relatively

insensitive to changes in the income distribution (especially in the tails of the distribution). When we also account for the redistribution in kind through effects on relative prices, the impacts on the richest and poorest groups are much more pronounced. In welfare terms, we find that for a removal of all tax/subsidy policies and a replacement by a yield preserving single rate commodity tax, the poorest decile of households suffers a welfare loss approximately equivalent to 20% of income (principally due to council house subsidies) while the top decile gains about the same amount (principally through the removal of the income tax).[4] This is different from the conventional view of the redistributive impacts of the tax system based on tax incidence calculations that the tax system has almost no impact on the household income distribution. Surprisingly, we find that the top 10% of income recipients gain half as much from an abolition of the local authority housing subsidies with replacement by the yield preserving alternative as they would from a yield preserving replacement of the income tax.

(7)   Our results indicate that the tax/subsidy system incorporates a substantial amount of redistribution in kind through what we term "specific egalitarianism". We also show that such redistributive objectives can be achieved by distorting taxes and subsidies (though at an aggregate welfare cost). We consider as an alternative policy regime the effects of subsidies to food and substantial taxes on owner-occupied housing, even though we would not advocate specific rather than broadly-based redistribution. We find that when these two policies are designed so as to raise no revenue on a net basis, it is possible to produce surprisingly large amounts of redistribution of 'real' income.

(8)   All of our model results depend on the choice of elasticities and other parameters (including tax rates) which we use. We follow literature and other estimates as far as we are able, but in some cases only limited information is available. We perform sensitivity analyses around our chosen model specifications but other problems remain. Elasticity estimates are in many instances sparse. We use

the same procedure followed by Harberger that (outside of
the income tax) averages tax rates computed from data are
also marginal tax rates that affect economic behaviour. This
procedure can be criticized, especially for analysis of the
effects of capital income taxation. We also base our calculations on 1973 data and their applicability to current tax
policy thus needs qualification. In particular, due to a
variety of features introduced into the UK corporate tax
over the last decade it is no longer a significant revenue
raising tax and almost certainly currently has considerably
smaller efficiency effects than our results suggest. It
should therefore be stated very clearly that different data,
elasticity values, and a different model could significantly
change the conclusions listed above.

In Part I of the study, we set out the structure of our
model together with our parameters and data. Part II
presents and interprets detailed results of our policy
calculations.

Notes

1. The results we generate depend critically on the choice
    of elasticity values in the functional forms we use for
    production and demand functions. We have relied heavily
    on literature searches as a way of choosing these
    values, supplemented by sensitivity analysis on key
    elasticities. For several of the required parameter
    values, however, literature estimates are sparse and in
    places somewhat contradictory, and the imprecise speci-
    fication of elasticity values is an important weakness
    to keep in mind in the discussion which follows.

2. A number of these assumptions have been relaxed in sub-
    sequent work. McLure (1969) has extended the model to
    cover interregional incidence, and has introduced
    immobile factors (1971). Thirsk (1972) has extended the
    analysis to the case of three goods, and Mieszkowski
    (1972) has considered the case of three factors.
    Anderson and Ballentine (1976) have extended the
    analysis to incorporate the case of monopoly. Finally,
    Vandendorpe and Friedlaender (1976) extend the Harberger
    formulation to encompass an initial situation with a
    number of distortionary taxes.

3. See Prest (1955).

4. The earlier summary of findings from the model presented
    in Piggott and Whalley (1981) emphasizes aggregate
    income distribution impacts in terms of the Gini coef-
    ficient without highlighting welfare impacts in the
    tails of the distribution. There is thus a difference in
    emphasis from our previous summary, and we discuss this
    in the text of Chapter 7.

PART I

THE GENERAL EQUILIBRIUM MODEL OF THE UK
- STRUCTURE, DATA AND MODEL SOLUTION

In Part I of our study we set out the structure of the general equilibrium model of the UK economy and tax/subsidy system that we have constructed. We also present the data used to calibrate the model and generate parameter values, along with a description of the methods used to obtain parameter values and solve the model for counter-factual equilibria.

In Chapter 1 we outline our approach to general equilibrium tax analysis stressing the basic analytical structure within which we work. In Chapter 2 we make this structure more concrete by specifying our model of the UK economy. We list the industry, commodity, and consumer groups we consider; and describe our functional forms, our treatment of government, external trade, savings and investment, and other features of the model. In Chapter 3 we discuss the UK tax/subsidy system, detailing its major distorting impacts and outlining our model treatment of each component of this system.

Chapter 4 describes the approach we have taken to calibration of the model in the generation of parameter values, and in Chapter 5 we give a complete description of the benchmark equilibrium data set which we have constructed for 1973 for use in calibration. Chapter 6 discusses the elasticity values which we have chosen in our functions. The appendices present an algebraic representation of the model, provide notes on data set construction, and report on our programming and computational experience.

CHAPTER 1

GENERAL EQUILIBRIUM ANALYSIS OF TAX AND SUBSIDY POLICIES

The general equilibrium model of the UK economy and
tax/subsidy system used in this study is a particular specification drawn from a general class of models widely used in
theoretical economics. In this chapter we outline the theoretical structure of general equilibrium tax models as a
prelude to the more specific model we describe later. Functional forms and parameter values used in the model appear
in later chapters.

1.1 General Equilibrium Analysis of Taxes in a Computational
    Framework

In this section we present a formulation of general equilibrium in the presence of taxes due to Shoven and Whalley
(1973). This generates no quantitative answers to policy
questions but provides a framework within which numerical
analysis of the impacts of several tax/subsidy policies can
be simultaneously investigated. This is the same framework
which we use in our model of the UK but is presented here at
a higher level of abstraction than the discussion in subsequent chapters.

We consider an economy with N commodities which may be
either consumed or used in production processes, each with a
single market price π_i; the vector of market prices being
denoted by (i=1,...,N). Economy-wide endowments w_i of each
commodity are treated as initially owned by consumers prior
to market trading, the vector w representing these endowments being given by (w=w_1,...,w_N). We consider Q consumers, w_i^q denoting the qth group's endowment of the ith
commodity.

A number of assumptions are made on production possibilities in the economy and the demand patterns of consumers.

Demand Assumptions

(1) Existence of market demand functions:

It is assumed that each commodity has a market demand function $\xi_i(\pi)$ ($i=1,\ldots,N$), which may be thought of as an aggregation over individual demand functions, i.e.,

$$\xi_i(\pi) = \sum_{q=1}^{Q} \xi_i^q(\pi).$$

(2) Non-negativity, continuity, and homogeneity of demand functions:

The $\xi_i(\pi)$ are assumed to be non-negative, continuous functions of π. This last assumption implies that demands for commodities depend only on relative prices; a doubling of all prices doubles both incomes and purchase prices so that physical quantities demanded remain unchanged. The assumption of homogeneity permits a normalization of prices to be used such that they sum to a constant such as unity, since relative prices rather than absolute prices are all that is important in a general equilibrium model. In the remainder of this chapter a normalization of unity is used,

i.e., $\sum_{i=1}^{N} \pi_i = 1.$

(3) Walras' Law:

A further assumption made on demand functions is a property conventionally known as Walras Law.[1] This states that the value of demands at any vector of prices (whether or not it is an equilibrium price vector) equals the value of consumer incomes.

$$\sum_{i=1}^{N} \pi_i \, \xi_i(\pi) = \sum_{i=1}^{N} \pi_i w_i.$$

This condition would be satisfied if all individual consumers were each on their budget constraint.

Production Assumptions

(1) <u>Existence of a set of productive activities:</u>[2]

It is assumed that there exists a set of techniques by which commodities can be used to produce other commodities. The use of the ith good in the jth activity when activity j is operated at a standardized level of intensity (defined as unity) is denoted by a_{ij}. It is assumed that there are a finite number, K, of possible activities, positive values of a_{ij} denote outputs from and negative values denote inputs into production processes.

(2) <u>Divisibility:</u> Any activity can be operated at any non-negative level of intensity X_j.

(3) <u>Irreversibility:</u> No activity can be operated in reverse, i.e. $X_j > 0$ for all j.

(4) <u>Costless disposal:</u> Any commodity can be disposed of costlessly, i.e., for each commodity j there exists an activity for which $a_{jj} = -1$ and $a_{ij} = 0$, $i \neq j$.

(5) <u>Linear homogeneity:</u>[3] The vector of outputs obtained by operating the jth activity at any non-negative level X_j is the vector $a_{ij} X_j$.

(6) <u>Boundedness:</u> Given fixed resource availabilities for the economy, it is not possible to produce infinite amounts of any good, i.e., the values of X_j for which $\sum_{j=1}^{K} a_{ij} X_j + w_i > 0$ for all i are contained in a bounded set.

With these assumptions, it is possible to define a state of <u>GENERAL EQUILIBRIUM</u> for the economy. Such a state is characterized by an equilibrium vector of market prices π^*, and activity levels X^* such that

(1) <u>Demands equal[4] supplies for all commodities</u>

$$\xi_i(\pi^*) = w_i + \sum_{j=1}^{K} a_{ij} X_j^* \quad (i=1,\ldots,N)$$

(2) <u>No activity yield positive profits</u>, with those in use
breaking even

$$\sum_{i=1}^{N} a_{ij} \pi_i^* < 0 \quad (= 0 \text{ if } X_j^* > 0) \quad (j=1,\ldots,k)$$

A general equilibrium can be conceived of as the outcome
of a process of search by production agents for fresh profit
opportunities. If any activity yields a per unit profit,
producers will expand production levels until profits are
competed away. If any activity yields a loss, producers will
close down and only resume production when costs are
covered. If demand exceeds supply for any commodity, producers will expand operations seeking fresh profits. If
supply exceeds demand for any commodity, producers will
contract output to avoid accumulation of unsold inventories.
As with the diagrammatic analysis in the introduction, the
Pareto optimality of competitive equilibria without taxation
can be simply demonstrated.

The integration of taxation and subsidy policies into this
analysis follows directly. Taxes and subsidies in either <u>ad
valorem</u> or some other form involve market interventions by
the government. These affect both the prices of commodities
and the incomes of consuming agents. The general equilibrium
implications of any tax are two-fold; the purchase price of
a taxed commodity will change, in turn causing further
changes in other prices, and the tax will generate revenue
for the government which will then be spent either as real
expenditures or as transfers.

The methods used to integrate these policies into the no
tax framework can be easily seen by considering a single tax
alone; we take the case of taxes on productive inputs. The
extensions of the approach to incorporate a whole tax system
are discussed later.

Taxes on the use of productive inputs may be represented
by a sequence of <u>ad valorem</u> tax rates t_{ij} on the use of the

i^{th} good in the jth activity. This implies that at prices π_i the tax collected for any activity j operated at unit intensity is given by r_j, where

$$r_j = \sum_i \pi_i \, t_{ij} \, a_{ij} \quad (j=1,\ldots,K)$$

In this section subsidies will be excluded by the restriction that $a_{ij} \, t_{ij} > 0$ for all i and j, although their incorporation will also be discussed later.

The major problem raised by the introduction of taxation into general equilibrium analysis is the treatment of tax revenues. Suppose we take the case where each individual has a fixed proportional share in revenues collected by the government. For any level of revenue, R, the transfer payment received by the qth individual will be

$$\alpha^q R \quad \text{where} \quad \sum_{q=1}^{Q} \alpha^q = 1, \; \alpha^q > 0. \quad ^5$$

Tax revenues pose a problem of simultaneity in decision making. Demands of consumer groups cannot be evaluated until tax revenues are known, since these are a component of income. On the other hand, tax revenues cannot be determined until demands are known, since the scale of operation of each industry, and hence tax collections, will be unknown.

Rather than restrict the analysis to N market prices π_i, - tax revenue R must therefore also be incorported as an endogenous feature of the analysis. The demand functions $\xi_i(\pi)$ - above must be modified to the demand functions $\xi_i(\pi,R)$, which are assumed continuous, nonnegative, and homogeneous of degree zero in (π,R). Zero homogeneity is interpreted, once again, as a property that doubling all prices and tax revenue doubles both incomes and purchase prices and leaves physical quantities demanded unaffected. This means that relative prices and tax revenue will be determined at an equilibrium, rather than relative prices alone. The normalization that prices sum to one, discussed above, must therefore be extended to include tax revenue:

$$\sum_{i=1}^{N} \pi_i + R = 1.$$

Walras' Law must include tax revenues as these appear in incomes:

$$\sum_{i=1}^{N} \pi_i \, \xi_i \, (\pi, R) = \sum_{i=1}^{N} \pi_i \, w_i + R$$

A general equilibrium in the presence of taxation must also be modified. Such an equilibrium is given by a vector (π^*, R^*, X^*) (rather than simply (π^*, X^*)) such that

(1) Demands equal supplies for all commodities

$$\xi_i \, (\pi, R) = w_i + \sum_{j=1}^{K} a_{ij} X_j^* \qquad (i=1,\ldots,N),$$

and

(2) No activity yields positive profit net of taxes, with those in use breaking even

$$\sum_{i=1}^{N} a_{ij} \pi_i^* - \sum_{i=1}^{N} a_{ij} t_{ij} \pi_i^* \leq 0 \qquad (= 0 \text{ if } X_j^* > 0)$$
$$(j = 1,\ldots,K).$$

These modifications define the formal general equilibrium model in the presence of taxation policies which can then be extended to include a wide range of tax and subsidy policies.

We also note two important properties of a general equilibrium incorporating taxation. The first is that it need not be Pareto optimal. This follows by an argument similar to that in the diagrammatic treatment of taxes in the introduction.

A second property is that, in equilibrium, the government budget must be balanced. This can be demonstrated by multiplying the equilibrium demand supply equalities by π_i^* and summing, and the equilibrium zero profit conditions by X_j^* and summing. This yields

$$\sum_{i=1}^{N} \pi_i^* \xi_i (\pi^*, R^*) = \sum_{i=1}^{N} \pi_i^* w_i + \sum_{i=1}^{N} \sum_{j=1}^{K} \pi_i^* a_{ij} X_j^*$$

and

$$\sum_{i-1}^{N} \sum_{j=1}^{K} \pi_i^* a_{ij} X_j^* - \sum_{i=1}^{N} \sum_{j=1}^{K} \pi_i^* a_{ij} t_{ij} X_j^* = 0$$

which implies

$$\sum_{i=1}^{N} \pi_i^* \xi_i (\pi^*, R^*) = \sum_{i=1}^{N} \pi_i^* w_i + \sum_{i=1}^{N} \sum_{j=1}^{K} \pi_i^* a_{ij} t_{ij} X_j^*$$

Using Walras' Law, this gives

$$R^* = \sum_{i=1}^{N} \sum_{j=1}^{K} \pi_i^* a_{ij} t_{ij} X_j^*$$

i.e. the government budget must be balanced in equilibrium.

The existence of a general equilibrium with taxes has been demonstrated by Shoven and Whalley (1973) in a computational general equilibrium framework using Scarf's algorithm. There is, however, no guarantee that a general equilibrium with taxes will be unique. This means that investigations of the effects of tax policies with this methodology face the possibility that there may be a number of solutions to the general equilibrium problem. This issue of non-uniqueness is returned to later.[6]

1.2 General Equilibrium Analysis of Complete Tax/Subsidy Systems

The preceding section has described how conventional general equilibrium analysis can be modified to include taxes on productive activities. To become an operational tool for policy analysis, this capability needs to be extended for the additional taxes and subsidies which are part of a typical tax/subsidy system. In addition to the production taxes considered in the previous section, it is possible to include consumer expenditure taxes, income taxes, subsidies, tariffs, and real government expenditures in the analysis. We consider each in turn.

(i) Consumer Expenditure Taxes

With these taxes each of the q individuals is assumed to face a non-negative vector of <u>ad valorem</u> tax rates $e^q (e^q = e^q_1, \ldots, e^q_N)$ on purchases of each of the N commodities. At any vector (π, R) the total expenditure tax revenue generated is given by

$$E = \sum_{q=1}^{Q} \sum_{i=1}^{N} e^q_i \pi_i \xi^q_i(\pi, R).$$

Walras' Law must be modified to include expenditure tax collections

$$\sum_{i=1}^{N} \pi_i \xi_i(\pi, R) + E = \sum_{i=1}^{N} \pi_i w_i + R.$$

The conditions for a competitive equilibrium are similar to the preceding section. The government budget balance property of a competitive equilibrium still prevails and expenditure taxes are included with production taxes as a government receipt.

(ii) Consumer Income Taxes

With these taxes a non-negative income tax function $t^q(I^q)$ can be incorporated for each consumer, where I^q is the gross of tax income of household q,

$$\sum_{i=1}^{N} \pi_i w^q_i + \alpha^q R.$$

The functions $t^q(I^q)$ must be homogeneous of degree one in (π, R), and therefore apply to real and not nominal incomes. This is necessary to retain the zero homogeneity property of the demand functions $\xi_i(\pi, R)$ as consumer incomes net of income taxes will finance demands and those incomes must be homogeneous of degree one in (π, R). The complexity of the form of the functions $t^q(I^q)$ depends upon how much richness of institutional detail is sought in the modelling of the tax system; increasing marginal and average tax rates across income classes, tax free allowances, and deductions from the tax base for particular expenditure items can all be incorporated.

As in the case of expenditure taxes, the conditions for a competitive equilibrium are unchanged but a further modification to Walras' Law is necessary to include income taxes

$$\sum_{i=1}^{N} \pi_i \xi_i (\pi, R) + E + T = \sum_{i=1}^{N} \pi_i w_i + R$$

where

$$T = \sum_{q=1}^{Q} t^q (\sum_{i=1}^{N} \pi_i w_i^q + \alpha^q R)$$

The government budget balance property of a competitive equilibrium will incorporate income tax receipts.

(iii) Subsidies

The incorporation of subsidies into the analysis from a formal point of view is simple. Production subsidies are incorporated by relaxing the condition that $a_{ij} t_{ij} \geq 0$ for all i,j, consumer expenditure subsidies by relaxing the non-negativity of the vectors e^q, and consumer income subsidies by relaxing the non-negativity of the functions $t^q(I^q)$.

The existence proof for competitive equilibria with taxes given in Shoven and Whalley (1973) does not incorporate subsidies. A perhaps more serious point is that agreeing on what does or does not constitute a subsidy is in practice sometimes difficult (see Prest [1974]), and data are scarce. Meaningful general equilibrium analysis of their impacts is for this reason more difficult than tax policy.

(iv) Tariffs and International Trade

Tariffs may be incorporated directly as part of the consumer expenditure taxes and production taxes discussed earlier. Tariffs on imports for final use would enter as the former, while tariffs on imports for intermediate use would enter as the latter. The treatment of international transactions in general equilibrium tax models is largely outside the scope of the present study[7], but a few observations are appropriate. If more than one country enters the model, an additional property of a competitive equilibrium will be a zero trade balance in each country, since the total value of imports plus capital outflows equals the value of exports plus capital inflows. Moreover, if each country operates a tax system, more than one tax authority will appear in the model. This means that a competitive equilibrium will involve not a single value of tax revenues, but one for each country. Such systems can be developed and are discussed by Shoven and Whalley [1974], but are notationally complex and are not developed here. A corollary of this treatment by Shoven and Whalley is the ability to consider multiple tax jurisdictions within a country.

(v) Real Government Expenditures

By considering the government to be one of the Q consuming groups, a value of α^q for the government can be selected to reflect the portion of tax collections retained by the government for real expenditures. The real expenditures by government will form part of the market demand functions $\xi_i(\pi,R)$. The terms α^q can, in fact, be replaced by the non-negative functions

$$\alpha^q(\pi,R); \quad \sum_{q=1}^{Q} \alpha^q(\pi,R) = 1$$

to allow for variations in redistributive policy as prices vary. The device of treating the government sector as one of the Q consumers in the economy can also be extended to other 'non-personal' sectors, such as the business investment and external sectors. In chapter 9 we describe model extensions to allow for the endogenous determination of real government expenditures, taking into account household preferences towards public goods.

The modifications and extensions (i)-(v) thus allow for a wide range of government tax and subsidy policies to be incorporated into the general equilibrium framework and allow for analysis and comparison between tax alternatives considered as packages rather than as separate proposals.

1.3 Equal Tax Yield Comparisons Between General Equilibria

In cases where all tax rates in the economy are given, equilibrium is characterized by an endogenous level of tax revenues. For many tax modification or reform proposals, a problem often posed is to choose rates of tax such that the current tax yield will be unchanged under the new tax scheme. Given the total yield from an existing tax system and the properties of a replacement tax system, the yield preserving tax rate or rates then become part of the general equilibrium solution.

An extension to the analysis of Sections 1.2 and 1.3 presented in Shoven and Whalley (1977) is that of a tax replacement equilibrium, under which a yield preserving broadly-based tax can be used to evaluate existing tax arrangements. In this case equilibria are considered in which the preserved yield is a "real" yield requiring correction for changes in relative prices. We use this equilibrium concept extensively in our analysis and so a description at this point may be helpful.

As Shoven and Whalley note, there are several definitions of tax yield equality which can be used in such an analysis. If the government is simply a tax collecting and transfer payment disposing agency, then an approporiate concept for determining "real" equality requires a price index which uses quantity weights. The issue then becomes the appropriate selection of these weights. We suppose that for the existing tax system, the equilibrium price revenue vector (π^{*0}, R^{*0}) has been determined along with equilibrium quantities X^{*0}. Two possible definitions for revenue R^1 equalling R^{*0} in real terms are

$$R^1 = R^{*0} \frac{\sum\limits_{i=1}^{N} \pi_i^1 \xi_i(\pi^{*0}, R^{*0})}{\sum\limits_{i=1}^{N} \pi_i^{*0} \xi_i(\pi^{*0}, R^{*0})} \qquad (L)$$

$$R^1 = R*^0 \frac{\sum\limits_{i=1}^{N} \pi_i^1 \xi_i(\pi^1, R^1)}{\sum\limits_{i=1}^{N} \pi_i^{*0} \xi_i(\pi^1, R^1)} \qquad (P)$$

where (π^1, R^1) refers to a new price and revenue vector. Either the Laspeyres price index (L) or the Paasche price index (P) can be used and applied as a correction to $R*^0$. More detailed indices are also possible. Each consumer's Laspeyres and Paasche cost of living indices can be calculated, for example, and weighted according to the fraction of government revenue to which the consumer has claim.

Equal yield equilibria are extensively considered in this study in the results appearing later. An important characteristic they possess is the ability to approximately preserve the size of the public sector in any tax modification experiments considered so that the impacts of changes in the level of public sector expenditures can be removed from impacts of changes in the structure of policies. A change in the relative size of the public and private sectors induced through a tax change can have a pronounced effect on results if the government is not treated as taxing itself for its own use of resources in the production of services which it provides.[7] As there is a single market price for each commodity at an equilibrium, the net of tax price received by sellers in the private sector is equal to the purchase price of the commodity to the public sector. The gross of tax price in the private sector, however, reflects the potential increase in the value of private sector production through use of an extra unit of resources. Thus, reducing or abolishing a tax and causing a resource flow from the public to the private sector can give the appearance of a substantial social gain if government is treated as paying no taxes on its resource use. In such circumstances, it seems clear that equal tax yield equilibria are more appropriate for evaluating alternative tax regimes than the equilibria for given tax rates described in earlier sections. Shoven and Whalley suggest that replacement schemes are easier to work with computationally if the rate or rates to be determined can be characterized by a single number. This number can be a multiplicative factor by which all (or some) of the tax rates are scaled or it can be one of the rates itself. In the latter case, there is some arbitrariness as to which rates are taken as given and which are to be determined. The endogenous rate may, however, be a base rate on which the other taxes (or surtaxes) are "floated". In contrast with non-equal yield equilibria (Shoven and Whalley, 1973), there is no guarantee that an equilibrium exists matching a given replacement tax scheme to a particular previously observed real yield. Our experience indicates, however, that these procedures always work when comparing relevant, realistic tax substitution possibilities.

1.4 Partition of the Commodities into Goods and Factors in General Equilibrium Models

The feature which characterizes two sector general equilibrium literature,[9] as distinct from the more general framework outlined in sections 1.2 - 1.4, is the partition of the list of commodities into goods and factors. In the two sector literature a limitation to two goods and two factors enables a diagrammatic treatment of general equilibrium to proceed.

Our model of the UK economy and tax system also incorporates this partition although we do not limit the dimensionality of the model as in traditional two sector literature. There are a number of computational and data reasons for introducing this distinction into our model. Because this is a more specific formulation than the general discussion in sections 1.2 - 1.4, we feel that it is important to clarify this point at this stage.

The characteristic of a good is that there is no initial endowment; goods are produced from factors and other goods. Factors are non-produced goods of which there is a positive initial endowment. A feature common to both the two sector literature and our model is that substitution possibilities between inputs are limited to factors; goods cannot be substituted for other goods in production.

There are a number of practical advantages which flow from
the incorporation of this distinction, and which simplify
the general equilibrium computations. As there are only
initial endowments of factors, consumer incomes can be
determined on the basis of factor prices alone once the
endowments of productive factors are given. Moreover, the
limitation of production substitution possibilities to factors enables zero profit good prices to be generated from
factor prices alone. As will be seen later, these two
features of the model yield substantial computational
advantages as an equilibrium involving all prices can be
sought by examining only candidate factor price vectors.

A further reason for making this distinction is that it is
also one which appears in national accounts both in the
division of factor incomes, and the decomposition of value
added by industry. Because of the reliance we place on this
type of data in calibrating our model, it would be difficult
to avoid this distinction even were these computational
advantages not present. This partition is prominent in the
description of the UK model presented in the next chapter.

1.5 Computational Solution of General Equilibrium Tax Policy Models

Computational methods for general equilibrium analysis,
though a relatively recent development in a technical sense,
reflect a long-standing interest of economists. The problem
is to find a set of equilibrium prices for which demands
equal supplies for all commodities, and no positive profits
occur in any of the available activities. Using the homogeneity property of demand functions, prices can be normalized to sum to a constant, and the search for candidate
equilibrium price vectors restricted to the unit price simplex. For models incorporating taxation, this price simplex
must be augmented to include an additional dimension for tax
revenue as indicated previously.

There are two types of search procedures which are currently used to solve general equilibrium models, Newton
methods and simplicial subdivision methods. With each of
these, a search procedure across the augmented simplex is
used for a model incorporating taxes.

In the case of Newton's method, the search involves a movement across the simplex in directions indicated by the local behavior of excess demand functions at any point under consideration. Steps can be large or small and there is no guarantee that the search procedure will terminate with an equilibrium solution.

With simplicial subdivision methods the search procedure involves the subdivision of a unit simplex into a finite number of pieces which are themselves simplices. Instead of taking steps of variable size across the unit simplex, movements are made to neighboring smaller simplices in the subdivision. The finiteness of the number of smaller simplices comprising the unit simplex that can be examined, along with a no-cycling argument, guarantees that an approximation to an equilibrium solution will eventually be found. This approximation becomes exact as the number of simplices considered in the subdivision becomes large.

Scarf's original formulation [1967a,b,c] of his computational algorithm contained the argument which guaranteed convergence (and which can also be used to prove existence of an equilibrium) but proved to be somewhat slow computationally. The reasons for this were twofold. Firstly, to preserve the convergence argument it was necessary to begin the procedure in a "corner" of the simplex being examined. No use could be made of prior information which could, in practice, substantially reduce the amount of time required to find a solution. Secondly, since simplicial subdivision methods (or indeed any numerical method) will only find an approximate solution, Scarf's original formulation required that any subsequent refinement of an approximate solution use the same procedure over again with a finer grid of points on the simplex. If the convergence argument was to be preserved it was necessary to restart once again in a corner rather than in the neighborhood of the approximate solution just found.

In recent years there have been a number of extensions of Scarf's original algorithm which remove both of these difficulties. Merrill [1971], Eaves [1972], and others have developed methods which allow for continual refinement of the approximation until an answer of desired accuracy is achieved and allow initiation of solution procedures on the face of the simplex rather than in a corner. These extensions thus make simplicial subdivision methods more competitive with Newton methods in terms of computational speed. A recent advance by van der Laan and Talman (1979) suggests a further substantial reduction in computational execution times for simplicial subdivision methods. Scarf (1977) has recently provided a survey of general equilibrium solution techniques, and for this reason, we do not discuss the computational aspects of applied general equilibrium in detail in this monograph.

To solve our model of the UK economy and tax system, we use a Newton method. Our computational experience with the Newton method has been good, although we have not investigated comparative execution times using Merrill's algorithm or other simplicial subdivision methods. We outline our computational experience in Appendix C.

Notes

1. This is a condition appearing in much of the post-war mathematical economics literature (see Arrow and Hahn (1971) and Scarf (1973)).

2. In the model of the UK to be described later, production functions incorporating continuous substitutability between activities are considered in place of a finite list of activities.

3. Although linear homogeneity is assumed here, it is common in more general treatments to also include the possibility of decreasing returns being present [see Debreu (1959)].

4. As the list of activities includes the disposal activities an equality will define a competitive equilibrium, rather than the inequality that demand must be less than or equal to supply. A commodity with a zero price for which supply exceeds demand will be costlessly disposed of.

5. The government can be treated as one of the individuals in this distribution scheme, and the proportion of government revenues retained for real expenditures on goods and services appears as one of the α^q. In Chapter 9 we present an alternative formulaton of government intervention where public goods appear in household utility functions. Government revenues are set at the level needed to finance provision of public goods such that the sum of the marginal rates of substitution between public and private goods equals the marginal rate of transformation between them.

6. Recently, Kehoe and Whalley [1982] have established uniqueness of equilibrium in a numerical general equilibrium model of the US economy and tax system used by Fullerton, Shoven, and Whalley [1980] and related to that discussed in this monograph. While this does not unambiguously establish uniqueness in the present model, it is highly suggestive that this will be the case.

7. See Whalley [1980].

8. This issue, and the wider set of issues of the treatment
    of government decision-making, are taken up in more
    detail later.
9. See, for example, Johnson [1971], Krauss and Johnson
    [1974].

CHAPTER 2

THE BASIC VARIANT GENERAL EQUILIBRIUM MODEL

The general equilibrium analysis of taxes and subsidies in
the preceding chapter gives little indication as to how such
a framework can be made operational. For a model of an
actual economy to be used to analyze policy alternatives, a
specific structure along with functional forms must be
chosen, and parameter values selected. In this chapter the
model of the UK is discussed. It is calibrated (or
benchmarked) to a 1973 'equilibrium' data set, the latest
year available for much of the data at the time of its construction (1975-1977).[1] The methods used to determine parameter values are discussed in Chapter 4.

The basic variant is a fixed factor supply, static general
equilibrium model which abstracts from intertemporal tax
distortions and distortions of labour supply. In Chapter 9
we describe a number of model extensions which analyze tax
distortions of labour supply and savings. Chapter 9 also
includes a model variant where government expenditures reflect household preferences towards public goods.

Results portray tax distortions of factor supplies as
being relatively mild (in terms of distorting costs) compared to some of the commodity and industry tax distortions.
Welfare loss estimates from savings distortions, however,
are dependent on assumptions about inflation and savings
elasticities, and in recent literature (such as Summers
[1980]) large effects from this distortion were reported.
The combination of convenience and model results provide the
reasons for partitioning our model presentation in this way,
with a basic structure presented here and the various model
extensions later. Appendix A provides a formal algebraic
statement of the basic variant model.

2.1 An Overview of the Basic Variant Model

The basic variant (static, fixed factor supply) model incorporates 33 UK industries and a similar number of commodities. There are two primary factors: capital and labour

services, and one hundred private sector household types, stratified by income, occupation, and family type. Additional "consuming agents" are modelled to represent government, investment, and foreign sector activity. All capital and labour services are owned by these 103 agents, who receive the income generated from their use. Industry production possibilities are represented by substitutable production functions describing requirements of primary factors, and by fixed intermediate production coefficients. Joint production by industries is explicitly included.

The price endogeneity in the model covers both goods and factors. Zero profit conditions by industry link goods and factor prices. At any set of factor prices, factor incomes of any agent can be determined. Along with transfers received these enter the individual agent's budget constraint and finance desired commodity demands. Each agent maximizes a utility function subject to its budget constraint to generate commodity demands. Agents' demands are aggregated to generate market demands. In equilibrium demands equal supplies for both goods and factors.

The UK tax/subsidy system is incorporated into the model by representing each legal tax in model equivalent (post-1973[2]) form. Corporate and property taxes are treated as differential taxes on use of capital services by industry, specific excises and customs duties as <u>ad valorem</u> taxes on both the final and intermediate use of products, the value added tax as a tax on producer costs with appropriate rebates, and income taxes as charges on household incomes. Some more minor taxes such as stamp duty, capital gains tax, and capital transfer tax are also integrated into the analysis. Subsidies include pricing policies towards nationalized industries, agriculture, and local authority housing as well as regional subsidies. The characteristics of each of these, and the way they are built into the model are taken up in Chapter 3.

The structure of the model is summarized in Figure 2.1 where the central role of the price system is emphasized. Changes in taxes and subsidies induce changes in demands and supplies so that the static competitive equilibrium is

Figure 2.1
Structure of the General Equilibrium Model
of the U.K. Economy and Tax System

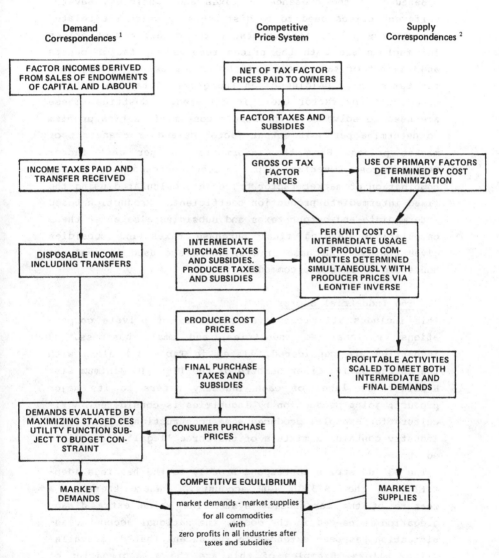

[1]100 household types are identified in the U.K. personal sector representing a three way stratification by income class, occupation of household head, and household composition. This is the most detailed classification available from budget data given a contraint that no cell should represent a sample of less than 10 from a total sample of 7,126 households in 1973. Demand patterns are also considered for the government and external sectors.

[2]33 products produced in the U.K. are considered which include outputs of nationalized industries. In addition, 27 foreign products are identified which are both imported into the U.K. and consumed abroad.

changed. Equilibrium solutions of the model under different policy situations allows us to compare alternative policy regimes. We calculate various summary statistics from these comparisons to measure welfare, distributional, and adjustment effects.

Because of the presence of taxes and subsidies, several different prices need to be distinguished which are related through the policy instruments in the model. Market prices for factors are both the prices received by factor owners and the net of tax prices paid by factor users. Adding factor taxes and subsidies gives the gross of tax and subsidy prices paid by factor users in different industries. These are used to solve each industry's cost minimization problem to determine per unit output factor demands for any set of market prices. From the information on per unit factor demands, cost covering output prices corresponding to any combination of market factor prices are calculated using the fixed intermediate production coefficients. Production based intermediate and output taxes and subsidies also enter these calculations. Adding final purchase taxes and subsidies gives consumer purchase prices, which are used to evaluate household demands for commodities.

2.2 The Industrial Sector

This includes all productive activities of private corporations, nationalized industries, and small business. 33 industries are considered, listed in Table 2.1 along with the corresponding Order Numbers of the 1968 SIC Minimum List Heading. The label of each industry refers to its major product; joint production by industries is considered. Agriculture for example, produces some construction output. Each industry contains a mixture of the three 'legal' forms listed above.[3]

The 33 industries correspond broadly to the headings identified in the 1973 UK GDP accounts.[4] Where there is a feature of the tax/subsidy system for which extra disaggregation is needed in the model, the national account classification has been extended to the extent that data availability allows. Examples of this are the disaggregation of 'food, drink, and tobacco' and the disaggregation of housing into 'housing services (private)' and 'housing services (local authority)'. In each of these cases, important tax and subsidy effects exist which cannot be adequately evaluated without the further disaggregation.

Not all of the industries in Table 2.1 correspond to identifiable consumer goods. In the cases of retail and wholesale trade, and to a lesser extent transportation, the primary output of the industry is part of a joint purchase by consumers along with outputs of other industries. Data are not available which allow these joint purchases to be accurately represented, and so the model treats as separate items products which are, in practice, not separately demanded.[5]

Several capital good and intermediate product industries appear in Table 2.1 even though their outputs are not purchased by households for current consumption. In the basic variant model, capital goods (excluding residential construction) are purchased by the business sector from retained earnings and household savings transferred to corporations through financial intermediation. These expenditures are incorporated into the model through the investment demands of the business sector. These are, in practice, financed primarily through household savings (if retained earnings are included as stockholder savings). We assume each household transfers a constant fraction of income to the business sector and thus no interest elasticity of savings enters the basic variant model. We relax this treatment and consider interest rate endogeneity of savings decisions as one of our model extensions discussed later.

The UK tax/subsidy system introduces a number of distortions between the industries considered. Manufacturing industry, being heavily incorporated, is relatively heavily taxed through the corporate tax, while private sector housing services (especially those originating from owner occupation) are lightly taxed with local authority housing receiving substantial subsidies.

Table 2.1

Structure of the Industrial Sector in the Model

U.K. Industries[1]	1968 U.K. Standard Industrial Classification Minimum List Heading[2]
1. Agriculture, forestry, fishing	001, 002, 003
2. Coal mining	101
3. Other mining and quarrying	102-104, 109
4. Food	211-219, 221, 229, 232
5. Drink	231, 239
6. Tobacco	240
7. Mineral oils	262, 263
8. Other coal and petroleum products	261
9. Chemicals	271-279
10. Metals	311-313, 321-323, 390-396, 399
11. Mechanical engineering	331-339, 343, 349
12. Instrumental engineering	351-354
13. Electrical engineering	361-369
14. Shipbuilding	370
15. Vehicles	380-385
16. Textiles	411-419, 421-423, 429
17. Clothing and footwear	441-446, 449 (part), 450

Table 2.1

U.K. Industries[1]	1968 U.K. Standard Industrial Classification Minimum List Heading[2]
18. Leather, leather goods, fur	431-433
19. Timber, furniture, etc.	471-475, 479
20. Paper, printing, publishing	481-489
21. Manufacturing not elsewhere specified	441-446, 449 (part), 450, 491-496, 499
22. Construction	500
23. Gas, electricity, and water	601-603
24. Transport	701-709
25. Communications	708
26. Retail trade	820-821
27. Wholesale trade	810-812, 831, 832
28. Banking, insurance, and finance	860-866
29. Housing services (private)	No MLH[3]
30. Housing services (local authority)	No MLH[3]
31. Public services	875
32. Professional services	871-874, 876, 879
33. Other services	881-889, 899

1. The model considers the same number of commodities as industries, industries being defined by their principal output.

2. 'Standard Industrial Classification' (Central Statistical Office, U.K., 1968, 3rd Edition).

3. No entries are given under the SIC but these industries appear in the U.K. GDP accounts.

Drink, tobacco, and mineral oils are items heavily taxed by specific excises. Coal, metals, gas, electricity and water, and transportation are all recipients of nationalized industry subsidies. Food is zero rated in the VAT system while a special tax applies to cars (vehicles). Construction, professional and other services (and to a lesser extent retail trade) are lightly incorporated and more lightly taxed than other industries. Certain industries (most notably shipbuilding) are regionally concentrated and receive regional subsidies. Some industries are heavier payers of rates than others because their use of capital services is structure intensive (housing services is the obvious case but this feature is also important for retail and wholesale trade). The level of detail captures all these features.

In modelling the production possibilities for each industry, the distinction between produced commodities and non-produced factors is extensively used. The economy has no initial endowment of a produced commodity prior to production, while for factors positive initial endowments occur. Two productive factors, capital and labour services, are considered in addition to the 33 produced commodities listed in Table 2.1.

Factors enter industry production processes with substitution between factors according to CES value added functions.[6] Intermediate production enters the model in two separate ways. Both joint production and intermediate use of goods by industries appear. Both of these portions of the intermediate production structure assume fixed coefficients. Value added cost functions can be derived from the CES value added functions and the minimum cost requirements of capital and labour needed to operate each industry at unit intensity can be calculated for any factor prices.[7]

Capital services are measured as the annual service flow yielded by the underlying capital asset (net of costs necessary to preserve 'capital intact'). A unit of capital services is defined as that amount whose market price (net of capital taxes) is unity in the 1973 equilibrium data we use to parameterize our model. A fixed total amount of capital services is assumed to be available for use in all industries. Capital services are thus treated as homogeneous and perfectly shiftable between industries, but in fixed aggregate supply. This is not an unreasonable treatment for a model interpreted as providing long-run counterfactual analysis[8], but in a model providing short-run projections is clearly unrealistic.

This treatment of capital services allows the capital endowment of the economy to be measured in terms of the profit type return from National Accounts data[9] and avoids the complex accounting issue of integrating balance sheet data (which for the UK are sparse) with National Accounts flow data.[10] Capital stock data by industry are available and provide an alternative source for measurement of capital use by industry; use is made of this data source in sensitivity analysis on the model.

Labour services are measured analogously to capital in service flow units. Because we use National Accounts data to provide a flow measure of the return to labour we are unable to link our data directly to employment by industry measured in numbers of employees. We use a units convention for labour services comparable to that for capital, a unit being that amount with a market price of unity (net of labour factor taxes), in our 1973 equilibrium data. In the basic variant model the economy has a fixed labour endowment all of which is used in production.

2.3 The Personal Sector

One hundred consumer groups appear in the personal sector in the model.[11] Each group owns income earning assets, receives transfers from the government, pays taxes, and has a preference ordering defined over the model commodities. Groups are identified as reporting households in Family Expenditure Survey (FES) data[12] classified by income, family circumstances (marital status and number of children), and occupation, and are listed in Table 2.2. Each group corresponds to a reporting cell in the FES.

The model classification of households is motivated by a concern to as much detail as possible in examining tax incidence issues within a price endogenous general equilibrium model. The number of households incorporated is considerably smaller than those considered in detailed tax incidence studies which do not use an explicit behavioural model.[13]

A feature of this treatment is the difference in income characteristics and preference patterns which are introduced into the model. Retired households, for instance, are large owners of capital assets even though many of them are in the lower deciles of the income distribution. Thus, tax changes which improve capital's share only mildly worsen the personal distribution of incomes. Differences by family characteristics in expenditures on drink, food, and other commodities are especially pronounced. Expenditure data from the FES are used to generate preference parameters, and the differences in parameters by household are especially important in the analysis of specific excise taxes.

Each household group is assumed to have a nested CES type utility function.[14] These functions have constant elasticities of substitution between groups of commodities. We choose elasticity values for the various nests to calibrate to literature estimates of own price elasticities of commodity groups.[15] An important feature of literature estimates is that they are not differentiated by household. We therefore largely use the same elasticity values within any nest for all households. Demands for commodities by each household are determined from utility maximization subject to a net of tax budget constraint. Household demands for commodities are summed to determine the total demands of the personal sector.

Similar 'foreign' and 'domestically' produced goods are treated in the model as heterogeneous commodities and appear in the nesting structure within preferences. A convenient feature of the nested functions is that it is possible to include similar domestic and foreign goods within the same nest, and specify a high elasticity of substitution between them with a lower elasticity of substitution across nests. Thus when the labour/leisure choice of households is incorporated (in Chapter 9), nesting structure within preference functions enables estimates of labour supply elasticities to be used through implied elasticity values in the nested utility functions.

The nesting approach can be extended to large numbers of levels of nesting, but as this is done more parameters must be specified in the utility function for each household. Execution times to solve the model rise with the added functional complexity. For these reasons the complexity of the partition of commodities into nests is restricted to a manageable level structure.

Consumer demand functions correspond to maximization of each household's nested utility function. Price indices for the 'composite goods' which any nest represents are constructed. A sequential procedure is used of first determining expenditures on nests, and then expenditures within nests. This procedure can be interpreted as one of first finding the demands for composite goods using the associated price indices, and then demands for commodities within nests.

The gross of tax incomes of consumer groups are derived from three sources, ownership of capital and labour services, and transfers received from government. Consumer groups pay income taxes on their gross incomes leaving disposable incomes which finance commodity demands.[16] The endowments of each household are determined using data on incomes by source and by household in the Family Expenditure Survey. These endowments are scaled to make them consistent with totals for the personal sector obtained from national accounts data.[17] The income tax functions faced by household groups are discussed in Chapter 3.

2.4 Treatment of Investment Expenditures in the Basic Variant Model

In the basic variant model financial savings by households are not considered as a decision variable. Real expenditures on newly produced capital goods by enterprises financed by household savings enter as a separate demand category in the model. A single set of preferences for investment expenditures by commodity replaces the separate savings functions of households. Households saving are a fixed portion of income, automatically transferred from households to the business sector. Investment expenditures by commodity (net

TABLE 2.2

Household Groups Considered in the U.K. Personal Sector

(Groups Identified by 1973 Family Expenditure Survey[1,2])

A. Households comprising one adult with or without children

I. Occupational group of head of household = manual employee; Weekly Income[3] Ranges ≤ £20, £20-30, £30-40, > £40

II. Occupational group of head of household = non-manual employee; Weekly Income Ranges ≤ £20, £20-30, £30-40, £40-50, £50-60, £60-70, > £70

III. Occupational group of head of household = self-employed; Weekly Income Ranges ≤ £20, £20-40, > £40

IV. Occupational group of head of household = retired; Weekly Income Ranges ≤ £10, £10-20, £20-30, £30-40, £40-50, > £50

V. Occupational group of head of household = unoccupied; Weekly Income Ranges ≤ £10, £10-20, £20-30, > £30

B. Households comprising two adults or two adults and one child

I. Occupation as A(I); Weekly Income Ranges ≤ £20, £20-30, £30-40, £40-50, £50-60, £60-70, £70-80, £80-90, > £90

II. Occupation as A(II); Weekly Income Ranges ≤ £30, £30-40, £40-50, £50-60, £60-70, £70-80, £80-90, £90-100, > £100

III. Occupation as A(III); Weekly Income Ranges ≤ £20, £20-30, £30-40, £40-50, £50-60, £60-70, £70-90, > £90

IV. Occupation as A(IV); Weekly Income Ranges ≤ £20, £20-30, £30-40, £40-50, £50-60, £60-70, £70-90, > £90

V. Occupation as A(V); Weekly Income Ranges ≤ £20, £20-30, £30-40, £40-60, > £60

C. All other households

I.   Occupation as A(I); Weekly Income Ranges $\leq$ £30, £30-40, £40-50, £50-60, £60-70, £70-80, £80-90, £90-100, > £100

II. Occupation as A(II); Weekly Income Ranges $\leq$ £40, £40-50, £50-60, £60-70, £70-80, £80-90, £90-100, > £100

III. Occupation as A(III); Weekly Income Ranges $\leq$ £30, £30-40, £40-50, £50-60, £60-70, £70-80, £80-90, £90-100, > £100

IV. Occupation as A(IV); Weekly Income Ranges $\leq$ £30, £30-40, £40-50, £50-60, £60-70, £70-80, > £80

V.   Occupation as A(V); Weekly Income Ranges $\leq$ £30, £30-40, £40-60, $\geq$ £60

1. Family Expenditure Survey: Report for 1973: HMSO

2. The disaggregation by income range is the maximum available given an imposed constraint that no data are released for a cell with less than 10 households. The 1973 FES contains 7,126 households whose distribution by cell is projected onto a population-wide basis for the U.K.

3. Income ranges in the FES do not correspond exactly with incomes in the model due to changes in treatment of particular items. The correspondence remains reasonably close enough for distributional indications to be meaningful.

of real depreciation) thus reflect a separate decision-making process outside the household sector. An additional agent (the 'business investor') makes decisions on the composition of investment expenditures. Maximization of a nested CES utility function determines these demands. The pattern of investment expenditures is derived from data in Input-Ouput tables.

This treatment incorporates a limited degree of price endogeneity into one of the final demand columns associated with an input-output table. Total household savings are given but their allocation among investment categories depends upon relative prices.

We use this as our treatment in the basic variant model to simplify our analysis. It abstracts entirely from inter-temporal tax distortions. Households savings do not respond to changes in the expected rate of return on investments. Savings are allocated among capital goods only on the basis of acquisition prices of capital goods. In equilibrium these will be production side determined cost covering prices, and do not necessarily reflect the discounted present value of the expected earnings stream from the capital asset involved.

To incorporate intertemporal decision making and distortions through taxes into our analysis, we use an extension to the basic variant model (described in Chapter 9) in which household utility functions include the expected future annuity stream generated by saving today. We use an expectations formation hypothesis which links the current rental price of capital to current savings decision, and incorporate savings endogeneity for households. In this model extension, the artificial construct of a separate demand pattern for investment expenditures is removed as is all financial intermediation, with households (as stock-holders and savers) making investment decisions. Our formulation is based on that used by Fullerton, Shoven, and Whalley (forthcoming 1983) in work on the US. They model intertemporal tax distortions using a sequence of equilibria with savings decisions depending upon the real return on capital. We do not consider the same sequence of equilibria approach, but are able to compare balanced growth paths through computation of equivalent one-period equilibrium problems.[18] This is discussed more fully in Chapter 9.

2.5 The Public Sector

The UK public sector enters the model through the tax, subsidy, transfer, and real expenditure interventions of central and local governments. The treatment of the public sector in the model is outlined in Table 2.3.

The public sector receives net revenues from the tax/subsidy system to which it adds income received from publicly owned assets.[19] Transfers are made predominantly to the private sector, and real expenditures on goods and services include both current and capital expenditures. These are broken down into real expenditures on goods produced by the industrial sector, and expenditures on a single public good (public services) for which there is no direct articulation of private sector demands. Decisions on the composition of public sector expenditures are modelled as a process of public sector utility maximization subject to the public sector budget constraint.[20]

The public sector includes the activities of the combined central and local authorities[21] plus certain non-commercial activities classified in the personal sector of the UK national accounts. The public sector therefore covers central government, local authorities, and related agencies of a non-commercial type (including universities and other publicly-supported educational establishments).

UK nationalized industries[22] are treated as outside the public sector and as part of the industrial sector. The appropriate model treatment for nationalized industries is contentious. Price, output, hiring, investment, and other decisions of nationalized industries are all interfered with to some extent by the central government.[23] On the other hand, these agencies differ from other public sector agencies in providing marketable outputs sold at (something

TABLE 2.3

The Treatment of the U.K. Public Sector in the Model

A. Tax Subsidy System

1. Corporation Tax
2. Rates
3. Regional Development Grants
4. Capital write-offs and cheap loans to Nationalized Industries
5. National Insurance and related contributions
6. Regional Employment Premium
7. Value Added Tax
8. Petrol Duty
9. Motor vehicle licences
10. Stamp Duty
11. Car Tax
12. Nationalized Industry Subsidies in Cash
13. Other industry subsidies
14. Income Tax
15. Capital Gains Tax
16. Capital Transfer Tax
17. Specific excise duties (non-petrol)
18. Protective duties
19. Subsidies to council housing

B. Transfers to Personal Sector

1. Social Security Benefits
   National Insurance
   Supplementary Benefits
   Family Allowances
   Other benefits
2. Education Scholarships
   Other grants
3. Local authority grants
   Rent rebates and allowances
   Other capital gains

C. Expenditures

1. Current central government expenditures on goods and services
2. Gross domestic fixed capital formation of central government
3. Current and capital expenditures of local government
4. [Debt interest and financial transactions discussed in later section.]

Model Sub-systems

Factor taxation and subsidies 1, 2, 3, 4, 5, 6, part of 13.

Producer output taxes and subsidies 7, part of 8 and 9, 10, 11, 12, part of 13.

Consumer output taxes and subsidies part of 8 and 9, 17, 18, 19.

Income taxation 14, 15, 16

Notes to Table 2.3

1. Public sector income accrues not only from taxation but from income from government assets and financial transactions. Government assets cover the capital stock of nationalized industries and the capital stock (including military equipment) employed by central and local government.

2. Income from real assets accruing to government covers only the distributed portion of nationalized industry surpluses and the imputed income from the central and local government capital stock.

3. Imputed expenditures on services of wholly-owned capital items are included in expenditures.

4. Capital expenditures of nationalized industries are treated as commodity purchases by the industrial sector. Lending to public corporations is included in public sector financial transactions as is the writing-off of nationalized industry debt.

5. Public sector commodity expenditures are broken down partly on a commodity basis using a recent Central Statistical Office commodity analysis. Residual expenditures (a majority) are treated as expenditures on a single public good which does not directly enter utility functions of consuming groups.

approaching) commercial prices. Nationalized industries are therefore treated as part of the industrial sector. This does not, however, prevent an extensive treatment of subsidy policy to nationalized industries. Public sector ownership of equity in these enterprises is incorporated into the model.

All financing and expenditure activities reported in the combined (capital and current) accounts of UK central and local authorities enter the model[24], with the coverage extending in some cases beyond these accounts. This is particularly the case with the national accounts treatment of subsidies, and of the imputed public sector incomes and expenditures associated with publicly-owned durable goods (especially military equipment).

The taxes collected by the public sector are the income tax, corporation tax, rates, value added tax, car tax, motor vehicle licence duties, excise duties (drink, tobacco, hydrocarbon oil), national insurance contributions (both employer and employee), capital gains tax, estate duty (which has since been replaced by the capital transfer tax) and tariff duties. All of these are treated in the model as ad valorem taxes paid on outlays or receipts by the appropriate economic agents. Petroleum Revenue Tax was not in operation in 1973, and is excluded from our calculations. This treatment in ad valorem form is open to objection for nearly all of these taxes, and the issues involved are discussed in more detail in Chapter 3. The model attempts to analyze the post 1973 taxation system and so the new taxes introduced in 1973 are included in the model, and treated as if they operated in full for the calendar year 1973.

In addition to tax policies, subsidies are also considered in the model in ad valorem form. These cover nationalized industries, local authority housing, agricultural support policy, and aspects of regional policy.[25] Data on payments of subsidies are in places poor, reflecting the absence of a 'legal' subsidy system in the UK. Some care is needed in defining what is meant by the term subsidy and these issues are discussed later.

The expenditure side of public sector activity covers both transfers and real expenditures. Transfers are made primarily to the personal sector but also (to a lesser extent) to the corporate and external sectors. Real expenditures cover both major items (health, defence, education) and minor items (parks, museums, etc.) and in addition capital expenditures on public sector construction products (e.g., highways). A CSO analysis[26] of central government expenditures by type of commodity rather than by function is used to obtain data on government commodity purchases.

2.6 The External Sector

In an open economy such as the UK, no empirical analysis of taxes and subsidies can ignore the external sector. Because of the empirical observation of similar commodities being both imported and exported by the UK, a second country ('rest of the world') is identified which produces commodities which are comparable but qualitatively different from UK products. These are close substitutes in demand.[27] Twenty-seven additional commodities are identified corresponding to the traded goods from the list of the thirty-three UK commodities in Table 1. Some of the imports are primarily for final demand, and others are largely for intermediate use. This treatment of the external sector partly dictates the choice of functional form for household demand functions since 'similar' UK and foreign products are close substitutes. The total of sixty commodities are partitioned into thirty-three nests for the staged utility functions from which the demand functions are derived.

The rest of the world trades with the UK and imports and exports traded goods. Six products produced in the UK are non-traded goods.[28] The rest of the world is represented as an economy which is large relative to the UK. As a result changes in the UK taxes and subsidies do not affect relative prices of world products (UK imports).

This external sector treatment has a major impact on the behaviour of the model under tax policy changes in the UK. If high degrees of substitutability between comparable domestic and foreign products are specified, then because the rest of the world is large relative prices of UK commodities can only change slightly in response to domestic tax changes. Implausibly large changes in production may occur in response to small policy changes. If lower degrees of substitutability are specified, then domestic and foreign prices are less closely related. This reflects the fact that the classical tax incidence problem in a small, open, price-taking economy is not a complete general equilibrium problem since some relative prices are set externally and remain unaffected by changes in domestic taxes. In practice, quota and other trade distorting policies operate even in the most open economies, and relative domestic prices can and do adjust to domestic policies while domestic and foreign produced commodities remain as close substitutes in demand.

The extent to which the UK is insulated from price changes abroad is reflected in estimates of trade elasticities. If domestic and foreign goods are perfect substitutes, the UK should face a high export price elasticity and have a high import demand elasticity. Empirical literature suggests that both these elasticities are low, in the region of -1.0 or below (in absolute value).[29] To reflect this, we use different values for the elasticity of substitution between comparable domestic and foreign produced goods in both foreign and domestic demand functions. Different assumptions on the degree of openness of the economy are accommodated in the calculations reported later.

Capital movements between the UK and the rest of the world appear in the model, but only in a crude form which closes the model. In equilibrium there must be a zero overall external sector balance for the UK, and capital movements are included in the model to remove the need for artificial adjustments to merchandise trade figures. Investment income paid abroad and received from abroad is represented by foreign ownership of UK capital, and UK ownership of foreign capital respectively. Capital outflows are treated as purchases of foreign capital goods, and capital inflows as foreign purchases of UK capital goods. Capital expenditures abroad are made primarily by the UK industrial sector, and capital inflows into the UK are invested by the UK indus-

trial sector on behalf of foreigners in capital goods produced in the UK.

A further issue with the model treatment of the external
sector concerns implicit border tax adjustments. The UK tax
structure as modelled embodies a particular border tax
structure reflecting the balance of direct and indirect
taxation. Direct taxes (income, corporate, property, and
social security taxes) can be considered to be origin-based
taxes in that they appear in export costs, are not rebated,
and are not charged on imports. Indirect taxes (and in particular the value-added tax) are generally destination-based
taxes being rebated on exports and applied to imports. This
treatment means that any large scale tax modification
coupled with a replacement of existing taxes by a single,
yield preserving tax can produce substantial variations in
relative import and export prices. This is because neither a
single destination (nor origin-based) tax accurately reflects the existing border tax treatment inherent in the tax
system.

Terms of trade gains or losses will be associated with the
implicit border tax arrangements of the existing tax structure, and terms of trade effects may accompany tax change
experiments. While border adjustments for general taxes can
be treated as monetary phenomena with no real effects,[30]
their appearance for discriminatory taxes can substantially
affect results. For this reason, in the calculations
reported later an attempt is made to allow for this by
having two replacement taxes. One is a general sales tax on
a destination basis, and the other a terms-of-trade preserving export tax or subsidy.

2.7 Equilibrium Solutions for the Model

Once specified, the model is used to calculate equilibrium
solutions under a number of alternative tax/subsidy arrangements. The model is calibrated to a given set of data generated under the existing tax arrangements, and an equilibrium
in the presence of these taxes computed. When a tax change
is introduced into the model a new equilibrium is computed.
Comparisons can then be made between equilibria using alternative summary statistics.

Two types of equilibria are examined and it is important to differentiate them. We refer to these as BENCHMARK EQUILIBRIA and REPLACEMENT EQUILIBRIA. A benchmark equilibrium is one represented by the data generated under existing taxes and subsidies, adjusted to correct for any violations of model equilibrium conditions occurring in the basic data.[31] In such an equilibrium zero profits (net of taxes) prevail in all industries, demands equal supplies for all goods and factors, the government budget is balanced, and there is zero external balance. This may be thought of as the 'observed' equilibrium generated by the economy in the presence of the policies corresponding to the data period examined.

A replacement equilibrium is the counterfactual equilibrium obtained from the model using alternative (and typically hypothetical) tax and subsidy policies. The alternative set of taxes is thought of as a 'replacement' for existing policies. Any one of a number of replacement alternatives may be involved; replacing rates by a VAT surcharge, eliminating corporate taxes, reforming income taxes, and many others. For all of these, the procedure followed is that the new tax policy to be considered is expressed in model equivalent form, introduced into the model in place of the existing policies, and the new equilibrium computed.

A replacement equilibrium is usually calculated in one of two ways. The new tax rates may be taken as given and the new equilibrium computed, even though this may involve a change in government revenues. Alternatively, a replacement tax or subsidy can be considered which preserves government revenue from the benchmark equilibrium in real terms. Once the structure of the replacement tax is specified (e.g., a broadly based sales tax), the tax or subsidy rate necessary to preserve government revenue can be calculated as part of the equilibrium.

Equal yield equilibria with broadly based sales taxes as the replacement tax are the most commonly used replacement equilibria for the policy changes analyzed in Part II. The reason for this is that the evaluations of taxes and subsidies attempt to examine effects on relative prices. If the

size of the public sector changes as taxes change, this can
affect results and does not provide a way of assessing the
relative merits of alternative taxes independently of the
level of public sector expenditures.

2.8 Dating the Model

Data for 1973 are used to construct the benchmark equilibrium for the model. This data set is used to calibrate
the basic variant of the model and its various extensions.
Calibration involves choosing parameter values for functions
in the model such that the model exactly reproduces benchmark data as an equilibrium solution.

At the time of model construction, this was the latest
year for which it was possible to assemble a consistent
benchmark equilibrium data set, although since its construction (during 1975-1977) considerably more recent data
has become available. 1973 was a high employment year, with
lower inflation than the following three years, and the
disruptions of the Middle East war were apparent only at the
end of the year. A major problem with using data for 1973
are the tax changes introduced that year. It can be argued
for instance, that equilibrium adjustments to these tax
changes were incomplete.

While this must be the case to some extent, it may also be
argued that the changes were announced some two years
earlier and adjustments would have proceeded in anticipation
of the introduction of the changes. In spite of this difficulty with this choice of year, the disadvantages involved
in using earlier years data were considered at the time of
construction of the benchmark data to be outweighed by the
benefits of working with data generated under the tax regime
we wished to analyze. Ideally, one would wish to average
data over a number of years to smooth out fluctuations in
individual years and the construction of data sets for years
later than 1973 would be desirable (even though we have not
thus far carried out such an exercise). Although some
averaging was done by Whalley (1977) in his earlier work on
the UK for the period 1968-70 using a smaller model than
that discussed here, this has not proved possible for the

present larger model. Transforming one year's data into a
form suitable for use in the model involves substantial work
over a long period. In Chapter 7, we report the results of
limited sensitivity analysis to large changes in some of the
more significant elements in our data set.

A further important issue concerns changes in the UK tax
system between the year of our study (1973) and the present.
We discuss this in Chapter 3, but it is worthwhile to high-
light the changes in corporate taxes which have significantly reduced the revenue importance of this tax. Analysis
of taxes with the model thus refers to the 1973 rather than
the current tax structure.

Notes

1. A large amount of effort was involved in constructing
   this data set after which our efforts turned to model
   development and use. We have unfortunately not had sufficient time to return to our data to update it. This
   means that our model and findings are somewhat dated
   even before publication, an unfortunate but inevitable
   feature of work of this type.

2. The term 'post-1973' indicates the UK tax system incorporating the major changes which took place in 1973. At
   this time a value added tax (VAT) was introduced, purchase tax and selective employment tax were eliminated,
   corporation tax was changed from a 'classical' to an
   'imputation' system, and the income tax was changed. All
   of these changes are reflected in the model specification of the tax system, although some data difficulties arose with the value added tax when the model and
   data set were being constructed. UK tax changes since
   1973 have changed the structure of the tax system,
   especially through rate variations. An important trend
   from 1973 to 1979 was the increasing proportion of tax
   collections occurring through the income tax because of
   the non-indexed progressive rate structure of the tax
   and high inflation rates. This has been partially reversed by the recent budgets of the Thatcher government.
   Possible impacts of these more recent tax changes on our
   modelling are discussed in Chapter 3.

3. The interpretation of industry groups containing
   nationalized industries is that they receive government
   subsidies in such a way that they accrue equally to all
   firms in the industry rather than to the nationalized
   components only. This is clearly unrealistic, but given
   that most industry groups affected are dominated by
   nationalized components, it does not seem to us to be an
   overly severe restriction on interpretation of subsequent results.

4. National Income and Expenditure 1964-1974, HMSO, Tables
   18 and 19.

5. A more desirable procedure would be to use separate
    consumer and producer good classifications with a link
    between the two given by a matrix of production coef-
    ficients. This would enable the trade and transportation
    industry outputs to be apportioned between the consumer
    goods considered and a classification used which fits
    that appearing in consumer expenditure data more
    closely. This is the procedure used by Fullerton,
    Shoven, and Whalley [1978] in their general equilibrium
    tax model for the US. A table is available for this
    purpose from the 1967 US Input-Output Tables (Survey of
    Current Business February 1974, Bureau of Census, US
    Government). The closest thing to such a table for the
    UK (Table 0, Input-Output Tables for the United Kingdom,
    1968, Central Statistical Office, 1973) does not contain
    the allocation of trade and transportation by consumer
    product given in the US data and is thus of limited
    value for this purpose.

6. See Appendix A.

7. These cost functions are adopted in the search procedure
    used to solve the model. Discussion of the parameter
    values used in the functions for each industry appears
    in Chapter 4.

8. Although the dynamic time path of the economy would, in
    all probability, be changed by an alteration in
    policies.

9. In the data used in the model profit type return is
    measured on a net of production tax basis as the sum of
    (i) trading profits of corporations net of 'true'
    depreciation and corporate taxes and excluding stock
    appreciation (ii) interest payments (iii) rent (includ-
    ing the imputed rent on owner occupied homes and govern-
    ment owned assets), and (iv) the portion of small
    business income attributed as a return to capital. This
    concept differs from that reported in the National
    Accounts, but figures on this basis can, with adjust-
    ments, be derived from national accounts sources. This
    treatment, along with a discussion of concepts and
    sources, is more fully described in Chapter 5. This

procedure follows that adopted by Harberger [1959, 1962, 1964], Shoven and Whalley [1972] and others.

10. Although the Revised UN System of National Accounts [1968 Rev. F] suggests the integration of balance sheet and national accounting data, official UK statistics fall far short of this goal. Recently official balance sheet data have been published; prior to this estimates were available in Revell [1967] and updated by Revell and Roe [1971] and the Royal Commission on the distribution of Income and Wealth [1975]. These data provide aggregates rather than industry subaggregates and cannot be easily used in the model.

11. The model differs from the UK National Accounts in the treatment of so-called "communal persons". Non-profit making bodies such as universities and churches are included in the personal sector in UK National Accounts, but for the purposes of the model are included with the public sector.

12. Family Expenditure Survey: Report for 1973; HMSO.

13. See, for example, Pechman and Okner [1974].

14. The properties of these functions are described in Sato [1967], Keller [1976], and Brown and Heien [1972].

15. The partitions of commodities into nests along with the elasticity parameters are discussed in Chapters 5 and 6.

16. The treatment of consumer income allocated to savings is discussed later.

17. The details of these adjustments are discussed in Chapter 4.

18. A more detailed discussion of this extension appears in Chapter 9.

19. In the model much of this is imputed public sector income from publicly-owned structures and military equipment; this is largely excluded from the UK National Accounts. This imputed income results in corresponding imputed expenditures. The effect of this treatment is to increase the relative size of the public sector as it is represented in national income accounts.

20. We later consider a model extension in which we replace this treatment of the expenditure side with one where public goods appear as an argument of household utility functions. We consider equilibria in which the sum of marginal rates of substitution between public and private goods across households equals the marginal rate of transformation, with public goods production financed through lump sum poll taxes.

21. See the definition of these in Rita Maurice [ed.], "National Accounts: Sources and Methods [1967, HMSO), pp. 320-321.

22. These 'industries' are broadly those enterprises taking the form of a public corporation, established with a board of control for which there is ministerial power of appointment but limited ministerial control of day to day policy. A list of these corporations (accurate as of 1967] is given by Rita Maurice (op.cit.), p.249. Major public corporations cover the following industries: coal, gas, electricity, railways, air transportation, communications, steel, and, to a limited extent, road transportation. Water boards and hospital management boards while having a similar legal structure are regarded not as nationalized industries but as part of the public sector.

23. Varying both over particular corporations and over time.

24. See Table 52 of National Income and Expenditure 1964-74, HMSO, 197.

25. Food subsidies were not operative in 1973 and are not considered although they could be integrated into the general approach.

26. "Commodity Analysis of Central Government Current Expenditure on Goods and Services," Economic Trends, August 1971, pp. (v)-(x). In the use made of these figures, it is assumed that the composition of all government commodity expenditures is the same as central government expenditures. This is not wholly accurate, but no other data exist for this purpose.

27. This is a procedure common in much recent applied general equilibrium modelling; it is usually associated with the work of Armington [1969].

28. These goods are Gas, Electricity, and Water; Retail Trade; Housing Services (private); Housing Services (local authority); Public Services and Professional Services.

29. See the recent compendium by Stern et al. [1976] where an export price elasticity value of -0.48, and an import price elasticity of -0.65 is suggested for the UK.

30. A classic proposition in public finance is that a movement from an origin to a destination basis (or vice versa) for a general (non-distorting) tax will be offset by a movement in exchange rates in a flexible rate regime or in domestic price levels in a fixed rate regime such that real trade flows will remain unchanged; see Johnson and Krauss [1974]. The taxes considered in the model are not general and so the proposition does not apply in simple form; there is no presumption that with a non-general tax the variation between tax bases will be largely offset by a monetary accommodation with limited real effects.

31. These conditions are discussed in more detail in Chapters 4 and 5, and involve demand supply equalities for all goods and factors as well as zero profit conditions by industry, government budget balance and zero external balance.

CHAPTER 3

MODEL TREATMENT OF UK TAXES, SUBSIDIES
AND GOVERNMENT EXPENDITURE

As indicated in Chapter 2 all major taxes and subsidies
operating in the UK (post April 1973) enter our model. This
chapter discusses the treatment of each, and outlines their
major discriminatory features. Numerical values used for tax
rates are reported in Chapter 5.

3.1 An overview of the 1973 Tax/Subsidy System in the Model

In the 1973 public sector accounts used in the model gross
tax revenues are £25.0 billion and expenditures on subsidies
are £5.3 billion. UK NNP in our data for 1973 is £69.8
billion. 35.8% of NNP is collected in taxes and 7.6% paid in
subsidies. The major taxes are income tax (£7.3 billion in
1973), specific excises (chiefly on hydrocarbon oil,
tobacco, and drink; a combined total of £3.9 billion),
national insurance and related contributions (£3.9 billion),
corporation tax (£3.2 billion), rates (£2.6 billion), and
value added tax (£2.2 billion). The major subsidies are
those to local authority housing (£3.1 billion) and
nationalized industries (£1.4billion). These are listed in
Table 3.1 along with the major features of each and their
treatment in the model.

Each of these is treated as an ad valorem tax or subsidy.
Some are treated as taxes on factor use with differential
rates by industry, some are production taxes on intermediate
use, some are consumer taxes on commodity purchases, and
some tax incomes of consumers. The model treatment adopted
for each tax and subsidy is motivated primarily by the discriminatory features which each introduces.

As the description in the remainder of this chapter will
make clear, the appropriateness of the model treatment
adopted for a number of these taxes and subsidies can be
queried on theoretical grounds. In the public finance literature there is considerable debate on a number of these
taxes, and the treatment adopted here does not imply that

these debates are resolved. There is discussion as to
whether to treat the property tax (rates) as an excise tax
or a profits tax[1] (a differential tax on capital use by
industry); and discussion on whether to treat the corporate
tax as a lump sum tax, a tax on particular financing instruments available to firms, or a tax on capital services used
by each industry.[2] With national insurance contributions
there has been discussion of whether they are a tax at all.[3]

The majority of legal taxes enter the model as a single
model equivalent tax. Where more than one model equivalent
tax (or subsidy) exists, these are aggregated to form a
single model sub-system. Certain legal taxes enter more than
one model sub-system and are first split into their model
equivalent forms. An example is excise taxes on hydro-carbon
oil which are treated partly as taxes on consumer purchases
(petrol for final use), and partly as taxes on intermediate
use (petrol for use by producers). A similar treatment is
followed with protective duties. Rates, on the other hand,
are treated solely as a tax on use of capital services by
industry, the domestic rate appearing as a tax on capital
services in both private and local authority housing services.

While the revenue raised by each tax in the model is taken
as the totals appearing in national accounts, this is not
the case with subsidies. This stems from a dissatisfaction
with the national accounts treatment of subsidies which
follows from an adherence in UK accounts to the UN convention of including only cash subsidies. In our opinion,
there is a substantial understatement of local authority
housing subsidies in UK national accounts. These points
reflect those already made by others describing UK data in
this area.[4] The revisions made to national account figures
substantially affect the measure of subsidies for 1973.
National accounts report a total for 1973 of £1.5 billion
in contrast to the figure used here of £5.3 billion.

One further point is that in the UK national accounts a
distinction is made between capital and other taxes; subsidies also appear as both current and capital expenditures.
This distinction has been dispensed with in the model treat-

TABLE 3.1

Components of the 1973 U.K. Tax/Subsidy System: Discriminatory Features and Model Treatment

A. The U.K. Tax System

Tax	Main Features	Treatment in the Model	Tax Collections in 1973[1] (£ mill)
1. Income Tax	Tax on annual incomes of tax units. Important features are large annual deductions, the non-taxation of imputed income of owner-occupied house, and a tax surcharge on investment income.	Ad valorem tax on annual income embodying features referred to in column at left.	7271
2. National Insurance and Related Contributions	Combined employer and employee contributions to 'finance' retirement pensions and other welfare benefits.	Ad valorem tax on labour services used by industry.	3905
3. Specific Excises	Taxes on drink, tobacco, hydrocarbon oil, and minor miscellaneous items such as betting.	Ad valorem taxes on both final consumption and (in the case of hydrocarbon oil) on intermediate usage.	3875
4. Corporation Tax	Tax on company trading profits with (i) deductibility of interest (ii) acceleration of the depreciation provisions	Ad valorem tax on use of capital services by industry	3224
5. Rates	Tax on assessed rental value of both residential and commercial structures	Ad valorem tax on use of capital services by industry.	2617
6. Value Added Tax	Tax on value added at each stage of the production process. Food is 'zero rated' and other commodities zero rated or exempt.	Ad valorem sales tax using effective rates calculated from zero rates and exemptions as they apply to intermediate production.	2155

	Main Features	Treatment in the Model	
7. Motor Vehicle Taxes	Annual registration fee on motor vehicles plus tax on purchase of cars.	Ad valorem tax on intermediate and final purchases of motor vehicles.	626
8. Protective Duties	Tariffs on imported products.	Ad valorem taxes on purchases of intermediate and final use.	429
9. Estate Duty	Tax on the value of estates passing in year.	Treated as part of the income tax system, being 'paid' out of investment income.	420
10. Capital Gains Tax	Tax (at the lower of the basic rate or 1/2 the taxpayer's marginal income tax rate) on net realized gains in the year.	Treated as part of the income tax on investment income.	304
11. Stamp Duty	Registration fee on financial transactions.	Ad valorem tax on both intermediate and final purchases of financial services.	205
12. Total Tax Collection			25,031

B. The U.K. Subsidy System

Subsidy	Main Features	Treatment in the Model	Subsidies Paid in 1973 (£ mill)
1. Local Authority Housing Subsidies	Artificially low rent charged on dwellings provided to council tenants.	Ad valorem consumption subsidy on local authority housing services.	3136
2. Nationalized Industry Subsidies	Cash grants, debt write-off, plus cheap credit facilities.	Ad valorem subsidies on both production and capital use by industry.	1597
3. Agricultural Support Policies	Payments made under annual price guarantee arrangements.	Ad valorem production subsidy to agriculture.	287
4. Regional Employment Premiums	Payment to employers on the basis of the number of employees in manufacturing industry in qualifying regions.	Ad valorem subsidy on use of labour by industry.	114

TABLE 3.1 (cont'd.)

B. The U.K. Subsidy System (cont'd.)

Subsidy	Main Features	Treatment in the Model	Subsidies Paid in 1973[1] (£ mill)
5. Regional Development Grants	Cost shared investment expenditures by manufacturing industries in qualifying regions.	Ad valorem subsidy on use of capital services by industry.	64
6. Miscellaneous Capital	Entry on public sector accounts; miscellaneous research, development and other industry assistance.	Ad valorem subsidy on use of capital services by industry.	83
7. Total Subsidies Paid			5,281
C. Collections of Taxes Less Subsidies			19,750
D. Model Value for NNP at Factor Cost			£69.8 bill.
E. Taxes Less Subsidies as a Percentage of NNP			28.3%

1. The data reported are as they appear in our benchmark data set, and not as they are reported in National Accounts. Some important differences occur, most notably with subsidies. These are explained in Chapter 6.

ment. Capital taxes in the 1973 national accounts include both capital gains taxes and estate duty (since replaced by capital transfer tax). They are treated in the national accounts in this way since they are considered to be paid out of capital and not out of income. In the model they are both treated as taxes on investment income.[5] Subsidies treated as capital expenditures appear as part of general government expenditures and are used by recipients to subsidize use of capital services (chiefly the nationalized industries).

3.2 The 1973 UK Tax System

In this section the structure of each of the major UK taxes is described, and their treatment in the model outlined.[6]

1. Income Taxation

The UK income tax is an annual tax at progressive rates on incomes of 'taxable units'. A taxable unit is either a single individual or a married couple (depending on the circumstances of the household), although a limited amount of income splitting now takes place. Annual tax free allowances are given which vary both by family size (a single person's allowance and an additional special 'married person's' allowance being given along with an allowance for each child depending on age), and the working character- istics of the wife (a wife's earned income allowance being given). Additional deductions besides the personal allow- ances are allowed for mortgage interest payments and one- half of life insurance premiums.

The main feature of the rate structure of the tax is a constant marginal rate bracket (the basic rate), which in the late 1960's and early 1970's covered the majority of income recipients. The basic rate is also the initial mar- ginal tax bracket. In the tax year 1972-73 this rate of (effectively) 30% applied to all taxable incomes up to (approximately[7]) £4,500 and covered 98% of taxable units.[8] Only after this wide initial rate bracket do marginal tax rates begin to increase. The subsequent rise in marginal rates is rapid, in 1977 reaching a top marginal rate of 83% on earned incomes over £20,000 and (also in 1977) 98% on investment income over this amount. The Thatcher government has reduced these top rates quite sharply.[9]

Investment incomes (over £2,000 per year in 1974) are subject to an investment income surcharge of 15% (10% applying on investment incomes from £1,000 to £2,000). In addition, a dividend tax credit has been given since 1973, structured such that an individual in the basic rate bracket pays no further income tax on dividends received (a credit of 3/7ths of dividends received was given in 1974 when the basic rate was 30%, the credit itself being included in the income tax base). As with most countries, the imputed income from owner-occupied housing is not included in the tax base nor are gifts and inheritances received. A separate capital gains tax operates on a realization basis taxing gains at the basic rate or one-half the marginal tax rate, whichever is lower. Capital gains on principal residences and on government bonds are exempt.

In the model, the income tax is treated as the dominant part of a model equivalent income tax system in which income tax, capital gains tax, and estate duty are considered to operate as a single system of personal taxation. Since the income of each household is determined by valuing its ownership of factors (labour and capital) at current factor prices and adding in transfers received, taxable income is calculated by deducting the personal allowances of each household along with other deductible expenses.[10] A 15% surcharge is applied to taxable investment income over £2,000 per household, and the dividend tax credit is also incorporated.

The calculation of taxable income determines the marginal tax rate faced by each household. Where taxable income falls below the exemption level, a zero rate is used. For all other households, a basic marginal rate of 30% is assumed. The average tax rate for each household is derived from FES data on tax payments.[11]

Under this treatment, households face a constant marginal tax rate. This weakens the progression of marginal rates from that in the true system as no household will be in a higher marginal rate bracket if its income rises. Relative

income positions of households may also change as prices
change in the model, but in spite of this, relative marginal
tax rates of households will not vary. The use of the constant marginal tax rate assumption reflects the width of the
basic rate bracket in the UK income tax and the low
thresholds for the top open-ended income ranges in FES data.

Average and marginal tax rates by household are reported
in Table 3.2. Two groups have average tax rates above marginal rates. We maintain the top income ranges with marginal
tax rates of 30% since the small number of households with
marginal rates above 30% do not appear in FES data as a
homogeneous group due to the open-ended top income ranges
used.

2. National Insurance and Related Contributions (Social
   Security)

Like most market type economies, the UK operates a system of
social security taxes, which is loosely tied to benefits
paid to qualifying individuals (retired, unemployed,
disadvantaged). Employers, employees, self-employed persons,
and non-employed persons are liable for contributions to
government operated funds which finance benefits. In the
model all these contributions are treated as ad valorem
taxes on use of labour services by industry.[12] This treatment is somewhat contentious because of the extensive discussion as to whether these contributions are really a tax.
It is frequently argued that, unlike other taxes, there is a
direct quid pro quo involved with these contributions and,
although collected by the government, monies go into a
separate fund out of which payments to beneficiaries are
made.

The treatment as a tax seems to us to be justified for a
number of reasons. Payments are not benefit related in that
any given individual is not actuarially guaranteed to get
back the value of his contributions. Furthermore, contribution levels vary with no change in benefits and benefit
levels change with no change in contributions.

TABLE 3.2

Average and Marginal Income Tax Rates by Household
(Classified using 1973 Family Expenditure Survey (FES) Data)

Household Description (FES Classification)		Percentage Marginal Income Tax Rate t_T^c Used in the Model	Average Tax Rate
Type I	Manual	< £20	0.0	3.2
		£20-30	30.0	11.9
		£30-40	30.0	15.7
		> £40	30.0	17.6
Type I	Non-Manual	< £20	30.0	3.7
		£20-30	30.0	12.6
		£30-40	30.0	15.2
		£40-50	30.0	15.8
		£50-60	30.0	16.4
		£60-70	30.0	23.8
		> £70	30.0	28.7
Type I	Self-Employed	< £20	30.0	5.9
		£20-40	30.0	5.6
		> £40	30.0	16.3
Type I	Retired	< £10	0.0	0.2
		£10-20	0.0	1.6
		£20-30	30.0	7.0
		£30-40	30.0	9.3
		£40-50	30.0	21.5
		> £50	30.0	35.8
Type I	Unoccupied	< £10	0.0	0.0
		£10-20	0.0	1.2
		£20-30	0.0	3.3
		> £30	30.0	26.3
Type II	Manual	< £20	0.0	1.5
		£20-30	30.0	5.7
		£30-40	30.0	10.7
		£40-50	30.0	12.8
		£50-60	30.0	14.8
		£60-70	30.0	15.3
		£70-80	30.0	17.4
		£80-90	30.0	18.8
		> £90	30.0	23.6
Type II	Non-Manual	< £30	30.0	6.8
		£30-40	30.0	9.5
		£40-50	30.0	10.5
		£50-60	30.0	13.6
		£60-70	30.0	13.9
		£70-80	30.0	16.3
		£80-90	30.0	15.7
		£90-100	30.0	18.2
		> £100	30.0	25.1
Type II	Self-Employed	< £20	0.0	0.0
		£20-30	30.0	7.2
		£30-40	30.0	6.8
		£40-50	30.0	8.1
		£50-60	30.0	7.6
		£60-70	30.0	9.6
		£70-90	30.0	9.6
		> £90		

1. 1973 Income Taxes as a percentage of gross household income.

Household Description (FES Classification)			Percentage Marginal Income Tax Rate t_T^c Used in the Model	Average Tax Rate
Type II	Retired	< £20	0.0	0.3
		£20-30	0.0	2.4
		£30-40	30.0	6.8
		£40-50	30.0	10.1
		£50-60	30.0	16.0
		£60-70	30.0	17.7
		£70-90	30.0	20.5
		> £90	30.0	42.9
Type II	Unoccupied	< £20	0.0	0.0
		£20-30	30.0	1.7
		£30-40	30.0	6.6
		£40-60	30.0	11.6
		> £60	30.0	22.0
Type III	Manual	< £30	30.0	2.1
		£30-40	30.0	5.3
		£40-50	30.0	9.6
		£50-60	30.0	11.0
		£60-70	30.0	12.3
		£70-80	30.0	13.2
		£80-90	30.0	13.5
		£90-100	30.0	14.8
		> £100	30.0	16.1
Type III	Non-Manual	< £40	30.0	5.6
		£40-50	30.0	9.0
		£50-60	30.0	10.1
		£60-70	30.0	11.9
		£70-80	30.0	13.2
		£80-90	30.0	14.4
		£90-100	30.0	15.2
		> £100	30.0	19.8
Type III	Self-Employed	< £30	0.0	0.0
		£30-40	30.0	3.3
		£40-50	30.0	4.7
		£50-60	30.0	5.6
		£60-70	30.0	7.1
		£70-80	30.0	7.2
		£80-90	30.0	10.3
		£90-100	30.0	10.0
		> £100	30.0	16.3
Type III	Retired	< £30	0.0	1.2
		£30-40	30.0	4.0
		£40-50	30.0	9.5
		£50-60	30.0	9.4
		£60-70	30.0	10.4
		£70-80	30.0	12.4
		> £80	30.0	16.3
Type III	Unoccupied	< £30	0.0	0.0
		£30-40	0.0	0.0
		£40-60	30.0	6.8
		> £60	30.0	14.9

The model treatment of these contributions as <u>ad valorem</u> taxes on the use of labour services by industry reflects a characterization of national insurance and related contributions as a payroll tax. The effects of these taxes on intertemporal allocation are not modelled although they are heavily stressed in recent journal literature (see Feldstein [1974]). We have no later model extension capturing the intertemporal substitution between private savings and anticipated future social security receipts.

A further point is that the <u>ad valorem</u> treatment is not wholly appropriate since age and sex characteristics affect contributions, and different contribution levels are set for self-employed persons. As the composition of the labour force and degree of incorporation changes by industry, so will the tax rate which these contributions represent. Our treatment of these contributions allows the inter-industry distortions produced to be analyzed under the assumption that the composition of the labour force by industry does not change as other taxes in the model vary. As can be seen from Table 5.4 in Chapter 5, the industry differentials involved are small compared to other components of the tax system. Even though these mild distortions apply to a major portion of the factor inputs of the whole economy, they nonetheless produce distortionary costs which are small in comparison with the rest of the tax/subsidy system.

3. Specific Excises

Specific excise taxes in the UK are heavily concentrated on three major groups of products - tobacco, drink, and hydrocarbon oils - although some other less important duties (such as betting duty) also exist. In aggregate they account for a significant portion of total tax receipts. In the past these taxes have had bases defined in terms of physical characteristics (weight, volume, specific gravity, moisture content, etc.). Within these broad groups a substantial diversity of treatment exists (beer, wines and spirits, for instance, are differentially taxed and further variations occur within these sub-groups). More recently, a process of 'ad valorization' of these taxes has been initiated in response to EEC directives reflecting moves to harmonize indirect taxes in the EEC.

In the model these taxes are all treated as _ad valorem_ taxes paid on purchases of taxed products. Both intermediate and final purchases of goods are taxed. Identical rates are used for comparable domestically produced and imported items. The tax rates used in the model for these items are large and severely discriminatory. These large rates pose a special difficulty with the modelling of consumer response to a hypothetical removal of the distortions these taxes introduce. As the model uses demand functions derived from continuously substitutable utility functions, substantial increases in the consumption of drink and tobacco are obtained if these taxes are removed and large welfare gains accrue from the removal of the distortions. The strength of the substitution effect for such a large price change must remain uncertain and in the discussion of results this feature is stressed.

Further complications arise with the interpretation of these taxes simply as distorting taxes rather than as congestion, externality correcting, or benefit related taxes. The high tax on hydrocarbon oils (which we model as sharply distortionary) can be partially or wholly justified as a congestion or road use tax. Equally, high taxes on tobacco and drink can be defended as externality based taxes reflecting the marginal costs of extra tobacco consumption to non-smokers and the marginal costs to non-drinkers of increased alcohol consumption. These features are excluded from our model but should be borne in mind in interpreting the significant welfare costs of these distorting taxes which our results produce.

A similar treatment to that used for excise taxes is adopted for customs duties. These were also based on physical characteristics of products prior to the adoption of the EEC common external tariff on entry to Europe, but are modelled in terms of _ad valorem_ equivalents. Customs duties cover a wider range of commodities than the specific excises and apply to imports for both final and intermediate uses.

4. Corporation Tax

Corporation tax is a flat rate annual tax on the trading and other profits of UK companies. In the model corporate taxes are treated as ad valorem taxes paid on the value of capital services used by various industries. This involves the calculation of effective tax rates derived from tax payments by industry and uses an assumption common in much of the corporate tax literature (Harberger [1959, 1962, 1966] and the literature which follows) that average and marginal tax rates are the same within each industry.[13] Lightly incorporated industries pay smaller amounts of corporation tax and have lower ad valorem tax rates on capital service inputs than heavily incorporated industries. This treatment ignores all complications that arise from the interaction between corporate taxes and financial policies of firms.

Since 1973 an imputation system has operated under which shareholders receiving dividends also get a fractional dividend tax credit. This imputes through to shareholders a portion of the corporate tax paid. The credit is structured so that shareholders in the basic income tax rate bracket pay no further tax. The income tax in the model includes the dividend tax credit, but this treatment does not fully capture the interindustry effects which the credit causes. A further feature of the current system is advanced corporation tax, also introduced in 1973, which accelerates the payment of corporation tax relative to earlier pre-1973 arrangements. Although this tax is important for the external sector it is regarded here solely as a withholding tax and is not explicitly included in the model.

The tax treatment of depreciation and stock appreciation introduce additional features of industrial differentiation in the model equivalent tax rates beyond that implied simply by the existence of the corporate tax. The treatment of stock appreciation in particular produces high effective tax rates. Over the years depreciation allowances in the UK have become progressively more generous in the acceleration they allow relative to true depreciation. In recent years 100% first year depreciation has been allowed for expenditures on plant and machinery and 40% on structures. The economic

measure of the tax base used in the model from which effective tax rates are calculated allows deductibility only for
true depreciation, and the differential effects of these
acceleration provisions across industries are captured.

Before December 1974 under the stock appreciation
provisions nominal capital gains on inventory holdings were
taxed on an accrual basis. In calendar year 1974 approximately 50% of (tax definition) trading profits of companies
were accounted for by stock appreciation alone.[14] This led
to a change in the law under which a ceiling of 10% was
placed on the ratio of taxable profits from this source to
total taxable profits. Because stock appreciation is treated
here as a purely inflationary capital gain, it is not
included in the tax base used to calculate effective rates
(the value of capital services used by industry) but the
taxes paid appear in the numerator. This raises effective
capital tax rates above legal rates in some cases, and we
consider the alternative treatment of removing those taxes
on inflationary gains as a variation on our central case
analysis in the results reported later. This treatment also
makes our effective corporate tax rates dependent on the
inflation rate. Furthermore, the stock relief provisions
which have operated since 1974 have sharply reduced
effective tax rates. Once again, it is important to
emphasize that our data are not directly applicable to current corporate tax distortions in the UK.

With the corporate tax, more so than with any other tax in
the model, the model assumption of constant and equal
average and marginal tax rates is open to criticism. Our
treatment ignores all complications that arise from the
interaction between corporate taxes and financial policies
of firms. This follows the treatment assumed in Harberger
(1962) but ignores much of the more recent literature on the
corporate tax. This stresses that under the corporate tax
interest payments are deductible from the tax base, and
companies will typically choose a debt-equity ratio which
minimizes the sum of shareholders' personal taxes and corporation taxes subject to other constraints given by the
risk of bankruptcy or takeover. Retention of profits with an

anticipated capital gain resulting from invested funds may also be advantageous to shareholders in high marginal income tax brackets. Changes in the corporate tax rate will thus typically give companies incentives to reorganize their financial structure, and a correct accounting for this would require an adjustment to measured marginal tax rates.[15]

Little of this literature can be directly integrated into the general equilibrium approach used here since financial policies of corporations do not appear. The model is thus to be interpreted as assuming that corporate financial policies of firms are unchanged as tax rates vary, and the equality of average and marginal tax rates holds. For any change considered in the legal structure of the tax we recalculate the model equivalent average and marginal tax rates which are then used in place of existing values.

In our calculations reported later, the corporate tax appears as one of the major sources of distortion in the tax system. A significant portion of the welfare cost we report reflects our treatment of stock appreciation, and we emphasize this in our later discussion of model results.

5. Rates

Rates are the UK form of property tax used to finance local government expenditures (along with central government grants). They are an annual tax on all property based on assessed annual letting values of property (not on the capital market values of assets as used in most countries). All property is covered with the exception of churches and agricultural buildings, and a differential treatment applies to domestic and non-domestic property.

In the model rates are treated as ad valorem taxes paid by industries on use of capital services. Both private and local authorities' housing service industries pay domestic rates on capital service use; other industries pay commercial rates. Industries intensive in structures in their capital use (such as retail and wholesale trade) thus have higher ad valorem tax rates on capital services than other industries, and industrial differentiation in model equivalent tax rates on capital use enters through this feature.

Lags and errors in assessments of rental values also cause differentiation by industry.

Whether it is more appropriate to treat property taxes as taxes on profits (as done here) or as excise taxes on the sale of services of structures has been extensively debated in recent years.[16] As the data used in the model do not satisfactorily identify industrial use of structures from other physical assets, the excise tax treatment seems to us less satisfactory for our purposes.

6. Value-Added Tax (VAT)

The value-added tax (which has operated in the UK since Britain joined the EEC in 1973) is a tax on value added at each stage of production. In broad terms, producers are taxable on the gross value of sales but are able to claim as a credit taxes paid on intermediate inputs. The introduction of VAT is a European response to the problems of cascade (or turnover) taxes which existed in most Western European states (but not the UK) in the period immediately after the second world war. One attraction of VAT is that a broadly based single rate VAT in a closed competitive economy is equivalent to a broadly based single rate sales tax. The tax is often projected as an administratively preferable way of operating a sales tax. The tax is sometimes supported as being easier to collect than a retail sales tax due to the concentration of large producers at early stages in the production process. There is also greater flexibility in exempting producers from the tax than is the case with traditional sales taxes,[17] and it can be operated on an origin basis, while the sales tax cannot.[18] There are also administrative arguments against the VAT which we do not go into here.

In practice the tax in the UK, as in all European countries, is neither broadly based nor charged at a single rate. There is also an important difference in the UK compared to other West European countries in the way in which commodities are 'removed' from the VAT system. Two methods are used, known as 'exempting' and 'zero rating'. A 'zero rated' commodity has a zero VAT rate on its sale but still qualifies for a rebate of taxes paid on inputs; 'exempt' commodities are entirely removed from the tax system and are not eligible for a tax rebate. In the UK food (importantly) is zero rated, and a number of financial transactions are exempt. A further feature of VAT is the treatment of the external sector: in the UK tax the destination basis is currently used and taxes are rebated on exports but imports are taxed.[19]

In the model, VAT is treated as an ad valorem tax on final sales because of the complexities in explicitly modelling all of the features of the tax as it applies to intermediate transactions. Exports are free of tax, and the tax is applied to imports for final' use. Effective tax rates are calculated using the input-output data from the model assuming producers are taxed on the portion of sales neither zero-rated nor exempt, with a rebate being given on the portion of taxes paid on inputs corresponding to the non-exempt output of the producer. A special 10% car tax was introduced in 1973 along with VAT to make good a revenue loss from the removal of the existing purchase tax on cars. This tax enters the model directly as an ad valorem sales tax on motor vehicles and is not included in the calculation of effective commodity tax rates implied by VAT.

Only limited differentiation in effective commodity tax rates occurs compared to distortions elsewhere in the tax system and only mild distortionary costs are encountered.

7. Other Taxes

In addition to the taxes discussed above, there are a number of smaller taxes which enter the model. Motor vehicle licence duties and stamp duties are both modelled as ad valorem equivalent expenditure taxes. Only expenditures on new vehicles enter the model, and no imputation is made for the value of the consumption stream of existing owned vehicles (unlike the case of home ownership). In treating the licence tax as an ad valorem tax on vehicles, the assumption is that new purchases constitute the same fraction of the stock of vehicles used for each industry and consumer group. Stamp duty is also included in the model and

treated as an <u>ad valorem</u> tax on purchases of financial services. Capital gains tax and estate duty are discussed under
the section on income taxation.

3.3 The 1973 UK Subsidy System

In addition to the tax system, we also capture the distorting effects of subsidies in the model. Unlike taxes, subsidies generally have no legislative form from which clear
definitions of components of a UK subsidy system naturally
follow. The official concept of a subsidy which appears in
National Accounts follows from a UN convention which is not
adequate for the model.[20] Each of the subsidy elements is
treated in <u>ad valorem</u> form and affects relative prices of
commodities. The list is as follows:

1. <u>Local Authority Housing subsidies</u>. This item covers the
subsidization of council tenancies (preferences towards
owner-occupiers are captured in the model treatment of the
tax system). They are calculated as an <u>ad valorem</u> subsidy on
purchases of the services of council housing. We impute a
rate of return to the capitalized value of the stock of
council houses, subtract payment of rent and rates by
tenants and divide by the value of the service flow. Our
treatment abstracts from the complex procedure of allocation
of council tenancies by queue (a system of quantity constraints). Also, we do not incorporate the reduced regional
mobility of labour which the limited transferability of
tenancies causes.

Our measure of the subsidy produces a figure substantially
larger than that reported in the Housing Subsidies Account
in the UK National Accounts[21], and this largely explains why
our welfare cost estimate for this subsidy is so large. The
National Accounts subsidy figure is £446 million in 1973,
whereas the figure used here is £3136 million. The details
of the way this latter figure has been calculated are given
in Chapter 5, but the source of this large discrepancy is
that the national accounts calculate these subsidies largely
using historical rather than replacement cost data. The
national accounts calculation essentially takes the dif-

ference between rent receipts and maintenance and interest charges on loans of local authorities for housing finance.[22] In our view, this is inappropriate not only because some houses are owned outright by local authorities, but because substantial capital gains have accrued on much of the local authority housing stock since its original purchase. A more reasonable calculation of the subsidy seems to us to involve taking the difference between receipts of controlled rents by local authorities and the rentals which could have been obtained in a free market (reflecting the opportunity cost to local authorities of artificially low rents). This approach is followed in developing the subsidy estimates used in the model. Through this use of the data, local authority housing subsidies become the largest of the subsidies examined here.

2. Nationalized industry subsidies. In the model these subsidies comprise cash payments to Nationalized Industries along with the subsidy elements inherent in debt written off and cheap credit available to Nationalized Industries because of their ability to borrow under government guarantee. Each of these components is separately estimated and differently treated in the model. Of all the components of the subsidy system, it is in this area that the most difficulty is encountered with data (which are in places very poor). Furthermore, the situation for 1973 discussed here has changed substantially in recent years with increased pressures on nationalized industries to cover costs.

Aggregate cash payments to Nationalized Industries are given on a yearly basis in the National Accounts,[23] and individual industry figures have been obtained from unpublished worksheets provided by the C.S.O. These payments are treated as ad valorem output subsidies to these industries.

The writing-off of debt is a more complex matter. The conceptual basis for valuing the subsidy component involved is to take the discounted present value (at the point the loan is granted) of the expected write-off of any loan made, after allowing for the cheap interest element. An accurate estimate of the subsidy element on this basis can only be obtained by tracing the complete history of all nationalized industry financial transactions on an industry by industry basis as the interest rate paid on loans by nationalized industries differs both over time and between industries. This involves going to the individual accounts of Nationalized Industries, and even in these accounts the necessary financial information is only available on an incomplete basis. Even if this information was available, this procedure would make the choice of a particular year unduly critical as individual industry loan write-offs show substantial variation over time.

The procedure which is adopted is to take the real value of debt written-off (in 1973 prices) over the eleven year period 1963-73 by industry, and to take one-eleventh of this figure as the annual subsidy estimate for that industry. This overestimates subsidies to the extent that the differential in interest paid from commercial rates prior to write-off is ignored, and underestimates subsidies to the extent that there has been a tendency for write-offs to increase over the time period considered. Government subscriptions to "Public Dividend Capital" (over the same eleven year period) are treated as debt written off since no dividends have ever been paid on these equity holdings.[24]

The calculation of the subsidy element received by nationalized industries in the form of cheap credit involves determining the structure of indebtedness of nationalized industries and estimating the reduction obtained on an 'appropriate' market interest rate both as a result of the government guarantee to the loan and any additional cheap interest element involved. The one-year debt position of nationalized industries classified by industrial type can be obtained from published sources[25] and these figures cover both loans make by the National Loans Fund and government guaranteed stock issues of public corporations. These figures exclude components of the National Debt which refer to original public corporation issues which have since been consolidated into the National Debt, either due to an organizational change or a write-off of public corporation indebtedness; some allowance is made for these.

Estimating the differential between the rate at which public corporations can borrow under government guarantee (or from the National Loans Fund) and the commercial rate at which Nationalized Industries could borrow in the absence of guarantee is a difficult matter. This differential should vary by industry, although no figures exist which enable this to be estimated. Given that some nationalized industries made losses for a number of years, one would think that private capital markets would not lend them funds even at sharply higher interest rates, and the value of the government guarantee itself is worth more than any small reduction in interest rates from those charged to large profitable corporations. The converse argument is that nationalized industries do not exercise their full monopoly power as would similarly placed private firms, and that price restraint dictated by government causes losses. Freed of these restraints loans could be serviced from current revenue. All this makes the choice of an interest differential very difficult. Even though there are grounds for believing this differential varies by industry a common figure of 2% has been adopted.[26]

There are two alternative treatments of subsidy payments to nationalized industries which can be claimed and which the model does not capture and these should be made clear. Firstly, if nationalized industries are viewed as natural monopolies which are subject to increasing returns to scale, subsidies can be interpreted as lump sum payments to compensate for the losses which result from government directed marginal cost pricing. Our model treats all industries as facing constant returns to scale since general equilibrium models incorporating scale economies are not yet developed to the point where they can be used for the policy evaluations considered here. Secondly, a portion of government payments to nationalized industries in the period 1973-74 represent explicit compensation for government restrictions on pricing policies of these industries.[27] The model assumes that producers maximize profits unhindered by price controls and receive ad valorem subsidies whatever prices are charged or whatever quantity is produced.

3. <u>Regional subsidies</u>. Both Regional Development Grants and
Regional Employment Premiums operating in 1973 are included
in the model as <u>ad valorem</u> subsidies; Development Grants as
capital subsidies and Employment Premiums as subsidies to
labour. Regional Development Grants are a cost-sharing programme of central government under which a fraction of
investment expenditures by firms in qualifying regions are
paid by the central government. Regional employment premiums
are payments on a per employee basis made to manufacturing
firms in qualifying regions.

Both of these subsidies, in aggregate, are small but to
the extent that certain recipient industries tend to be
regionally concentrated, they have the effect of being paid
on a differential basis by industry. Regions are not
separately identified in the model and this indirect treatment of regional policy is all the model, as currently con-
stituted, will allow. Information on receipts by industry
under these schemes is difficult to obtain and some approximation is necessary with the data used.

4. <u>Agricultural subsidies</u>. These subsidies are payments to
farmers made by central government under price guarantee
arrangements. These arrangements have changed since the
period covered by the model due to British entry into the
EEC. In aggregate these sums are small but they directly
affect one industry and are therefore potentially significant. Some year by year volatility occurs in this subsidy
and our analysis is therefore sensitive to the choice of
year.

In addition to the above, there are a number of features
of government policies, often referred to as 'subsidies',
which are not considered as such by the model. Many of these
are features of the tax policies which appear in the model
and thus require no further treatment. Important elements in
this category are 'subsidies' to homeownership through the
non-taxation of imputed income, 'subsidies' to corporations
through accelerated depreciation, 'subsidies' to food
through their zero-rating for VAT purposes, and 'subsidies'

to life insurance through the deductibility of one-half of life insurance premiums.[28]

Additional features not considered in the model are food subsidies, which did not operate for the period considered in the model, and 'subsidies' through publicly provided services (e.g., free roads being a 'subsidy' to road transportation).

3.4 The Treatment of Public Sector Expenditures

Although the primary objective of the model is to analyze the effects of the UK tax/subsidy system on resource allocation and distribution, a treatment has to be adopted in the model for the expenditures which the net receipts of the tax/subsidy system finance. Furthermore, taxes and subsidies do not comprise the only financing instruments of government, as debt financing is available as a substitute for tax financing.

The combined UK public authorities are treated in the model as making both real expenditures and transfers. The real expenditures reflect the provision of particular goods and services to the personal and corporate sectors of the economy, such as national defence, education, health and social services, maintenance of highways, police and fire protection, and judicial services. Government expenditures on capital account, such as the construction of highways, are also included.

These activities appear through public sector expenditures on commodities for the provision of these goods and services. Purchases of primary factor services (capital and labour services) by the public sector along with commodity purchases are treated as inputs into the production of a single public good for which there is no direct articulation of demands. The valuation of the output of the public good is determined as in the national accounts by the value of inputs. The composition of these inputs is determined from a public sector utility function which is maximized subject to a budget constraint given by the receipts not transferred to persons, plus income from publicly owned assets. In an extension to our basic variant model, described in Chapter

9, we also consider a model formulation in which public goods enter household utility functions. Households are charged lump sum taxes and government production is such that the sum over households of the marginal rate of substitution between public and private goods equals the marginal rate of transformation.

Transfer payments from the public sector to the private sector also enter the expenditure side of government and are substantial (£6.2 billion in 1973). The largest of these are payments made under the general heading of social security of which the majority are old age pensions. Other payments include unemployment and illness benefits, maternity supplementary assistance, and other similar payments. Interest payments on public sector debt are included as transfers as are a number of grants-in-aid made to the personal sector which are related to specific activities (such as student scholarships, and grants towards the improvement of substandard housing). Quantitatively, grants-in-aid are small.

All of these transfer payments are treated in the model as fixed distributions of total government receipts to individual household groups. The figures for these transfers are derived from Family Expenditure Survey data and are discussed more fully in Chapter 5. These transfers are treated as fixed proportions of total government revenues even though under some tax proposals considered by the model net of tax incomes of households may change substantially and eligibility for some transfers may end (or start). As modelled, transfers have no marginal effects and are not distorting, although for low income households income related transfers can produce high implicit tax rates. We consider one case in which high tax rates on low income groups are used to reflect this.

Non-tax receipts of government fall into two classes. As with households, the public sector is treated as receiving substantial imputed income from owned assets (structures and equipment, including military equipment). This income is used to buy the factor services which these assets provide. This has the effect of increasing both government receipts and expenditures from figures reported in National Accounts.[29]

The public sector also receives funds from the private sector as a result of net borrowing through the sale of bonds (net of redemptions). Bond issues are treated in the model as a resource transfer from the private to the public sector. The current income transferred to the public sector in practice, is made in return for the anticipated future income stream which government bonds offer, although this process is not captured in our model.

3.5 An Initial Overview of the Impact of the 1973 UK Tax/Subsidy System

Even though the model discussed here is used numerically to calculate the microeconomic impact of UK tax and subsidy policies, the particular treatments adopted both for individual taxes and subsidies and for the production and demand structure of the economy imply that a number of prominent features of our results can be anticipated prior to results being reported. It would be misleading to disguise the model dependence of some of our numerical results reported later, even though attempts have been made to assess sensitivity of the findings to model structure as well as numerical values of parameters. Before reporting general equilibrium calculations of the effects of these policies, a brief guide to some of these significant features is therefore helpful.

In broad terms, the legal components of the UK tax/subsidy system have been grouped into four model tax/subsidy subsystems. There are taxes and subsidies on factor inputs (capital and labour) differentiated by industry; industry producer taxes and subsidies on both outputs and intermedite usage of other industries' outputs; consumer taxes and subsidies on commodity expenditures; and taxes on household incomes.

Table 3.3 provides an overview of the major distortions in the tax/subsidy system on a highly aggregated basis. We examine the tax system in terms of its component parts as taxes on capital, labour, output and incomes.

In the capital tax system the heavy taxes on manufacturing industry are clearly displayed. As noted earlier in this chapter, this is to some extent a reflection of the par-

ticular year's data chosen. The negative tax rate for agricultural resources reflects the nationalized industry subsidies which accrue to the coal industry. The labour taxes
incorporate only small tax rate differentials across industries. Within the factor tax system, the major distortion
occurs with differential capital taxes between manufacturing
and other industries.

In the output tax system, major distortions occur with
excisable items (drink, tobacco and gasoline) and subsidies
to local authority housing. These distortions are large and,
given that in a partial equilibrium calculation the welfare
cost of a distortion varies with the square of the tax rate,
these distortions are likely candidates to be important
sources of welfare loss, a suggestion confirmed by our calculations reported later.

Within the income tax, average rates vary across the
household groups. A sample from the hundred household groups
identified in the model is reported in Table 3.3 and the
marginal tax rates used for these groups are also reported.
As previously mentioned, the structure of the UK income tax
is such that the large majority of taxpayers face a constant
marginal tax rate with only a small proportion of taxpayers
paying rates above the standard rate of 30%. We are unable
to identify such households within the groups that we work
with in our data.

The picture of the tax system which emerges from Table 3.3
is thus one of distorting capital taxes in the factor tax
system, sharply distorting output taxes and subsidies with
two items being particularly important - the excisable items
and local authority housing services - and an income tax
which has a number of features which are less readily
apparent as to their impacts.

TABLE 3.3

Aggregated Summary of Model Equivalent Tax Rates Used
to Represent 1973 U.K. Tax System

Factor Tax System

Percentage Tax Rates on Net of Tax Factor Rewards

Industry[1]	Capital Taxes[2]	Labour Taxes[3]
Agricultural and Resources	-8.3	8.7
Manufacturing	149.5	9.2
Construction Utilities, Services	29.5	8.7
Housing Services	14.6	6.1

Income Tax System

A Sample of Consumer Groups in the Model[5]	Average Tax Rates on Gross Income	Marginal Tax Rate Assumed
"Rich" (Non-Manual 2 person household, weekly income > £100 in 1973)	25.1	30.0
"Middle Income" (Manual 2 person household, weekly income > £30, < £40 in 1973)	12.8	30.0
"Poor" (Retired, 1 person, weekly income < £10 in 1973	0.2	0.0

1. These are aggregated over the categories appearing in Table 2.1
2. Corporate and Property taxes plus some nationalized industry
   subsidies.
3. Social security taxes plus some regional subsidies to labour.
4. Excises, VAT, plus subsidies.
5. The model considers 100 household types with a three way
   stratification by income, family size, and family characteristics.

Output Tax System

Percentage Tax Rates on Net of Tax Expenditures

Commodity Category	Output Taxes[4]
Food	0.9
Drink, Tobacco, Gasoline	137.0
Local Authority Housing Services	-78.0
Other	10.7

Model Also Incorporates the Following Features of the Personal Income Tax:

  (i)   imputed income on owner occupied housing accrues tax free;

 (ii)   expenditures on leisure from 'expanded' income (including leisure income)(discussed in Chapter 10);

(iii)   dividend tax credit and investment income surcharge;

 (iv)   tax distortion of savings (discussed in Chapter 10).

3.6 Developments in UK Taxes and Subsidies between 1973 and 1980

In our model we use data for 1973 to generate model parameters and effective tax rates. This was the latest year
available for much of our data at the time of model construction. We have not updated our data set to a more recent
year due to the volume of work involved and limited
resources. In this section, however, we provide an indication of major developments in tax/subsidy policies in the
UK since 1973, and indicate how our model might be modified
were these developments to be incorporated.

In Table 3.4 we outline the major developments in tax
policy in the UK between 1973 and 1980. It is important to
note that other policies (in particular expenditure patterns
and subsidies) were simultaneously changing. Nonetheless,
Table 3.4 provides an outline of the major developments
which are of relevance to our model. The main implications
can be summarized as follows:

1. Changes in the balance between direct and indirect
taxation. Over the period 1973 to 1980 there have been
noticeable changes in the balance between direct and indirect taxation. Under the Labour governments from 1974
through to 1979 the effect of increases in marginal tax
rates in the income tax system combined with inflation substantially increased the fraction of total taxes collected
through the income tax. This has been sharply reversed by
the Thatcher government in the 1979 and 1980 budgets, with
cuts in marginal income tax rates and an increase in the
value-added tax rate to 15%.

2. The role of VAT. Since its introduction in 1973 the
value-added tax has first expanded into a multiple rate tax
and then changed sharply under the Thatcher government into
a more substantial revenue raising tax. This somewhat
changes the perception of the value-added tax which comes
out of our calculations.

TABLE 3.4

Outline of Developments in U.K.
Tax Subsidy Policy Since 1973

1974   VAT rate cut to 8% - income tax basic rate raised to
            33% with top marginal tax rate on earned income of
            83% (on unearned income of 98%) - personal allowances
            in income tax increased - change in stock appreciation
            treatment in corporate tax - increase in employer
            contributions in national insurance

1975   Higher rate VAT on 'luxuries' of 25% - income tax basic
            rate raised to 35% - personal allowances in income tax
            raised - petroleum revenue tax rate (PRT) set at 45%
            - wealth tax announced but not introduced - annual
            licence fee on cars raised to £40 - employer contri-
            butions to national insurance raised - development
            land tax introduced

1976   Increase in allowances in the income tax - increase in
            excises on hydrocarbon oil, tobacco, and drink - annual
            licence fee on cars raised to £50

1977   Basic rate of income tax lowered to 34% - allowances
            raised in income tax - excises raised - new national
            insurance surcharge system introduced

1978   Basic rate of income tax lowered to 33% - allowances
            raised in income tax - rate of petroleum revenue tax
            raised to 60% - national insurance surcharge raised
            - 'luxury item' VAT rate cut to 12 1/2%

1979   Sharp cut in marginal tax rates in income tax - basic
            rate 30% (25% on first £750) top marginal tax rate
            on earned income of 60% - VAT raised to 15%

1980   Abolition of 25% rate band in income tax - increase in
            personal allowances in income tax - rate of PRT increased
            to 70% - increase in excises - annual car licence raised
            to £60

3.   The reduced significance of corporate taxes. With
expensing for plant and machinery expenditures and the stock
relief provisions of 1974 collections of corporate taxes are
currently a much smaller fraction of revenues than in 1973.
Distorting costs of the tax fall significantly since many
firms face a zero marginal corporate tax rate.

4.   The development of new taxes. Since 1973 three new taxes
have been developed. The petroleum revenue tax (PRT),
potentially a large revenue raiser in the 1980s, has been
introduced to tax rents on North Sea oil. In addition a
development land tax was introduced by the Labour government, along with a new system of surcharges on national
insurance contributions. These new taxes in total do not
currently constitute a major fraction of revenue and leave
the fundamental structure of the tax system largely
unchanged, although PRT will grow in importance through the
1980s.

5.   Developments in subsidy policy. Although not listed in
Table 3.4, two major developments in subsidy policies occurred in the 1970s. Firstly, under the Labour governments of
the middle 1970s, an attempt was made to reduce the cash
payments to nationalized industries and a phasing out of
nationalized industry subsidies occurred with a resulting
increase in the prices of services provided. This suggests
that our calculations overestimate the welfare cost of current nationalized industry subsidies. Simultaneously subsidies to local authority houses increased in the 1970's.
This follows from a number of attempts to freeze the rents
paid on local authority houses in nominal terms during
periods of rapid inflation.

   Lastly we note that all of our later calculations of welfare cost are presented as monetary magnitudes in £1973 ,
which in turn can be related to fractions of NNP making our
estimates reasonably transferable as an input into current
policy formulation.

Notes

1. See Mieszkowski [1972] and Aaron [1975].
2. See Harberger [1962], [1966], and Stiglitz [1973], [1976].
3. See Brittain [1973], Barro [1974].
4. See Prest [1974, 1975].
5. This may seem an unlikely treatment for estate duty. While any single household experiencing a family death could not necessarily meet estate duty out of current income, this is not true for the aggregated consumer groups considered in the model. The payment of this tax by all members of a group may be interpreted as an annual ex-ante tax (on account) based on the average current investment income of members of the group.
6. A more lengthy treatment of the tax system which takes up many conceptual issues glossed over here appears in the recent book by Kay and King [1978].
7. The word 'approximately' is inserted because up to 1973-74 the UK income tax consisted of two taxes, an income tax at a single rate and a progressive surtax. Liability for surtax in 1972-73 began at £3,000 but an additional earnings allowance was given for surtax (but not income tax) of the excess of earned income over £3,000 subject to a maximum of £2,000. To further complicate matters, the earnings allowance was calculated on earned income after reduction by earned income relief (a 2/9ths reduction up to a maximum of approximately £9,000). The starting point for surtax liability therefore depended on the composition of income as well as its amount.
8. Inland Revenue Statistics 1975 (HMSO), p.4.
9. The top marginal tax rate on earned income is now 60%.
10. Credits were calculated as 3/7ths of dividends, derived from the National Income and Expenditure Blue Book (NIBB), 1963-73, Table 32. The resulting £751 million is split between households using FES dividend receipts as weights. Investment income subject to surcharge was allocated according to Inland Revenue Statistics, to

income groups whose incomes are above £40 per week.
Aggregate personal capital gains tax liabilities were
calculated from NIBB 1963-73, Tables 29 and 49, and
were split between households in the model using unpublished IRS survey data. Aggregate estate duty liabilities were taken from NIBB 1963-73, Table 69. This
amount was split among households using data from
Atkinson and Harrison (1978) and Inland Revenue
Statistics.

11. The imputed income from ownership of dwellings is part
of the capital income of households, and 'expenditures'
on owner-occupied housing services are allowed as a tax
deduction as are one-half of payments of life insurance
premia (which are deductible only at the basic rate).
In practice, this last deduction is subject to an upper
limit of one-sixth of taxable income although this is
assumed not to be binding on any household.

12. Contributions by non-employed persons are small and are
distributed across industries proportionally with all
other types of contributions.

13. More recent literature has sharply challenged this
treatment, however. See Fullerton and Gordon [1981],
King [1974], Stiglitz [1973], and Flemming [1976].

14. National Income and Expenditure 1964-74, Table 32,
p.37.

15. Stiglitz [1973], for instance, has constructed a model
of a single firm which he has used to argue that the
corporation tax can be considered to be lump sum tax.
While firms face zero marginal taxes, their average tax
rates are positive. See, in addition, King [1974],
Stiglitz [1976], and Flemming [1976].

16. See Mieszkowski [1972]. The treatment as a tax on
capital inputs by industry corresponds to what Aaron
[1975] has termed the 'new view' on property taxation.

17. A traditional problem of sales taxes is the cascading
of the tax if producer goods are taxable. For some
goods it is difficult to distinguish between producer
and consumer purchases on the basis of the characteristics of the good alone. VAT, in taxing transactions,

allows for more flexibility in rebating the tax to producers even though the purchase of the same good for final consumption purposes is taxed.

18. This is basically the argument of the Neumark Committee [1963] which recommended VAT as a harmonization objective in the EEC. The argument is that an origin based tax is desirable to eliminate fiscal barriers (border posts at which taxes on exports are rebated, and taxes charged on imports); and that a retail sales tax on an origin basis is a contradiction. The VAT in the EEC will ultimately operate on the so-called 'restricted origin principle', with the origin principle applying for internal EEC trade between member countries and the destination principle for trade between member and non-member states.

19. Harmonization in the EEC calls eventually for an origin basis for internal EEC trade and a destination basis for extra EEC trade. The time-table for such a scheme has been delayed substantially from the original objective of 1978.

20. See Prest [1974]. The UN convention refers primarily to payments of cash and excludes such things as cheap government guaranteed credit, non-collection of (a fraction of) rental income on government-owned structures occupied by others, write-offs of debt owed to government, and other transactions.

21. National Income and Expenditure 1964-74, Table 54, p.60.

22. See Rita Maurice, op.cit., p. 312.

23. National Income and Expenditure 1963-73, Table 34.

24. The principal data source on debt write-offs are the National Accounts (NIBB 1963-73, Table 40). Estimates of Public Dividend Capital subscriptions are reported in the Annual Abstract, 1974, pp.334 ff.

25. Annual Abstract of Statistics 1974, p.34 ff.

26. This is to some extent supported by the notes to the 1973 issues of the Bank of England Quarterly Bulletin (Notes to the Statistical Annex to Table 27) which state that nationalized industries borrow at $\frac{1}{2}$% - 1%

above base rate, whereas commercial companies borrow at
1%-5% above depending on the nature of borrowing.

27. The term 'compensation for price restraint' is one that
appears in the nationalized industry accounts in the
National Income and Expenditure blue book. If other
types of government action are also taken into account
one can argue that transfers in the opposite direction
could be justified. For example, quotas on coal in the
UK represent a substantial government price support in
favour of the domestic coal industry.

28. These are all examples of so-called 'tax expenditures',
deviations from a broadly based tax system. The treatment of these as subsidies assumes that a broadly based
tax system is desirable and deviations from it are
subsidies to groups receiving the tax preferences. Much
of the work on tax expenditures follows Surrey [1973];
in the US there is now an annual requirement of
official publication of a tax expenditure budget.

29. It can be argued that it is misleading to consider
these transactions in the model as it amounts to the
public sector renting out their assets period by period
to themselves, and this activity diminishes the response in factor prices which the model will yield for
tax changes. On the other hand, to ignore these assets
understates measured GNP and treats government asym-
metrically from households. The proportion of these
assets that can be easily transferred to private sector
industries is unclear. Many are structures and transport vehicles which can be sold for use in other industries, but others are clearly more specialized (such as
military hardware).

CHAPTER 4
CALIBRATING THE MODEL

This chapter discusses the selection of parameter values for
the equations of our model. The approach followed is to use
the equilibrium solution concept of the model and adopt a
simple calibration procedure.[1] This calculates parameter
values consistent with an assumed equilibrium contained in
observed data after adjustments are made to it to ensure all
equilibrium conditions hold. We term this a 'benchmark equilibrium'.

The size of the model and its integrated structure make it
impossible to simultaneously estimate all parameter values
using conventional simultaneous equation econometric techniques. The number of exogenous variables is small, and
extensive use of excluded variables as identifying restrictions is not possible because of the general equilibrium
interdependence which the model captures. If, as an alternative, single equation estimation is used, parameter estimates will be obtained which do not necessarily generate an
equilibrium consistent with observed data. To achieve this
consistency, parameter values for equations are calculated
from observed data (after adjustments) using the equilibrium
conditions of the model. We utilize this data set along with
extraneous elasticity estimates required in our calibration
procedure.

Since the data used must simultaneously satisfy all model
equilibrium conditions, a large amount of work is involved
in the construction of a consistent equilibrium data set. In
addition, since this data set only yields observations on
expenditures, a time dependent units convention is used to
separate price and quantity observations. Our units convention makes it difficult to sequence observations for time
series estimation even were this feasible given the volume
of work involved.

Extraneous estimates of substitution elasticities for both
demand and production functions are selected on the basis of
a literature search of elasticities (see Chapter 6). These

enter our calibration procedure since our equilibrium observation only generates share parameters for the CES functions
we use. 'Second order' substitution parameters must be
determined in some other way. For our production function
elasticities we survey the literature and also do a limited
amount of single equation time series estimation. For our
demand functions we use literature surveys of estimates of
uncompensated own price elasticities, and choose elasticities of substitution consistent with these.

This approach to model estimation has important implications for the organization of the basic data used in the
study. Obtaining a detailed data set containing production
decisions   of   industries,   consumption   decisions   of
households, and taxes paid on transactions, all consistent
with the equilibrium solution concept of the model, involves
a substantial extension and reorganization of UK economic
statistics as currently reported. Some difficulties are
associated with collecting raw data in sufficiently disag-
gregated form. Others reflect present government collection
of economic data which (in the UK as elsewhere), is heavily
oriented towards macroeconomic concerns. While detailed
information is separately available in input-output tables,
budget studies, income distribution statistics and other
sources, the absence of integrated detailed microeconomic
data on consistent classifications is a major difficulty in
a study of this sort. Also, taxation and subsidies are relatively neglected in these data, and in places limited detail
is available.

4.1   The Choice of Functional Forms for the Behavioural
Equations in the Model

Before discussing the estimation of parameter values for the
model equations, the considerations involved in the choice
of particular functional forms for demand and production
functions should be explained. The functional form used in
the model must be consistent with the basic model assumptions, and the maximizing responses of agents must be simple
enough to make repeated solution in the sequences of calculations involved in equilibrium computations feasible. Trac-

table functional forms, therefore, must obviously be used to
describe behaviour patterns of both producers and consumers.
Household utility maximization problems must be readily
soluble, as must industry cost minimization problems.[2]

   Inevitably, in practice the well-known family of convenient functional forms provides the candidate specifications
for general equilibrium policy models of the type used here.
Demand and cost functions derived from Cobb-Douglas, Stone-
Geary, and CES (either single stage or nested) utility and
production functions tend to be used. More complex variants
(such as Generalized Leontief functions) may also be considered although such functions raise more difficult estimation problems and substantially increase execution times
required for equilibrium calculations. The choice of CES
functions used in this study reflects the trade-off between
complexity (and hopefully added realism) and tractability.
The use of CES functions (on the demand side nested CES
functions) allows corresponding Cobb-Douglas functions to be
separately considered as special cases. The CES function is
a directly additive function which implies certain restrictions on the corresponding demand functions. We use nested
CES utility functions (additive functions of additive functions) to derive demand functions which modify the nature of
these restrictions somewhat but they still apply within
nests. The derived CES demand functions imply unitary income
elasticities. This could be relaxed through use of a Stone-
Geary variant of CES but we have not incorporated this extension. These points are discussed more fully in Chapter 6
where the choice of substitution elasticities is also discussed.

4.2 Alternative Approaches to Parameter Selection
In the model considered here, utility and production functions yield household demand and industry cost functions
which depend upon all prices. If we think of a reduced form
for the model represented by interdependent excess demand
functions, estimation of a conventional form becomes difficult. For the parameters of any particular structural
equation to be identified a large number of excluded exo-

genous variables or other identifying restrictions are required.[3] This makes identification of all equations in the model by conventional methods (such as zero or other parameter value restrictions) impractical.

One approach to overcome these problems is to partition the model. Production and demand (utility) functions could be separately estimated, and the parameter values introduced into the model. Alternatively a literature search could be used for parameter selection for some or all portions of the model (such as the demand functions). The major difficulty with this type of procedure is that in estimating production and demand equations the exogeneity of variables not central to the equation(s) being considered is assumed; and the estimates so determined are then used in a model which explicitly recognizes their joint endogeneity. There is no guarantee that a model estimated in this way will generate an equilibrium that is at all plausible. In a model which is to be regarded as representative of an actual economy, some overall criterion of reasonableness directly linked to the equilibrium solution concept of the model seems desirable. In the division and reassembly involved in the partitioning of the model for estimation to proceed, no such criterion can be incorporated. It is quite possible, for instance, that an equilibrium could be generated by the model from the estimated parameters in which 30 percent of the labour force is employed in agriculture, when the published statistics suggest that the figure is closer to, say, 12 percent. In addition, partitioning produces difficulties with the compatibility of units used in the general equilibrium model and separate estimation exercises.[4]

For all these reasons, partitioning and separate estimation alone is not adopted here as an approach to parameter selection. Instead, the equilibrium solution concept of the model is used as the primary restriction in the process of parameter selection.

The fundamental assumption made in 'calibrating' the model is that the economy is in equilibrium in a particular year. By modifying the National Accounts and other blocks of data for that year, a data set is generated in which all equilibrium conditions inherent in the model are satisfied. This is termed a 'benchmark equilibrium' data set. The requirement that the set of parameter values used in the model be capable of replicating this 'observed equilibrium' as an equilibrium solution to the model is then imposed as a restriction in the process of parameter selection.

Parameter values are determined in a non-stochastic manner by solving the equations which represent the equilibrium conditions of the model. We use the data on prices and quantities which characterize the benchmark equilibrium.[5] Whether the observed equilibrium alone is sufficient to uniquely determine the parameter values depends upon the functional forms used. For example, Cobb-Douglas functions imply constant shares. The benchmark equilibrium data set, which contains equilibrium share observations, can therefore be generated by only one set of Cobb-Douglas functions. In using CES production and demand functions extraneous estimates of elasticities of substitution (which are unit free) are incorporated into the procedure, serving together with the equilibrium replication requirement as identifying restrictions on the model.[6]

We describe parameter selection in the CES case in Section 4.6.

4.3 The Construction of a Benchmark Equilibrium Data Set

The assumption that an economy is in equilibrium implies that the model equilibrium conditions must be satisfied in any data used to determine parameter values. In a benchmark equilibrium data set all equilibrium conditions are satisfied. Demands equal supplies for all goods and factors, and non-positive profits are made in all industries.

In order for these equilibrium conditions to be satisifed by the data, various adjustments are necessary. The blocks of data we use are available separately in National Accounts and related sources but are not arranged on any synchronized basis. These data sets are modified so as to become mutually consistent with each other.[7] In certain cases prior changes are made to basic data clearly at variance with the model before mutual consistency adjustments to data blocks are undertaken. Table 4.1 presents an example of a simplified benchmark data set in which the model equilibrium conditions are satisfied; demands equal supplies and zero profit conditions are satisfied by industry. In Chapter 5, we report on the construction of a high dimensional analogue of this numerical example using UK National Accounts and other data for 1973. We incorporate all tax and subsidy policies into this data set, along with public sector activity.

The data requirements for our benchmark equilibrium data set are extensive and a substantial amount of work is involved in constructing such a set. Data are needed on the use of productive inputs by industry, including the use of both domestic and imported commodities. On the demand side information is required on the expenditure patterns of different consumer groups, and on the composition of their incomes. To incorporate the public sector into the model, data are required on tax revenues, tax payments by agent, subsidy receipts, and transfers; and all as they relate to each producer, commodity, and consumer. Data on government expenditures on goods and services and foreign trade data are also required.

The sources for these data are generally the publications or unpublished records of government agencies and the methods of manipulation and adjustment are frequently complex. Adjustments are needed for a number of reasons, such as unsuitable stock flow distinctions appearing in the published accounts, incomplete detail on taxes and subsidies, differences of definition between source materials and concepts appearing in the model, and classification incompatibilities between the model and basic data sources.

The most critical adjustments occur when inconsistent classifications are matched. Information on commodity expenditures by different household groups obtained from survey data is collected on a commodity basis different from either the Standard Industrial Classification, on which National Accounts are based, or the Standard International Trade Classification on which foreign trade statistics are based.[8] No concordance links the expenditure survey data classification to either of the others. The underlying clas-

TABLE 4.1[1]

A Simple Example of a Benchmark Equilibrium Data Set

DEMAND SIDE

1) Purchases of Products by Consumer Groups at Consumer Prices

	Consumer Groups A	B	C	Value of Purchases at Consumer Prices
Products 1	4	2	1	7
2	2	3	1	6
3	4	1	3	8
4	1	3	4	8
Disposable Incomes	11	9	9	29

PRODUCTION SIDE

1) Inter-Industry Transactions

	Industries 1	2	3	4	Output for Intermediate Use	Final Consumer Demands
Products 1	2	1	2	3	8	6
2	4	3	1	2	10	4
3	2	1	1	1	5	7
4	2	1	1	0	4	5
Intermediate Costs	10	6	5	6	27	22
Factor Value Added	4	8	7	3		

PUBLIC SECTOR

Receipts		Expenditures		
Consumer Purchase Taxes	7	Transfers to Groups	A	6
Income Taxes	7		B	7
Business Taxes	5		C	6
	19			19

CONSISTENCY CONDITIONS SATISFIED BY DATA

1. Demands equal supplies for all products.
2. Each industry's total costs equal total sales.
3. Each consumer's group purchases equals disposable income for the group.
4. The endowments of consumers match factor usage.
5. The government's budget is balanced.
6. The value of final demands equals the sum of value added.

2) Consumer Disposable Incomes

	Consumer Groups A	B	C	Total
Income from Capital	5	1	1	7
Labour Income	3	3	4	10
Transfers Received	6	7	6	19
less Income Tax Paid	3	2	2	7
Disposable Incomes	11	9	9	29

2) Composition of Value Added by Industry

	Industries 1	2	3	4	Total
Capital Service Usage	1	2	3	1	7
Labour Service Usage	2	4	3	1	10
Indirect Business Taxes	1	2	1	1	5
Total	4	8	7	3	22

3) Consumer Taxes Paid

	Value of Purchases at Consumer Prices	Consumer Taxes	Value of Purchases at Producer Prices
Products 1	7	1	6
2	6	2	4
3	8	1	7
4	8	3	5
Total	29	7	22

---

[1] A number of features not included in this example must be incorporated into the data set used in the model such as: 1) Real Government Expenditures; 2) Foreign Trade; 3) Consumer Savings; 4) Investments by Business, Consumers and Government; 5) Depreciation; 6) Inventory Accumulation; 7) Financial Transactions between the Personal Business, Public and External Sectors; 8) more complex taxation and subsidy arrangements e.g., a value-added tax.

sification of industry factor cost data differs from that of
the input-output table and classification adjustments are
therefore also necessary to production data.

The full documentation of the sources and resulting manipulation of data is given in the following chapter. To a
considerable extent, these data difficulties arise because
government economic statistics of economy-wide activity are
constructed primarily with macroeconomic and not micro-
economic policy analysis in mind. A more widespread use of
general equilibrium policy models will ultimately require an
orientation for National Accounting practices reflecting
this general approach.[9]

4.4 Units Conventions and the Use of the Benchmark Equilibrium Data Set

The benchmark equilibrium data set obtained by adjusting
diverse data sets into a mutually consistent form provides
observations on equilibrium transactions in value terms. To
obtain information separately on equilibrium prices and
quantities, a units convention must be adopted to separate
observations on price quantity combinations into component
parts.

As factors of production are treated in the model as perfectly mobile between alternative uses, the allocation of
factors by industry in equilibrium will equalize the returns
received net of taxes and gross of subsidies in all industries. It is therefore convenient to adopt a definition of
physical units for all factors as that amount of a factor
that can, in equilibrium, earn a reward of £1 net of taxes,
and after receipt of subsidies, in any of its alternative
uses. Units for commodities are similarly defined as those
amounts which, in equilibrium, sell for £1 net of all consumer taxes and subsidies.

The assumption that marginal revenue products of factors
are equalized in all uses in equilibrium permits this convention to translate factor payments data by industry into
observations on physical quantities for use in the determination of parameters for the model.[10] In this way observed
equilibrium transactions (products of prices and quantities)

are separated out into price and quantity observations. An observed equilibrium is characterized by an equilibrium price vector of unity, and ownership of a unit of labour or capital services yields a net income of £1.

One significant departure from this procedure arises from the impossibility of obtaining data on sales of inputs by individual household groups to particular industries. Because of this constraint, the units for factors are defined in terms of factor rewards net of factor taxes but gross of income taxes. Even though consumer groups face different marginal income tax rates, this is a procedure consistent with the use of a quantity associated with a market price as a units definition, if the income tax does not discriminate between types of incomes on the basis of industry of origin. Factor rewards are, however, differently treated in the income tax system depending upon the industry of origin. The most important example is the imputed income from owner-occupied housing. In addition, capital gains accrue more heavily in some industries than others (depending on corporate retention policies) and are differently taxed from other income. As it is more reasonable to argue that at a competitive equilibrium factors are allocated between industries so as to equalize returns net of all taxes rather than just factor taxes, the industry specific features of the income tax imply that no equal proportional relationship exists between gross and net of income tax returns for all industries. We attempt to make some allowance for this issue as it affects capital use in owner-occupied housing when we perform alternative sensitivity analyses on our model and data.

4.5   Consistency Adjustments in the Construction of a Benchmark Equilibrium

Consistency adjustments to basic data are necessary since the benchmark equilibrium data set must satisfy the general equilibrium conditions of the model and diverse data sets adjusted only for inconsistent classifications and definitions will not be consistent with conditions for a general equilibrium. Consumer expenditures will not equal disposable

incomes for each consumer group, household sector incomes by
type will not equal factor rewards originating in the industrial sector, and consumer demands for products will not
equal the supply of products from the industrial sector.

A number of alternative adjustment procedures are possible
as inconsistencies can be reconciled by adjusting either or
both of two discrepant data sets. The procedure used predominantly in this study is to adopt totals derived from
1973 UK National Accounts as the basis for adjustments. The
details of these consistency adjustments which preserve
national accounts totals are explained in Chapter 5, and a
broad outline only is provided at this stage.

After adjusting gross domestic product accounts by industry for such items as the treatment of self-employment,
rents, and interest paid, an estimate of the profit-type
return and labour income by industry is obtained. These
figures provide estimates of use of primary factors by
industry, and together with taxes paid by industry comprise
value added. From National Accounts estimates of personal
consumption expenditures, private net fixed capital formation,[11] inventory accumulation, and exports it is possible
to obtain a total figure for final UK demands for products.
The composition of components of final demand by product is
obtained from the input-output tables. The sum of final
demands valued at producer prices must, for general equilibrium consistency, equal the sum of value added by industry
and a scaling procedure is used to ensure this condition
holds. Final demand and value added figures are then used to
adjust intermediate transactions accounts contained in
input-output tables.

In their published form, the input-output accounts are
produced on a different classification from that used in the
model and for a different year from the rest of the data
set, and inconsistencies therefore appear. If final demand
and value added figures are crudely combined with the input-
output accounts, the value of industry outputs (for both
final and intermediate use) does not equal the value of
inputs (both intermediate and primary inputs). Adjustments
to intermediate transactions in the input-out tables restore

these conditions through alternate iterations on rows and columns of the input-output matrix until the conditions are satisfied. This procedure is formally equivalent to the RAS procedure described in Bacharach [1970], for updating input-output tables to later year factor cost and final demand data.[12]

As the final demands for products contain the final demands of the household sector, the value of these demands must equal the total disposable income of the household sector. The aggregate incomes of the household sector by type (capital-type return, labour income, and transfers) among consumer groups are determined using distributional information given in the Family Expenditure Survey.[13] Each of these components of income, when summed across households, equals the corresponding total elsewhere in the data set. Factor ownership of households equals the economy endowment less that of government, corporations and foreigners. Transfers sum to the amount assumed in the public sector accounts. As the sum of value added equals the sum of final demands household incomes in aggregate equal household purchases.

The unadjusted expenditure survey data on products purchased by household reveals a further source of inconsistency. Expenditures for any given household group will not sum to that group's disposable income less savings, and the sum of expenditures on any given product will not equal the available supply to the personal sector.[14] An iterative procedure on the rows and columns of the expenditure matrix is also performed until these conditions are satisfied; this procedure is similar to the RAS method of updating input-output tables described above.

Other inconsistencies in the data set also require adjustments. The budget of the government must be brought into balance and financial transactions of the public sector incorporated as real transactions involving resource transfers. The foreign trade deficit in the data set for 1973 is accommodated by integrating into the data set both inflows and outflows of investment as purchases of capital goods produced in the UK and abroad along with dividend and interest flows and transfers. An outline of these adjustments is given in Table 4.2.

4.6 Determining Parameter Values from the Benchmark Equilibrium Data Set

Once constructed, the benchmark equilibrium data set is used to determine parameter values for production and demand functions using a simple non-stochastic calibration procedure. The requirement placed on the set of estimated parameter values is that they be capable of reproducing the complete benchmark equilibrium data set as an equilibrium solution to the model. The estimation procedure thus uses the equilibrium solution to the model and the benchmark equilibrium data set to solve for parameter estimates.

Once functional forms are chosen for production functions, it is possible to calculate the associated distribution parameters by using the benchmark equilibrium observations of capital and labour services used in each industry. The CES value added functions for each industry are given by[15]

$$Y_j = \gamma \left[\delta_j K_j^{-\rho_j} + (1-\delta_j) L_j^{-\rho_j} \right]^{-\frac{1}{\rho_j}} \quad j=1,\ldots,33 \text{ (U.K. industries)}$$

where γ_j is a constant defining units of measurement, δ_j is a weighting parameter, and $\sigma_j \ (= \frac{1}{1+\rho_j})$ is the elasticity of substitution.

From the benchmark equilibrium data set, values for K_i and L_i can be obtained and factor tax rates t_i^K and t_i^L calculated. As units are chosen for productive factors such that $P_K = P_L = 1$ (where P_K and P_L refer to the net of tax factor prices) at the benchmark equilibrium, prices associated with the equilibrium quantities are known.

Once a value of σ_j is selected for each industry,[16] the values of δ_j are given by

$$\delta_j = \left[\frac{K_j^{\frac{1}{\sigma_j}} (1 + t_j^K)}{L_j^{\frac{1}{\sigma_j}} (1 + t_j^L)} \right] \Bigg/ \left[1 + \frac{K_j^{\frac{1}{\sigma_j}} (1 + t_j^K)}{L_j^{\frac{1}{\sigma_j}} (1 + t_j^L)} \right]$$

Values for γ_j are then derived from the zero profit conditions for each industry (given the units definition for outputs).

Parameters for household demand functions are calculated in a similar manner, from the benchmark equilibrium data on purchases of commodities by households. The procedure is analogous to that for production functions, except that individual consumer demand functions rather than first order conditions from cost minimization are used to estimate parameter values.

Taking a two nested variant of CES consumer demand functions, the ratio of expenditures by household q on any two commodities i, j, which are members of some higher nest ℓ, gives an equation involving the bottom level weighting parameters in each household utility function:

$$\frac{P_i X_i^q}{P_j X_j^q} = \frac{(b_i^q)^{\sigma_\ell} \cdot P_j^{(\sigma_\ell - 1)}}{(b_j^q)^{\sigma_\ell} \cdot P_i^{(\sigma_\ell - 1)}}$$

where the P's are consumer prices and X_i^q represents the qth individual's benchmark demands, b's are distribution parameters in the utility function and σ^ℓ is the value of the elasticity of substitution within the ℓth nest.

Once the elasticity values within nests are selected,[17] the ratios of the parameters b_i^q and b_j^q can be calculated and by normalizing the parameters associated with the elements of each nest to sum to unity, their individual values can be obtained. This procedure is repeated for each lower level nest.

TABLE 4.2

Consistency Adjustments Made in Constructing the Benchmark Equilibrium Data Set

Modifications to Production Side Data		Modifications to Demand Side Data	
Input-Output Transactions Accounts	Final Demand for Products	Household Sector Final Products	Household Expenditure Matrix (Including Savings)
1971 Basic Data updated, and aggregated onto a differing classification for use in the model	1) Consumer Expenditures 2) Capital Formation 3) Government Expenditures 4) Inventory Accumulation 5) Exports Source - National Accounts and Input-Output Data	Source - Component of Final Demands for Products (from production side data)	Aggregated from 1973 Family Expenditure Survey Data

- Value Added by Industry

(i) profit type return
(ii) labour costs
(iii) production taxes

- Source – National Accounts (with adjustments)

Production Side Consistency Conditions

1) Sum of value added equals sum of final demands at production prices

2) For each industry total sales equal to total costs

Demand Side Consistency Conditions

1) Aggregate budget balance at consumer prices

2) For each household group expenditures equal disposable income

Household Disposable Incomes

- Source – Allocation of production side totals by income type using household survey data

Consistency Difficulty

For each industry the value of sales (to both final and intermediate users) does not equal total costs (both value added and intermediate costs). RAS iterative procedure applied.

Consistency Difficulty

Disposable income of each household does not equal its expenditures. The sum of expenditures on each commodity does not equal the total implicit in final demands of households. RAS iterative procedure applied.

Other Inconsistencies

1. A government deficit or surplus is inconsistent with general equilibrium budget balance. A deficit or surplus is interpreted as requiring a real resource transfer between government and other sectors for it to be brought into balance.

2. A foreign trade deficit or surplus is offset by inward and outward investment flows, interest and dividends paid and received from abroad, and transfers.

For top level utility weighting parameters, the benchmark data on the sum of expenditures on components of the category can be used. $\bar{P}_\ell^q \bar{X}_\ell^q$ is the expenditure by household q on the category ℓ where $\bar{P}_\ell^q$ is a true cost of living index for the qth household calculated using the prices associated with elements within the ℓth nest, and $\bar{X}_\ell^q$ is the quantity of the associated composite commodity bought by the qth household. The ratio of expenditures on any two categories ℓ, ℓ' gives a similar equation involving weighting parameters:

$$\frac{\bar{P}_\ell^q \ \bar{X}_\ell^q}{\bar{P}_{\ell'}^q \ \bar{X}_{\ell'}^q} = \frac{(b_i^q)^\sigma \ \bar{P}_{\ell'}^q \,^{(\sigma-1)}}{(b_{\ell'}^q)^\sigma \ \bar{P}_\ell^q \,^{(\sigma-1)}}$$

A value σ for the elasticity of substitution across nests is selected, and the coefficients b_ℓ^q calculated subject to the constraint that they sum to one. This same procedure can be extended to the three level nested CES functions used in the model.

By using the complete benchmark equilibrium data set in this way to generate parameter values for production and demand functions, the equilibrium computed by the model before any policy changes will replicate the benchmark equilibrium data set exactly.[18] This is assured as the equilibrium conditions have been used directly in the determination of parameter values. A practical advantage of this procedure is that the equilibrium solution of the estimated model is known ex ante and its recalculation serves as a check on the correctness of programming and on error propagation difficulties.

Our procedure of parameter selection thus involves the construction of a benchmark equilibrium data set consistent with the model along with a set of extraneously chosen elasticities of substitution in demand and production functions. These two pieces of information are then combined with the requirement that the entire set of parameters chosen for the model equations produce an equilibrium solution identical in

all respects to the benchmark. These conditions require a
unique set of non-elasticity parameter values. In the next
two chapters we present our 1973 benchmark data set (Chapter
5) and discuss our selection of elasticity values (Chapter
6).

Notes

1.   A fuller discussion of both calibration and some of the
     difficulties with econometric estimation of general
     equilibrium systems appears in Mansur and Whalley
     [1981].

2.   In fact to determine equilibria computationally it is
     simpler to work directly with the consumer demand func-
     tions for commodities, and the per unit output factor
     demand functions of producers.

3.   Considerable industrial and household disaggregation is
     specified in the model in order to analyze the detail
     of taxation and subsidy policies. By limiting the size
     of model and coping with units problems in ways other
     than those adopted here, identification and estimation
     of equations by conventional methods can become prac-
     tical. Such an approach has been followed by Allingham
     [1973]. An important simplification in his work is the
     limitation to market rather than individual demand
     functions as well as a substantially smaller commodity
     listing than would be satisfactory for the policy
     issues considered here. Supply functions rather than
     production functions are also used and consequently
     questions of economic efficiency are not directly ad-
     dressed.

4.   Units of capital and labour services are defined in the
     model as those amounts capable of generating a return
     of one pound in any possible use net of taxes, and
     gross of subsidies. These units are defined for a par-
     ticular year for which the data is assumed to represent
     an equilibrium for the economy. While physical units
     are implied by such an assumption they cannot be speci-
     fied in a form that makes a conversion to other well-
     defined physical units (such as tons) possible. Single
     equation estimation which produces unit dependent esti-
     mates are of limited value in the model unless the
     units involved are capable of being converted from one
     to another.

5. A potential difficulty is that the model may exhibit
    multiplicity of equilibria, so that even if the test of
    replication is not satisfied there is no way to rule
    out the admissibility of a given specification. This is
    one of the several difficulties which the possibility
    of multiplicity of equilibria causes in the use of the
    model. As noted earlier, Kehoe and Whalley [1982] have
    recently demonstrated uniqueness of equilibrium in a
    similar general equilibrium tax model of the US economy
    suggesting that uniqueness may also apply here.

6. The choice of elasticity values critically affects
    results obtained with the model; the values chosen are
    discussed in Chapter 6.

7. While published input-output transactions are scaled
    for consistency with National Accounts aggregates, this
    is not done with other data such as taxation and family
    expenditure information. Furthermore, the synchron-
    ization at issue here is not just with respect to
    aggregates but for all matching sub-aggregates.

8. In recent years UK trade statistics have been reported
    on a SIC as well as a SITC basis. This practice has a
    longer history in the US.

9. Such an orientation is inherent in the social account-
    ing matrix approach which appears in Stone's work
    [1962] and has strongly influenced the most recent UN
    conventions on national accounting [1968]. In the case
    of the present data set there is something more clearly
    model-oriented than is the case with the UN conven-
    tions. The latest UN conventions have so far had only
    limited impact on actual accounting procedures followed
    in most countries and more detailed information on a
    consistent basis beyond conventional national accounts
    and related data is unlikely to be available in the
    near future. For a proposed set of national micro
    accounts, see Ruggles and Ruggles [1970].

10. While underlying physical units of measurement are
    implied by such a procedure, their physical dimensions
    remain undefined as there are no weight or volume
    measures one can appeal to. With labour services, for

instance, different people will be of different produc-
tivities and provide different quantities of labour
services and counting the number of workers in an
industry is an inappropriate measure of labour used by
industry.

11. The corresponding final demand column in the input-
output table is for private gross fixed capital formation. Incomes to capital owners are measured in the
model as net of depreciation, depreciation expenditures
being treated as an intermediate expenditure and final
demands as net of depreciation. After the consistency
adjustments to the input-output table, these depreciation expenditures appear in the intermediate transactions in the economy.

12. The RAS procedure can be shown to be optimal in the
sense of minimizing the loss function

$$\sum_i \sum_j \frac{(a_{ij}^0 - a_{ij}^*)^2}{a_{ij}^*},$$

where a_{ij}^0 is a representative element of the initial
matrix, and a_{ij}^* a representative element of the modified matrix. See Theil (1967) sections 2.5 and 10.1,
and the appendix to Chapter 10.

13. Family Expenditure Survey, 1973, Department of
Employment, H.M.S.O.

14. A further problem with these expenditure data is that
expenditures on imported and domestically produced
goods are not separately identified. It is assumed in
constructing the benchmark equilibrium data set that
for any household proportions of expenditures are given
by the ratio of domestically consumed production to
final imports for each good.

15. The notation used is the same as that in Appendix A.

16. The selection of these values is discussed in Chapter
6.

17. These values are also discussed in Chapter 6.

18. Ignoring the problem of non-uniqueness mentioned
earlier.

19. Assuming uniqueness of equilibrium.

CHAPTER 5
THE BENCHMARK EQUILIBRIUM DATA SET

A benchmark equilibrium data set for the UK economy and tax
system for use in calibrating the model for the year 1973
has been constructed along the lines outlined in Chapter
4. In this chapter the main features of this data set are
described.

A substantial volume of data has been drawn on from different sources and reorganized in a consistent manner for
our use here. In the process a data base has been generated
which has value outside of the immediate study, and so a
substantial amount of detail is provided in the tables which
follow to provide accessibility for other potential users of
the data set.

A benchmark equilibrium data set, as described in Chapter
4, is an adjusted set of basic data which meets all of the
equilibrium conditions of the model. These are that demands
equal supplies for all goods; no industry makes any abnormal
profit; external sector transactions balance; the government
budget is balanced; and lastly, household incomes equal
household expenditures.

Adjustments are necessary to basic data because the information available in the National Accounts and related
sources is primarily macro and production oriented. Thus, in
household expenditure data reporting expenditures and
incomes of individual household types, the total sum of
household factor incomes after scaling to an economy-wide
basis will not match the sum of factor rewards reported by
industry of origin in the National Accounts. The private
sector expenditures on each domestic good obtained by summing across household expenditure data will not equal the
value of final production less exports reported in National
Accounts production data. Other inconsistencies between data
sets are also present if unadjusted basic data alone are
used for the calibration procedures described in Chapter 4.

Further difficulties arise in constructing a consistent
data set besides the adjustments to blocks of data described
above. There are substantial areas where data are not available in a form in which they can be used directly in the
model. Data do not exist in a convenient form on payments of
taxes on use of factors by industry which enable calculations of effective factor tax rates to be made. Information
on subsidies paid by governments to individual industries is
also sparse. In other areas data are not available in a
model-admissible form, and so a number of prior calculations
are necessary before beginning the consistency adjustments
to other data sets. For example, self-employment income must
be split between returns to capital and labour before being
introduced into the benchmark data set. These problems
result in a data set containing information of varying
reliability; some data are directly available from published
sources, while some have had to be constructed using the
best information we have been able to obtain. We attempt to
list the sources of our data but the volume of information
involved necessitates a summary approach in most cases. The
documentation of sources for tables presented is given in
Appendix B at the end of the book.

Once constructed, the benchmark equilibrium data set is
used to generate parameter values for the equations used in
the model. This involves breaking the benchmark equilibrium
observations on the value of transactions into separate
observations on prices and quantities. For this purpose
units for physical quantities of both productive factors and
commodities are assumed to exist which correspond to the
amounts traded at an equilibrium market price of one pound.
This units convention enables the benchmark equilibrium data
to be used directly as quantity observations associated with
equilibrium market prices all of which are unity. This convention is reflected in the tables reported in this chapter
where measures of factor payments by industry have been
constructed on a net-of-tax, gross-of-subsidy basis. These
data are used to represent factor use by industry in the
benchmark equi·ibrium in physical terms. The net of tax
gross of subsidy measure is used since in equilibrium any

physical unit can move between alternative uses and receive the same rate of return (net of tax and gross of subsidies). A corresponding physical concept is also used for outputs, defined as that amount which, in equilibrium, can be sold for one pound before payment of consumer purchase taxes.

The major sources for the benchmark equilibrium data set are the national income accounts,[1] input-output data,[2] household expenditure data,[3] foreign trade,[4] and taxation data[5] (available primarily on an administrative basis). In constructing the benchmark equilibrium data, aggregate totals in these sources are reconciled as far as possible with the National Accounts. For instance, where industrial detail on collections of a particular tax is required the method of allocation by industry is chosen such that the total will reflect that appearing in National Accounts.

In Table 5.1 some of the major characteristics of the 1973 UK benchmark equilibrium data set in aggregated form are displayed. The value of capital and labour employed and production taxes paid by each industry are reported. The negative taxes in primary production reflect subsidies paid by government. The sum of production taxes, capital and labour give the total value added originating in the economy. The intermediate production structure reflects the use of products of each industry by other industries. Each industry also pays intermediate production taxes on its use of products. (These include motor vehicle licence duties, tariffs, and other charges.) There are also final production taxes which are paid on the value of production by industry.

Final demands of the economy are broken down by sector and by product. Personal sector consumption demands, net investment expenditures, government expenditures, and exports all appear. Each sector also has demands for imports.

The reconciliation of aggregate value added in this table with the total appearing in National Accounts is given in Table 5.2. It can be seen that a number of adjustments to National Accounts procedures are involved particularly for the value of the imputed income to owner-occupied housing, measurement of the income return to local authority housing, and the imputed income from government owned assets. These along with other adjustments are discussed more fully below.

TABLE 5.1

Summary Production and Demand Transactions Benchmark Equilibrium Data Set, UK 1973   £ millions*

Production

Domestic Commodities	(1) Profit-type Payments	+	(2) Labour Costs	(3) Net Capital Taxes	+	(4) Net Labour Taxes
Primary Production	598.2		1691.9	-50.2		148.4
Manufacturing	1085.1		13704.0	1635.5		1268.4
Non-Manufacturing	2407.7		14642.3	1425.8		1221.5
Government and Services	3933.7		12274.5	601.3		1135.9
Housing	8699.5		290.6	1276.2		17.6
Total	16724.2		42603.3	4888.7		3791.8

Demand

Domestic Commodities	(9) Total Output (Producer Prices)	-	(10) Intermediate Output (Gross of Intermediate Output Taxes)	+	(11) Intermediate Output Taxes	+	(12) Final Output Taxes
Primary Production	5214.5		3042.2		-		11.3
Manufacturing	57409.3		29508.3		822.7		3632.2
Non-Manufacturing	39623.5		16390.9		-		926.5
Government and Services	21175.8		4962.0		-		585.2
Housing	10226.4		-		-		-3136.0
Imported Commodities	16352.9		12910.7		297.8		810.1
Total	15002.4		66814.1		1120.5		2829.3

* Columns may not add to reported totals due to rounding. See special notes to the Table in Appendix C.

=	(5) Total Primary Costs	+	(6) Intermediate Use (including imports)	+	(7) Net Production Taxes	=	(8) Total Costs
	2388.2		3310.9		-448.0		525.1
	17693.1		40582.4		-6.0		58269.5
	19697.5		18591.5		-362.0		37927.0
	18546.7		3208.5		-		21153.9
	10283.9		-		-57.0		10226.9
	68008.1		65693.3		-873.0		132828.4

=	(13) Personal Sector Consumption Demands (Consumer Prices)	+	(14) Net Investment Expenditures (Consumer Prices)	+	(15) Government Expenditures (Consumer Prices)	+	(16) Exports (Producer Prices)
	1607.6		145.3		81.9		348.8
	13930.3		2293.9		3335.4		12796.3
	16798.2		1352.6		3544.0		2464.3
	3497.6		146.0		12915.3		240.1
	7090.7		-		-		-
	3015.6		1145.3		389.8		-
	45940.0		45940.0		20266.4		15849.5

TABLE 5.2

Reconciliation of Model Value Added with GDP at

Factor Cost Appearing in UK National Accounts

1. GDP at Factor Cost for 1973 as reported in the National
    Accounts,[1] £62.2 billion.

2. Adjustments to National Accounts Measure for Changes
    in Model Accounting System

    (a) less £ billion

           Capital Consumption   6.3
           Subsidies   0.4
                                        ────
                                              -6.7
                                              55.5
                                              ────

    (b) plus

           Financial Charges   1.5
           Imputed Public Sector   2.9
           Capital Income
           Additional Imputed   5.0
           Housing Income (Public
             and Private)
           Rent Paid by Industry   0.5
           Rates   2.6
                                        ────
                                             +12.5
                                              68.0
                                              ────

    Model Value Added = 68.0

1. NIBB 1963-1973, Table 11, p. 13.

Notes to table are given in Appendix B.

5.1 Profit Type Return by Industry

Calculations of profit type return by industry from 1973 are reported in Table 5.3. The 33 model industries appear in this table and the profit type return data involve a number of different components. Return to capital in the private sector includes trading profits of corporations gross of tax and depreciation. These are obtained from National Accounts sources and reflect the tax reporting of corporate profits in that they include stock appreciation (which is subtracted in column 10)[6] as well as the self employment income allocated as a return to capital. The self-employment income by industry is broken down into returns to capital and labour, and the return to capital is included in the measure of profit type return.[7]

The trading surpluses of public corporations gross of depreciation are added in to the overall profit type return by industry. These reflect the calculated profit of nationalized industries after subtraction of all of costs, including interest on debt held by the central government. The profit type return in public authority activity includes the return to capital used in providing local authority housing services (reflecting a calculation of the imputed value of the rental services from the stock of houses owned by local authorities), and the value of the profit type return in the provision of public services. This latter figure reflects an imputation of the income flow from the capital stock owned and employed in the public sector. The financial charge component[8] of interest payments paid by businesses are deducted from the profit type return since these are charges paid by businesses in the generation of their profit. The hire of plant and machinery is added into the profit type return of industries borrowing plant and machinery since the profit type return reflects an attempt to measure the value of capital services physically used in an industry. The sum across industries of this component of the profit type return is equal to zero.

TABLE 5.3

Profit-Type Return by Industry: U.K. 1973

	(1) +	(2) +	(3) −	(4) +	(5)
Industry	Return to Capital in Private Sector Gross of Tax and Depreciation	Trading Surpluses of Public Corporations Gross of Depreciation	Profit Type Return in Public Authority Activity	Financial Charges Paid by Business in Interest Payments	Industrial Reallocation of Hire of Plant and Machinery
Agriculture and Fishing	927.2		20.0	3.7	
Coal Mining	-	61.0			8.1
Other Mining and Quarrying	78.4			1.6	11.8
Food	359.3			10.1	5.7
Drink	518.8			20.7	1.1
Tobacco	47.2			3.7	0.4
Mineral Oils	20.6			1.2	1.4
Other Coal and Petroleum Products	19.1			1.1	3.6
Chemicals	645.4			25.1	8.4
Metals	352.6	146.0		17.3	13.8
Mech. Engineering	651.7			37.5	9.8
Instr. Engineering	61.3			6.2	0.8
Elec. Engineering	680.8			25.3	7.8
Shipbuilding	22.6			1.5	1.3
Vehicles	365.7			15.5	11.3
Textiles	384.5			7.7	3.9
Clothing	148.3			3.4	6.9
Leather, fur, etc.	24.7			1.3	0.3
Timber, Furniture, etc.	118.6			2.3	1.7
Paper, Printing, and Publishing	498.0			64.0	4.7
Manufacturing n.e.s.	795.3			24.0	8.6
Construction	819.9			18.2	
Gas, Electricity, and Water	15.0	1,030.0	81.0		5.7
Transport	560.0	280.0	36.0	35.2	
Communications	6.0	501.0			
Retail Trade	1,221.8	2.1		25.2	
Wholesale Trade	881.7	1.9		69.6	-117.1
Banking and Insurance, etc.	1,711.8		68.8		
Housing Services (Private)	155.5		6.2		
Housing Services (Local Auth.)	-		3,997.2		
Public Service	188.3		2,883.9		
Professional Services	515.9			2.9	
Other Services	785.7	29.0	8.0	28.2	
	13,581.7	2,051.0	7,101.1	452.5	0

Notes to tables are given in Appendix B.

(6) -	(7) -	(8) +	(9) -	(10) =	(11)
Rental Income Plus Reallocation of Rental Expense by Industry	Capital Consumption	Corporation Tax	Capital Type Subsidies	Stock Appreciation	Profit Type Return
111.0	300.0	21.1	0.3	290.0	443.7
1.8	45.0		115.0	3.5	137.4
1.8	57.4	17.2	1.3		17.1
6.8	99.8	90.3	7.6	100.2	79.0
9.1	133.3	164.2	3.7	132.7	81.8
	0.0	27.6	0.3	3.1	13.5
0.4	6.3	4.3	0.5	6.4	4.7
0.5	6.6	4.0	0.2	6.8	4.9
12.7	186.2	135.2	9.2	191.9	137.3
10.8	159.2	73.2	109.6	262.9	120.2
10.7	157.4	206.9	12.2	222.5	60.1
1.0	14.0	18.8	1.7	20.1	5.7
12.3	181.5	182.1	11.4	254.6	68.8
0.4	5.4	8.0	6.2	10.7	4.9
7.0	102.6	90.3	7.8	144.1	39.3
8.1	119.4	64.6	7.0	145.9	65.9
2.7	39.5	47.1	3.3	48.8	22.4
0.4	5.8	8.2	0.6	7.3	3.4
2.3	33.4	29.5	3.3	26.4	34.3
8.7	127.9	99.6	6.6	100.2	126.3
14.5	213.6	213.5	12.9	167.6	212.6
16.7	149.0	149.5	6.2	151.0	375.1
29.0	839.0		140.2	18.0	443.9
19.8	705.6	68.9	355.8	5.0	436.9
13.0	463.4		73.1		129.7
261.0	226.4	293.2	6.0	471.9	474.2
12.3	95.4	334.7	6.1	200.1	85.1
-491.8	234.0	605.2	13.2		462.8
5,440.6	583.0	55.0			4,964.3
	288.0		26.0		3,735.2
600.0	531.0				3,141.2
12.7	98.3	19.5			407.9
15.4	119.9	192.3	4.9	118	384.6
6,151.7	6,327.3	3,224.0	952.2	3,109.7	16,724.2

Rents paid by industry are added into the profit type return since these also reflect factor use. The largest portion is rent paid by the private housing industry; this number reflects an imputation made to the value of dwellings owned by the private sector. This figure is used in place of the reported income from owner-occupied housing in the UK National Accounts since it is felt that the latter figure is an underestimate.[9]

Capital consumption is subtracted in order to measure the profit type return by industry net of all expenses. Depreciation is treated as a cost of doing business. In the general equilibrium model in which the data are used, capital is allocated by industry so as to equalize the return in all uses after all costs, including depreciation. The capital consumption data are taken from the capital stock estimates in the National Accounts; tax depreciation is not used because of the substantial acceleration in depreciation allowances under the UK corporate tax code.

The National Accounts corporate tax total is made consistent with the data on payments of corporate taxes by individual industries from Inland Revenue sources. This tax is subtracted in the calculation of the profit type return since a net of tax measure is used. Nationalized industries, such as gas, electricity, and water, and the communications industry, pay little or no corporate tax.

Capital subsidies include subsidies received by nationalized industries, and also regional subsidies received by qualifying industries in particular regions of the country. Stock appreciation is subtracted in the calculation of the profit type return as it is treated as an inflationary capital gain on an accrual basis. It is included in the taxable profits of corporations under column 1 and should be excluded in a measure of the value of capital services used by industry. This treatment of stock appreciation makes a substantial difference both to the measure of the profit type return and to the calculated capital tax rates and is returned to below.

The aggregate profit type return reported in column 11 is approximately £17 billion. Of the total profit type return in the economy over half is accounted for by profit type return in the housing industries (private and local authority). Another 25 percent is accounted for by public service. In total, service industries account for some 85 percent of the total profit type return originating in the UK economy. This is a reflection both of the measurement procedure which is used,[10] and the relative profitability of UK manufacturing industry in recent years. If the industrial composition of the profit type return is compared to the industrial composition in the capital stock data by industry a somewhat different picture is obtained. These figures are discussed below where sensitivity exercises on the 1973 benchmark equilibrium data set are reported. We have chosen to use flow estimates in our benchmark because they give a direct measure of capital return.

5.2 Return to Labour by Industry

The return to labour by industry in the UK for 1973 is reported in Table 5.4. As with Table 5.3, figures are reported for the 33 industries considered in the model and the return to labour constructed from component parts. Labour income includes self employment income allocated as a return to labour and employment income which is taken primarily from national accounting sources with some extra disaggregation by industry using information from the input-output tables. Column 1 thus contains the major component of value added in the economy. As with the capital type return the industrial composition of income from employment is worth noting with services accounting once again for a majority of the total labour type return (especially public services).

Columns 2, 3 and 4 report combined employer and employee national insurance contributions paid by industry for 1973. These produce differential effective tax rates by industry since total contributions are a combination of separate flat-rate and income-related elements. Thus, in banking and insurance, which on average have more highly paid employees than other industries, smaller combined national insurance contributions per employee are paid than in other industries

TABLE 5.4

Return to Labour by Industry: UK (1973) (£ mill)

Industry	(1) Income from Employment and Self-employment Allocated as Return to Labour	(2) Combined National Insurance Contribution for Employees	(3) National Insurance Contributions for Self-employed	(4) National Health and Redundancy Funds	(5) Return to Labour
		−	−	− =	
Agriculture and Fishing	1107.6	58.9	18.7	6.2	1023.8
Coal Mining	636.0	50.9		4.1	581.0
Other Mining and Quarrying	96.6	9.0		0.7	86.9
Food	939.8	89.6	0.7	7.3	842.0
Drink	377.9	22.2		1.8	353.9
Tobacco	92.8	6.3		0.5	86.0
Mineral Oil	48.0	5.1		0.4	42.5
Other Coal and Petroleum Products	44.5	4.7		0.4	39.4
Chemicals	893.8	70.8		5.7	817.3
Metals	1095.1	99.4	0.1	8.0	987.6
Mech. Engineering	2120.5	74.6		14.0	1931.9
Instr. Engineering	304.1	23.5		1.9	278.7
Elec. Engineering	1380.2	129.8	0.5	10.4	1239.5
Shipbuilding	387.2	33.3	0.1	2.7	351.1
Vehicles	1871.0	140.8	0.4	11.3	1718.5
Textiles	871.5	88.3	0.3	7.1	775.8
Clothing	557.0	53.67	1.2	4.4	497.8
Leather, Fur, etc.	66.8	7.8		0.6	58.4
Timber, Furniture, etc.	548.5	40.1	0.7	3.3	504.4

Paper, Printing, and Publishing	1233.3	95.6	0.5	7.7	1129.5
Manufacturing n.e.s.	2252.6	186.2	1.5	15.1	1049.8
Construction	3760.1	269.7	25.9	23.7	3440.8
Gas, Electricity and Water	831.0	57.7	-	4.6	768.7
Transport	2966.0	179.7	4.8	14.8	2766.7
Communications	1116.0	72.3		5.8	1037.9
Retail Trade	2946.9	230.4	20.9	20.2	2675.4
Wholesale Trade	1739.6	126.1	4.1	10.4	1599.0
Banking and Insurance, etc.	2506.0	139.0	1.7	11.3	2354.0
Housing Services (Private)	227.7	12.6	0.2	1.0	213.9
Housing Services (Local Authority)	80.5	3.5		0.3	76.7
Public Service	8330.2	358.9	5.5	29.2	7936.6
Professional Services	2813.8	385.5	8.7	31.6	2388.0
Other Services	2266.4	269.4	23.6	23.5	1949.9
TOTAL	46509.0	3495.5	120.1	290.0	42603.4

Notes to tables are given in Appendix B.

TABLE 5.5

Production Taxes and Subsidies on Return to Labour and Profit-Type Return:
UK (1973) £ mill.

Industry	(1) + Combined National Insurance Contributions: Employees	(2) + National Insurance Contributions: Self-employed	(3) - National Health and Redundancy Funds	(4) = Labour Subsidies	(5) Net Labour Tax
Agriculture and Fishing	58.9	18.7	6.2	-	83.8
Coal Mining	50.9	-	4.1	-	55.0
Other Mining and Quarrying	9.0	-	0.7	0.1	9.6
Food	89.8	0.7	7.3	6.5	91.3
Drink	22.2	-	1.8	2.7	21.3
Tobacco	6.3	-	0.5	0.6	6.2
Mineral Oils	5.1	-	0.4	0.4	5.1
Other Coal and Petroleum Products	4.7	-	0.4	0.4	4.7
Chemicals	70.8	-	5.7	8.0	68.5
Metals	99.4	0.1	8.0	11.0	96.5
Mech. Engineering	174.6	-	14.0	14.8	173.8
Instr. Engineering	23.5	-	1.9	2.4	23.0
Elec. Engineering	129.8	0.5	10.4	10.7	130.0
Shipbuilding	33.3	0.1	2.7	10.8	25.3
Vehicles	140.8	0.4	11.3	8.7	143.8
Textiles	88.3	0.3	7.1	6.7	89.0
Clothing	53.6	1.2	4.4	4.0	55.2
Leather, Fur, etc.	7.8	-	0.6	0.9	7.5
Timber, Furniture, etc.	40.1	0.7	3.3	4.2	39.9
Paper, Printing and Publishing	95.6	0.5	7.7	5.9	97.9
Manufacturing n.e.s.	186.2	1.5	15.1	13.4	189.4
Construction	269.7	25.9	23.7	1.6	317.7
Gas, Electricity and Water	57.7	-	4.6	-	62.3
Transport	179.7	4.8	14.8	-	199.3
Communication	72.3	-	5.8	-	78.1
Retail Trade	230.4	20.9	20.2	-	271.5
Wholesale Trade	126.1	4.1	10.4	-	140.6
Banking and Insurance etc.	139.0	1.7	11.3	-	152.0
Housing Services (Private)	12.6	0.2	1.0	-	13.8
Housing Services (Local Authority)	3.5	-	0.3	-	3.8
Public Service	358.9	5.5	29.2	-	393.6
Professional Service	385.5	8.7	31.6	-	425.8
Other Services	269.4	23.6	23.5	-	316.5
	3495.5	120.1	290.0	113.8	3791.8

Notes to tables are given in Appendix B.

(6) Labour Tax Rate (in %)	(7) + Corporation Tax	(8) - Rates	(9) = Capital Subsidies	(10) Net Capital Tax	(11) Capital Tax Rate on Net of Tax Income (%)
8.2	21.1	7.7	.3	28.5	6.4
9.5	-	13.2	115.0	-101.8	-74.1
11.1	17.2	7.3	1.3	23.2	135.7
10.8	90.3	31.9	7.6	114.6	145.1
6.0	164.2	7.2	3.7	167.7	205.0
7.2	27.6	1.1	0.3	28.4	210.4
12.0	4.3	9.1	0.5	12.9	274.5
11.9	4.0	3.9	0.2	7.7	157.1
8.4	135.2	33.2	9.2	159.2	116.0
9.8	73.2	44.0	109.6	7.6	6.3
9.0	206.9	39.8	12.2	234.5	390.2
8.3	18.8	6.1	1.7	23.2	407.0
10.5	182.1	25.7	11.4	196.4	285.5
7.2	8.0	5.8	6.2	7.6	155.1
8.4	90.3	31.9	7.8	114.4	291.0
11.5	64.6	22.4	7.0	80.0	121.4
11.1	47.1	10.0	3.3	53.8	240.2
12.8	8.2	1.8	0.6	9.4	276.5
7.9	29.5	13.8	3.3	40.0	116.6
8.7	99.6	29.4	6.6	122.4	96.9
9.2	213.5	55.1	12.9	255.7	120.3
9.2	149.5	21.2	6.2	164.5	43.9
8.1	-	108.2	140.2	-32.0	-7.2
7.2	68.9	71.9	355.8	-215.0	-49.2
7.5	-	21.0	73.1	-52.1	-40.2
10.2	293.2	193.7	6.0	480.9	101.4
8.8	334.7	80.1	6.1	408.7	480.3
6.5	605.2	78.8	13.2	670.8	144.9
6.5	55.0	938.9		993.9	20.0
4.9	-	308.3	26.0	282.3	7.6
5.0	-	194.5		194.5	33.3
17.8	19.5	75.2		94.7	23.2
16.2	192.3	124.7	4.9	312.1	81.1
	3224.0	2617.0	952.2	4888.7	

because of the flat rate component. National insurance contributions are also sex differentiated and so industries
with high proportions of female labour (such as the textile
industry) will pay lower national insurance contributions.
To the national insurance contributions are added the
special contributions for self-employed and the contributions made under the National Health redundancy fund. The
return to labour is constructed as income from employment
plus the self-employment income attributed as a return to
labour less the sum of the national insurance contributions
(columns 2, 3, and 4).

5.3. Taxes and Subsidies on the Return to Labour and the Profit Type Return

The components of the taxes and subsidies on value added
appearing in Tables 5.3 and 5.4 are reported in Table 5.5.
These are separately broken down into taxes on labour and
capital, and the effective ad valorem tax rates used in the
model are also reported. The labour tax includes national
insurance contributions and labour subsidies. The labour
subsidies are regional employment payments to qualifying
industries (a residual of the selective employment tax
system abolished in the UK in 1973).

Taxes on capital contain three components: the corporate
taxes; rates (the UK property tax); and capital subsidies
paid to selected industries. The allocation of rates by
industry uses unpublished information from the input-output
tables for 1968. The capital subsidies are primarily subsidies paid by government to nationalized industries, but
also include some regional subsidies paid to qualifying
industries.

Capital tax rates are high, averaging around 200% for
manufacturing industries and at first sight they may appear
implausibly large. Three separate points need to be noted.
Firstly, these tax rates are on a net basis, and thus a 200%
tax rate corresponds to a tax rate at 66 2/3% on the gross
return. Secondly, capital taxes include both corporate and
property taxes, so combined tax rates will tend to exceed
the legal corporate tax rate. Thirdly, the significance of

stock appreciation in 1973 and its treatment as taxable
inflationary capital gains means the tax paid on this
appears in our tax rate calculation with no corresponding
entry in the tax base. This significantly raises calculated
tax rates.

We also note that capital tax rates are sharply differentiated by industry with high tax rates on manufacturing, low
rates on both housing industries, and substantial subsidies
on nationalized transportation and power industries.

5.4   Details of Costs of Production by Industry

Costs of production by industry are reported in Table 5.6.
The benchmark equilibrium costs associated with operating
production processes in each industry are broken down into
primary costs and costs of intermediate products purchased
for use in that industry. The intermediate costs reflect the
intermediate transactions which appear in the benchmark data
set; these are used to generate the input-output coefficients for the model. Total primary costs include the profit
type return, labour costs, taxes paid on value added, plus
net taxes on production (which may be negative). Net taxes
on production are output subsidies (cash payments) paid by
government to particular industries. In the case of banking,
insurance, and finance, stamp duties are treated as a
production tax. The total costs in Table 5.6 also measure
the gross value of output of each industry at factor cost,
because of the general equlibrium zero profit condition
satisfied in the benchmark data set for each industry where
the value of sales equals total costs.

5.5   Demands for Commodities

Demands for commodities are reported in Table 5.7. The commodities included are both UK produced and imported commodities. The demands are broken down by type and by sector.
Intermediate demands reflect row sums of intermediate transactions accounts gross of any intermediate purchase taxes.
All final demands reported are at producers' prices.

TABLE 5.6

Costs of Production by Industry: U.K. 1973   £ mill.

Industry	Profit-type Payments	Labour Costs	Net Capital Tax Payments	Net Labour Tax Payments
Agriculture (Including Forestry and Fishing)	443.7	1023.8	28.5	83.8
Coal Mining	137.4	581.0	-101.8	55.0
Other Mining and Quarrying	17.1	86.9	23.2	9.6
Food	79.0	842.0	114.6	91.3
Drink	81.8	353.9	167.7	21.3
Tobacco	13.5	86.0	28.4	6.2
Mineral Oils	4.7	42.5	12.9	5.1
Other Coal/Petroleum Product's	4.9	39.4	7.7	4.7
Chemicals	137.3	817.3	159.2	68.5
Metals	120.2	987.6	7.6	96.5
Mechanical Engineering	60.1	1931.9	234.5	173.8
Instrumental Engineering	5.7	278.7	23.2	23.0
Electrical Engineering	68.8	1239.5	196.4	130.0
Shipbuilding	4.9	351.1	7.6	25.3
Vehicles	39.3	1718.5	114.4	143.8
Textiles	65.9	775.8	80.0	89.0
Clothing and Footwear	22.4	497.8	53.8	55.2
Leather, Leather Goods and Fur	3.4	58.4	9.4	7.5
Timber, Furniture, etc.	34.3	504.4	40.0	39.9
Paper, Printing and Publishing	126.3	1129.5	122.4	97.9
Manufacturing n.e.s.	212.6	2049.8	255.7	189.4
Construction	375.1	3440.8	164.5	317.7
Gas, Electricity and Water	443.9	768.7	-32.0	62.3
Transport	436.9	2766.7	-215.0	199.3
Communications	129.7	1037.9	-52.1	78.1
Retail Trade	474.2	2675.4	480.9	271.5
Wholesale Trade	85.1	1599.0	408.7	140.6
Banking, Insurance and Finance	462.8	2354.0	670.8	152.0
Housing Services (Private)	4964.3	213.9	993.9	13.8
Housing Services (Local Authority)	3735.2	76.7	282.3	3.8
Public Service	3141.2	7936.6	194.5	393.6
Professional Services	407.9	2388.0	94.7	425.8
Other Services	384.6	1949.9	312.1	316.5
	16724.2	42603.4	4888.7	3791.8

Notes to tables are given in Appendix B.

Net Taxes on Production	Total Primary Cost	Cost of Intermediate Usage	Total Costs
-287.0	1292.8	2524.6	3817.4
-161.0	510.6	374.7	885.3
0.0	136.8	411.6	548.4
0.0	1126.9	6073.6	7200.5
0.0	624.7	733.5	1358.2
0.0	134.1	414.1	548.2
0.0	65.2	1673.3	1738.5
0.0	56.7	134.5	191.2
0.0	1182.3	3794.2	4976.5
-6.0	1205.9	3693.8	4899.7
0.0	2400.3	3906.1	6306.4
0.0	330.6	505.8	836.4
0.0	1634.7	3000.0	4634.7
0.0	388.9	522.5	911.4
0.0	2016.0	3884.8	5900.8
0.0	1010.7	2746.2	3756.9
0.0	629.2	1069.1	1698.3
0.0	78.7	211.0	289.7
0.0	618.6	1160.1	1778.7
0.0	1476.1	2460.9	3937.0
0.0	2707.5	4598.9	7306.4
0.0	4298.1	4971.6	9269.7
-151.0	1091.9	2579.0	3670.9
-207.0	2980.9	4094.9	7075.8
-209.0	984.6	967.8	1952.4
0.0	3902.0	2351.9	6253.9
0.0	2233.4	1217.7	3451.1
205.0	3844.6	2408.6	6253.2
0.0	6185.9	0.0	6185.9
-57.0	4041.0	0.0	4041.0
0.0	11665.9	0.0	11665.9
0.0	3316.4	1471.8	4788.2
0.0	2963.1	1736.7	4699.8
-873.0	67135.2	65693.3	132828.4

TABLE 5.7

Value of Demands for Commodities U.K. 1973

£ mill.

U.K. Commodities	Intermediate Demands Net of Intermediate Tax	Intermediate Taxes	Private Sector Consumption Expenditures	Investment Expenditures	Government Demands	Exports	Total Final Demands	Total Output
Agriculture (inc. For. and Fish)	1962.6	0.0	1395.7	144.0	30.4	270.5	1840.6	3803.2
Coal Mining	617.7	0.0	198.1	0.0	36.8	15.0	249.9	867.6
Other Mining and Quarrying	461.9	0.0	4.9	0.4	13.2	63.3	81.8	543.7
Food	1600.2	0.0	4706.4	0.3	107.5	413.2	5227.4	6827.6
Drink	164.6	0.0	578.4	68.3	0.4	397.7	1044.8	1209.4
Tobacco	89.8	0.0	387.7	3.5	0.3	64.8	456.3	546.1
Mineral Oils	1709.6	633.7	179.8	62.5	44.3	404.2	690.8	2400.4
Other Coal/Petroleum Products	119.1	0.0	61.0	7.6	24.6	57.0	150.2	269.3
Chemicals	2604.8	0.0	519.5	81.6	253.7	1359.4	2214.2	4819.0
Metals	3495.8	0.0	0.0	276.4	11.4	926.1	1213.9	4709.7
Mechanical Engineering	3133.7	0.0	10.1	537.9	541.7	2014.6	3104.3	6238.0
Instrumental Engineering	196.4	0.0	34.9	56.4	159.8	352.0	603.1	799.5
Electrical Engineering	1834.8	0.0	344.5	409.2	503.6	1215.4	2472.7	4307.5
Shipbuilding	370.5	0.0	0.0	89.0	279.3	204.7	573.0	943.5
Vehicles	2372.8	189.0	501.2	246.3	648.9	2071.7	3468.1	5840.9
Textiles	2016.9	0.0	885.2	0.0	26.2	782.0	1693.4	3710.3
Clothing and Footwear	450.1	0.0	1045.0	0.0	40.4	150.0	1235.4	1685.5
Leather, Leather Goods and Fur	126.2	0.0	59.9	0.0	0.0	97.0	156.9	283.1
Timber,Furniture, etc.	1058.6	0.0	406.0	83.3	58.8	101.1	649.2	1707.8
Paper Printing and Publishing	2888.1	0.0	570.0	0.0	163.1	252.0	985.1	3873.2
Manufacturing NES	4453.6	0.0	731.0	18.4	102.1	1933.4	2784.9	7238.5
Construction	3978.3	0.0	2191.4	1112.9	1613.4	696.2	5613.9	9592.2
Gas, Electricity and Water	1514.5	0.0	1725.2	13.8	188.7	7.1	1934.7	3449.2
Transport	5179.6	0.0	1756.8	8.5	120.0	804.3	2689.6	7869.2
Communications	1049.3	0.0	532.6	81.0	168.7	120.7	903.0	1952.3
Retail Trade	2328.2	0.0	4248.6	29.0	142.0	16.4	4436.0	6764.2
Wholesale Trade	923.5	0.0	2431.9	16.6	81.3	279.4	2809.2	3732.7
Banking,Insurance and Finance	1417.5	0.0	3076.0	82.0	1148.0	540.2	4846.2	6263.7
Housing Services (Private)	0.0	0.0	6185.6	0.0	0.0	0.0	6185.6	6185.6

Housing Services (Local Auth.)	0.0	0.0	4040.8	0.0	0.0	0.0	4040.8	4040.8
Public Service	0.0	0.0	0.0	0.0	11667.2	0.0	11667.2	11667.2
Professional Services	2490.2	0.0	1623.1	67.8	579.4	38.2	2308.5	4798.7
Other Services	2471.8	0.0	1455.8	60.8	519.6	201.9	2238.1	4709.9
Imported Commodities								
Agriculture (inc. For. and Fish)	978.6	4.2	291.5	0.0	14.1	0.0	305.6	1284.2
Coal Mining	13.8	0.0	5.3	0.0	0.0	0.0	5.3	19.1
Other Mining and Quarrying	1497.0	0.0	0.0	0.0	0.0	0.0	0.0	1497.0
Food	812.7	2.7	1052.4	0.0	57.5	0.0	1109.9	1922.6
Drink	100.0	0.0	113.0	0.0	0.0	0.0	113.0	213.0
Tobacco	2.3	0.0	12.7	0.0	0.0	0.0	12.7	15.0
Mineral Oils	425.2	162.3	62.9	0.0	12.4	0.0	75.3	500.5
Other Coal/Petroleum Products	13.4	0.0	7.6	0.0	0.0	0.0	7.6	21.0
Chemicals	844.3	6.1	12.6	0.0	19.2	0.0	31.8	876.1
Metals	957.2	11.2	0.0	249.5	0.0	0.0	249.5	1206.7
Mechanical Engineering	743.4	10.5	3.7	336.9	84.4	0.0	425.0	1168.4
Instrumental Engineering	189.8	3.4	43.4	75.9	21.7	0.0	141.0	330.8
Electrical Engineering	890.5	12.8	102.6	277.4	31.6	0.0	411.6	1302.1
Shipbuilding	70.5	0.0	0.0	44.2	11.5	0.0	55.7	126.2
Vehicles	727.3	66.0	152.4	38.8	46.7	0.0	237.9	965.2
Textiles	607.0	7.2	76.2	0.0	0.0	0.0	76.2	683.2
Clothing and Footwear	78.7	5.5	235.8	0.0	0.0	0.0	235.8	314.5
Leather, Leather Goods and Fur	67.8	0.2	10.4	0.0	0.0	0.0	10.4	78.2
Timber, Furniture, etc.	641.8	1.4	25.6	0.0	0.0	0.0	25.6	667.4
Paper, Printing and Publishing	590.4	2.1	25.7	0.0	0.0	0.0	25.7	616.1
Manufacturing NES	1263.0	2.2	114.5	1.2	0.8	0.0	116.5	1379.5
Construction	20.0	0.0	0.0	0.0	0.0	0.0	0.0	20.0
Transport	811.0	0.0	0.0	0.0	0.0	0.0	0.0	811.0
Communications	81.0	0.0	0.0	0.0	0.0	0.0	0.0	81.0
Banking, Insurance and Finance	91.6	0.0	32.5	0.0	0.0	0.0	32.5	124.1
Professional Services	32.4	0.0	12.6	0.0	0.0	0.0	12.6	45.0
Other Services	62.2	0.0	22.8	0.0	0.0	0.0	22.8	85.0
	65693.6	1120.5	44303.2	4581.4	19574.7	15849.5	84308.8	150002.4

Private sector demands reflect demands of the household sector, including residential construction. Small private sector demands occur for capital goods and items used primarily for intermediate purposes such as metals. Total final demands for UK products equal the sum of private sector consumption demands, investment expenditures, government demands, and exports. Final demands for imports in the UK appear as the final demands for consumption and capital goods, and include government expenditures on imported products.

5.6 Consumer Taxes and Subsidies

Consumer taxes and subsidies by product are reported in Table 5.8. These destination based taxes are charged on both domestically-produced and imported goods. Taxes are rebated on exports. As has already been mentioned (see Chapter 3), calculations are performed which include the value-added tax in this data set as an equivalent final sales tax rebated on exports.

The specific excise taxes are primarily on drink, tobacco, and mineral oils. They produce high rates of tax on these items (up to 400 percent) and so their removal produces substantial quantity responses in consumption of these items in the model.

The other items which appear as consumer taxes and subsidies derive from specific government interferences which are treated as ad valorem equivalent taxes and subsidies. The major item is the subsidy paid to tenants of local authority housing offered at controlled rents which are below the cost of provision of local authority housing services. The total of all these items is given in column 5 of Table 5.8.

5.7 Consumer Incomes and Income taxes

For all of the consumer groups in the model a number of components of consumer incomes are considered. These are reported on a weekly per household basis in Table 5.9 after all adjustments to the benchmark data set have been completed. In these adjustments the total profit type return of the private sector is allocated by household using information in the Family Expenditure Survey. This procedure

uses information on ownership of homes, interest and dividends received, and small business income. The total labour
income accruing to the household sector is similarly
allocated between household groups using data on wages and
salaries. Transfers received reflect old-age pensions,
unemployment compensation and other components of the extensive transfer system operating in the UK. Because incomes in
the model are defined differently from those in the Family
Expenditure Survey used to classify households, FES incomes
are often different from weekly disposable incomes implied
by the model data.

From gross income, income tax liabilities are subtracted
for each of the household types to yield weekly disposable
income. Annual income tax liabilities summed across households are calculated so as to be consistent with National
Accounts reported total income tax. As all tax receipts
collected by government appear in the model, additional
personal taxes are treated as components of an enlarged
income tax system along with the personal income tax. Thus
capital gains tax and estate duty are treated as components
of the model income tax system. As has already been mentioned, individual households are not separately identified
in the model but instead groups of households are treated;
estate duty is thus treated as a probabilistic tax, a payment 'on account' out of current income, with eventual
settlement at death.

Income tax liabilities by household are calculated using
FES information on income tax payments by each of the household types. The allocation of capital gains tax and estate
duty by individual income range follows a different procedure as explained in Chapter 3. The gross income minus the
income tax liabilities gives the measure of disposable
income which appears in column 6 of Table 5.9. From the
disposable incomes savings are subtracted to give expenditures on goods and services. Savings reflect resource
transfers from the private sector to other sectors of the
economy (most notably the corporate sector) as discussed
earlier.

TABLE 5.8

1973 U.K. Consumer Taxes and Subsidies: Collections by Product

in Benchmark Data Set

(£ mill.)

	(1) Specific Excise	(2) VAT	(3) Other	(4) Protective Duty (Final Output)	(5) Total	(6) Effective Tax Rate
DOMESTICALLY PRODUCED COMMODITIES						
Agriculture (including Forestry and Fishing)	–	9.5	–	–	9.5	0.6
Coal Mining	–	0.0	–	–	–	–
Other Mining and Quarrying	–	1.8	–	–	1.8	9.7
Food	–	35.1	–	–	35.1	0.7
Drink	845.5	68.1	–	–	913.6	141.2
Tobacco	1067.8	42.8	–	–	1110.6	283.7
Mineral Oils	686.5	0.0	–	–	686.5	239.5
Other Coal/Petroleum Products	–	1.8	–	–	1.8	1.9
Chemicals	–	70.5	–	–	70.5	8.2
Metals	–	0.1	–	–	0.1	0.0
Mechanical Engineering	–	0.0	–	–	0.3	0.0
Instrumental Engineering	–	0.0	–	–	–	–
Electrical Engineering	–	0.3	–	–	0.3	0.0
Shipbuilding	–	0.0	–	–	–	–
Vehicles	–	137.7	315.6	–	453.3	32.5
Textiles	–	92.9	–	–	92.9	10.2
Clothing and Footwear	–	91.8	–	–	91.8	8.5
Leather, Leather Goods and Fur	–	6.1	–	–	6.1	10.2
Timber, Furniture, etc.	–	55.4	–	–	55.4	10.1
Paper, Printing and Furnishing	–	27.5	–	–	27.5	3.8
Manufacturing n.e.s.	–	86.4	–	–	86.4	10.1
Construction	–	0.7	–	–	0.7	0.0
Gas, Electricity, and Water	–	0.6	–	–	0.6	0.0
Transport	–	0.4	–	–	0.4	0.0
Communications	–	1.1	–	–	1.1	0.1
Retail Trade	–	450.1	–	–	450.1	10.2
Wholesale Trade	–	257.5	–	–	257.5	10.2
Banking, Insurance, and Finance	–	216.1	–	–	216.1	5.0
Housing Services (Private)	–	0.0	–	–	–	–
Housing Services (Local Authority)	–	0.0	-3136.0	–	-3136.0	-77.6
Public Service	–	–	–	–	–	–
Professional Services	–	216.3	–	–	216.3	9.5
Other Services	–	184.9	184.0	–	368.9	18.1

IMPORTED COMMODITIES						
Agriculture (including Forestry and Fishing)	–	1.8	–	22.3	24.1	7.9
Coal Mining	–	0.0	–	0.0	–	–
Other Mining and Quarrying	–	0.0	–	0.0	–	–
Food	–	7.7	–	14.1	21.8	2.0
Drink	132.5	11.8	–	0.1	144.4	127.8
Tobacco	30.2	1.4	–	0.0	31.6	248.8
Mineral Oils	132.5	0.0	–	0.6	133.1	176.8
Other Coal/Petroleum Products	–	0.2	–	0.0	0.2	2.6
Chemicals	–	2.6	–	32.2	34.8	109.4
Metals	–	0.0	–	0.0	–	–
Mechanical Engineering	–	0.0	–	56.0	56.0	13.2
Instrumental Engineering	–	0.0	–	18.2	18.2	12.9
Electrical Engineering	–	0.0	–	67.8	67.8	16.5
Shipbuilding	–	0.0	–	0.0	–	–
Vehicles	–	23.8	63.4	42.2	129.4	54.4
Textiles	–	7.9	–	38.0	45.9	60.2
Clothing and Footwear	–	19.4	–	29.2	48.6	20.6
Leather, Leather Goods and Fur	–	1.1	–	1.2	2.3	22.1
Timber, Furniture, etc.	–	2.6	–	7.3	9.9	38.7
Paper, Printing and Publishing	–	1.0	–	11.1	12.1	47.1
Manufacturing n.e.s.	–	11.9	–	11.8	23.7	20.3
Construction	–	0.0	–	–	–	–
Transport	–	0.0	–	–	–	–
Communications	–	0.0	–	–	–	–
Banking, Insurance, and Finance	–	3.7	–	–	3.7	11.4
Professional Services	–	0.5	–	–	0.5	4.0
Other Services	–	2.0	–	–	2.0	8.8
Final Output Taxes	2895.0	2155.2	-2573.0	352.1	2829.3	
Intermediate Output Taxes	796.0	–	247.0	77.6	1120.6	
	3691.0	2155.2	-2326.0	429.7	3949.9	

Notes to tables are given in Appendix B.

TABLE 5.9

Components of Weekly Household Incomes in 1973 U.K. Benchmark Data Set

Household Description (FES Classification)		(1) Profit-type Return	(2) Labour Income	(3) Transfers	(4) Gross Income	(5) Income Tax Liabilities (inc. Capital Gains Tax and Estate Duty)	(6) = (4) - (5) Disposable Income	(7) Savings	(8) = (6) - 7 £/week Consumption Expenditure
Type I Manual	≤ £20	1.80	9.28	8.12	19.21	0.62	18.59	0.67	17.92
	£20-30	2.19	22.48	4.39	29.06	3.81	25.55	2.46	22.79
	£30-40	2.84	34.98	2.56	40.37	6.77	33.60	2.61	30.99
	> £40	4.48	47.29	0.62	52.39	10.47	41.92	2.76	39.16
Type I Non-Manual	≤ £20	1.77	11.77	6.54	20.99	1.48	18.61	2.16	16.45
	£20-30	2.26	23.02	2.31	29.59	4.48	23.11	0.52	22.59
	£30-40	3.84	32.90	1.58	38.32	7.36	30.96	1.86	29.10
	£40-50	7.83	41.78	2.40	52.00	9.83	42.17	4.99	37.18
	£50-60	9.32	49.16	3.20	61.68	13.04	48.64	1.49	47.15
	£60-70	7.79	61.30	0.85	69.94	19.13	50.81	1.42	49.39
	> £70	46.43	80.93	1.42	128.78	42.52	86.26	11.84	74.42
Type I Self-Employed	≤ £20	6.23	3.56	9.33	19.12	1.84	17.28	0.30	16.98
	£20-40	26.06	14.16	4.42	44.64	4.52	40.12	0.0	40.12
	> £40	57.09	34.84	2.17	94.10	18.19	75.91	4.77	71.14
Type I Retired	≤ £10	0.86	0.03	12.26	13.15	0.03	13.12	0.60	12.52
	£10-20	5.85	0.02	12.75	18.62	0.33	18.29	0.67	17.62
	£20-30	25.17	0.02	11.57	36.77	6.00	30.77	0.37	30.40
	£30-40	41.89	1.30	9.56	52.74	10.67	42.07	0.0	42.07
	£40-50	61.44	0.0	10.80	72.24	23.98	48.26	4.10	44.16
	> £50	106.40	0.0	10.70	117.16	64.48	52.68	0.0	52.68
Type I Unoccupied	≤ £10	0.85	0.06	7.94	8.85	0.0	8.85	0.30	8.55
	£10-20	1.45	0.91	14.58	16.93	0.20	16.73	0.40	16.33
	£20-30	6.81	2.14	14.90	23.85	0.92	22.93	0.0	22.93
	> £30	56.00	4.14	12.56	72.77	29.48	43.29	0.0	43.29
Type II Manual	≤ £20	2.14	13.41	13.02	28.57	0.43	28.14	0.52	27.62
	£20-30	2.89	22.35	7.05	32.28	2.55	29.73	1.34	28.39
	£30-40	2.62	36.23	2.65	41.50	5.12	36.38	2.38	34.00
	£40-50	2.97	48.35	1.63	52.95	7.28	45.67	3.72	41.95
	£50-60	4.35	62.05	1.58	67.98	9.97	58.01	8.79	49.22
	£60-70	4.92	72.56	1.10	78.58	12.24	66.34	9.16	57.18
	£70-80	6.64	79.31	0.43	86.38	16.20	70.18	5.96	64.22
	£80-90	6.74	94.81	0.37	101.92	19.33	82.59	10.88	71.71
	> £90	4.67	117.53	0.68	122.88	26.11	96.77	17.21	79.56

Type II Non-Manual

≤ £30	4.00	20.94	5.20	30.15	3.05	27.10	1.56	25.54
£30-40	4.16	36.41	1.38	41.95	5.06	36.89	2.98	33.91
£40-50	8.83	46.05	3.44	58.33	7.55	50.78	7.23	43.55
£50-60	7.90	55.20	1.09	64.19	10.79	53.40	2.98	50.42
£60-70	9.42	72.16	1.35	82.93	12.45	70.48	12.14	58.34
£70-80	11.18	75.84	0.69	87.72	17.02	70.70	5.07	65.63
£80-90	13.84	86.66	0.81	101.31	18.33	82.98	9.16	73.82
£90-100	10.30	105.95	0.18	116.42	21.98	94.44	15.42	79.02
≥ £100	36.13	164.33	0.81	201.27	50.59	150.68	29.35	121.33

Type II Self-Employed

≤ £20	8.73	6.61	6.34	21.68	0.0	21.68	1.04	20.64
£20-30	17.30	12.39	4.10	33.80	4.05	29.75	0.15	29.60
£30-40	22.25	22.15	1.69	46.09	4.16	41.93	1.34	40.59
£40-50	30.64	30.45	1.72	62.81	6.52	56.29	5.07	51.22
£50-60	35.68	34.69	1.50	71.87	7.42	64.45	2.09	62.36
£60-70	45.62	37.81	0.50	83.94	11.59	72.35	0.60	71.65
£70-90	49.96	47.51	1.86	99.33	11.96	87.37	1.86	85.51
> £90	116.94	96.62	2.02	195.58	44.14	151.44	0.82	150.62

Type II Retired

≤ £20	3.63	0.30	19.40	23.33	0.09	23.24	0.82	22.42
£20-30	13.78	2.71	18.94	35.44	0.99	34.45	1.12	33.33
£30-40	18.77	12.15	17.60	48.53	5.98	42.55	1.79	40.76
£40-50	23.53	22.08	14.90	60.51	8.99	51.52	2.53	48.99
£50-60	42.29	20.99	15.94	79.22	17.56	61.66	5.74	55.92
£60-70	66.07	22.45	19.43	107.95	24.37	83.58	16.84	66.74
£70-90	71.17	34.08	15.48	120.71	32.09	88.62	10.58	78.04
> £90	171.67	5.47	16.52	193.65	121.49	72.16	4.62	67.54

Tye II Unoccupied

≤ £20	4.12	1.13	13.53	18.77	0.0	18.77	0.37	18.40
£20-30	8.91	7.91	12.01	28.84	1.77	27.07	0.37	26.70
£30-40	20.74	13.58	9.05	43.37	4.97	38.40	0.15	38.25
£40-60	35.51	19.12	9.08	63.71	10.62	53.09	2.38	50.71
> £60	100.10	21.62	6.59	128.32	38.73	89.59	10.95	78.64

Type III Manual

≤ £30	0.75	24.93	12.46	38.14	1.38	36.76	1.64	35.12
£30-40	1.84	36.92	4.60	43.36	2.89	40.47	2.23	38.24
£40-50	2.46	48.76	4.20	55.41	5.67	49.74	5.51	44.23
£50-60	3.65	58.29	3.47	65.41	7.75	57.66	5.44	52.22
£60-70	3.73	69.75	4.32	77.81	9.88	67.93	7.52	60.41
£70-80	3.84	83.82	4.35	92.00	11.76	80.24	11.10	69.14
£80-90	6.09	97.54	4.50	108.14	13.65	94.49	14.97	79.52
£90-100	6.93	113.99	2.56	123.48	16.53	106.95	20.78	86.17
> £100	6.14	134.21	3.40	143.76	21.83	121.93	16.24	105.69

TABLE 5.9 (cont'd.)

Type III Non-Manual

≤ £40	3.38	30.37	5.03	38.79	3.47	35.32	0.97	34.35
£40-50	5.40	47.50	3.41	56.32	6.55	49.77	5.14	44.63
£50-60	7.91	56.44	3.00	67.34	8.62	58.72	6.11	52.61
£60-70	8.13	64.00	3.80	75.94	11.66	64.28	3.80	60.48
£70-80	9.34	79.82	3.02	92.18	13.94	78.24	9.53	68.71
£80-90	10.16	88.69	2.36	101.21	16.55	84.66	9.24	75.92
£90-100	11.10	96.19	2.20	109.49	19.46	90.03	5.74	84.29
> £100	28.31	143.51	2.89	174.71	36.63	138.08	21.60	116.48

Type III Self-Employed

≤ £30	16.04	14.76	2.63	33.44	1.01	32.43	1.86	30.57
£30-40	23.09	21.09	3.62	47.80	2.94	44.86	1.04	43.82
£40-50	27.28	31.59	2.95	61.82	3.64	58.18	4.77	53.41
£50-60	29.74	41.08	3.40	74.22	5.41	68.81	3.87	64.94
£60-70	36.25	46.29	5.12	87.67	8.14	79.53	6.11	73.42
£70-80	39.99	52.78	2.78	95.54	7.95	87.59	1.86	85.73
£80-90	39.83	59.87	3.07	102.77	13.21	89.56	0.0	89.56
£90-100	56.35	64.79	2.94	124.08	14.48	109.60	5.07	104.53
> £100	97.37	94.77	2.44	194.59	33.99	160.60	5.21	155.39

Type III Retired

≤ £30	5.58	3.72	25.48	34.79	0.45	34.34	0.37	33.97
£30-40	8.44	17.15	21.97	47.55	2.79	44.76	3.35	41.41
£40-50	8.62	29.23	22.79	60.65	6.35	54.30	5.21	49.09
£50-60	15.03	38.19	16.52	67.74	7.27	60.47	2.01	58.46
£60-70	12.29	56.23	19.39	87.91	9.47	78.44	12.37	66.07
£70-80	16.95	49.88	20.10	86.92	13.21	73.71	0.0	73.71
> £80	39.99	76.26	18.49	134.75	27.54	107.21	4.62	102.59

Type III Unoccupied

≤ £30	1.36	8.04	20.80	30.20	0.0	30.20	0.37	29.83
£30-40	1.92	16.38	14.69	32.99	0.0	32.99	0.52	32.47
£40-60	12.51	30.10	18.09	60.69	5.45	55.24	1.42	53.82
> £60	47.09	54.78	21.12	122.99	21.51	101.48	10.95	90.53

Notes to tables are given in Appendix B.

from the FES gross income ranges reported on the left hand side of the table. The major reason for this is the imputation of income from owner-occupied housing. In addition, the aggregate household capital income implied by FES data is less than that given by other (non-housing) data in the model. In the allocation of capital income between agents, therefore, those with relatively capital intensive endowments will have a relatively greater disparity between model incomes and FES incomes. These influences account for the disparities in self-employed and retired groups.

5.8 Major Categories of Expenditures by Households

Table 5.10 reports selected categories of expenditures in our adjusted data set by household on a weekly basis after aggregation across the various commodities in the model. As can be seen from this table expenditures on these items differ by group, especially income and family characteristics. These data thus particularly motivate the importance of disaggregation by household type in the model since these expenditure patterns are reflected in different preference parameters for the household groups in the model.

A large proportion of private sector consumption expenditures are devoted to services of various kinds (not reported in Table 5.10). These include Retail and Wholesale Trade, which account for about 15% of domestic household expenditures. This treatment has the effect of increasing to some extent the effective output tax rates on non-service items reported in Table 5.8, since the purchase of any commodity will include a distributive trades component.

5.9 The Public Sector Accounts for the Year 1973

Table 5.11 reports receipts and expenditures of the public sector in the model. Tax collections account for approximately 70 percent of total receipts: the income tax, national insurance contributions, specific excise taxes, the corporate tax, purchase taxes, and rates are major components. The government also receives income from its ownership of dwellings and imputed income from its own capital stock. This last item implies a corresponding expen-

TABLE 5.10

Selected Major Categories of Expenditures by Household

(expenditures per household, £ per week)

HOUSEHOLD DESCRIPTION (FES CLASSIFICATION BY GROSS WEEKLY HOUSEHOLD INCOME)			(1) Food	(2) Drink and Tobacco	(3) Fuel and Power	(4) Housing	(5) Vehicles	(6) Clothing and Apparel
TYPE I	MANUAL	≤ £20	3.66	.85	2.58	3.67	.17	.38
		£20-30	3.70	1.77	1.34	3.36	.35	.51
		£30-40	3.92	2.97	1.91	4.42	.62	.83
		>£40	3.39	3.31	2.04	7.12	.72	.69
TYPE I	NON-MANUAL	≤ £20	2.36	.50	1.11	3.39	.12	.51
		£20-30	2.99	1.50	1.30	4.69	.40	.69
		£30-40	3.11	1.58	1.73	7.10	.64	.73
		£40-50	3.14	1.37	1.77	8.78	.67	.83
		£50-60	3.93	1.28	2.56	13.92	.85	.96
		£60-70·	2.31	2.22	1.83	9.57	.95	2.35
		>£70	3.72	2.24	2.68	17.28	2.00	.94
TYPE I	SELF-EMPLOYED	≤ £20	2.72	1.56	1.03	3.22	.11	.18
		£20-40	5.44	2.95	1.72	9.25	.53	1.99
		>£40	4.13	6.31	2.65	17.83	1.02	2.40
TYPE I	RETIRED	≤ £10	3.42	.39	1.57	2.42	.09	.25
		£10-20	3.10	.48	1.43	5.41	.22	.30
		£20-30	4.02	1.04	1.76	9.93	.39	.58
		£30-40	4.53	1.09	2.58	14.18	.65	.36
		£40-50	3.70	.52	2.32	11.17	.56	.69
		>£50	2.43	.92	2.38	28.53	.57	.05
TYPE I	UNOCCUPIED	≤ £10	1.00	.39	.42	1.15	.04	.08
		£10-20	3.30	.91	1.33	3.04	.18	.37
		£20-30	3.45	.88	1.28	5.31	.32	.76
		>£30	4.63	.97	1.59	11.47	.60	2.11
TYPE II	MANUAL	≤ £20	6.39	2.62	2.36	3.99	.19	.45
		£20-30	6.56	2.34	2.11	4.13	.44	.80
		£30-40	6.53	2.98	2.29	5.27	.64	.98
		£40-50	7.38	3.63	2.54	5.88	.82	1.35
		£50-60	7.14	3.62	2.43	6.83	.97	1.39
		£60-70	7.22	4.04	2.75	8.79	1.12	1.59
		£70-80	8.04	3.83	3.11	11.88	1.56	2.39
		£80-90	6.72	4.69	2.88	11.42	1.53	2.13
		>£90	6.37	4.56	3.12	7.64	1.55	3.20
TYPE II	NON-MANUAL	≤ £30	4.61	1.76	1.77	4.66	.28	1.02
		£30-40	5.29	2.22	2.41	6.36	.61	.72
		£40-50	6.05	2.35	2.43	9.28	.78	1.37
		£50-60	6.32	2.17	2.67	15.73	.97	1.44
		£60-70	5.77	2.59	2.65	12.97	1.02	1.34
		£70-80	7.22	3.26	3.42	15.73	1.49	1.69
		£80-90	7.38	3.98	3.16	16.05	1.52	1.43
		£90-100	6.48	2.94	3.77	16.87	1.45	1.38
		>£100	8.48	3.47	4.24	31.74	1.97	2.60
TYPE II	SELF-EMPLOYED	≤ £20	3.23	1.31	1.61	3.71	.12	.45
		£20-30	5.73	2.77	1.98	6.35	.54	.80
		£30-40	7.48	2.92	2.59	7.22	.65	1.23
		£40-50	7.56	3.73	3.12	10.65	.86	1.31
		£50-60	8.25	5.60	2.98	12.01	1.38	1.73
		£60-70	11.13	3.54	3.22	14.90	1.59	2.41
		£70-90	9.22	4.53	5.25	14.64	1.84	3.23
		>£90	15.82	9.14	6.01	35.93	3.72	7.64

HOUSEHOLD DESCRIPTION (FES CLASSIFICATION BY GROSS WEEKLY HOUSEHOLD INCOME)		(1) Food	(2) Drink and Tobacco	(3) Fuel and Power	(4) Housing	(5) Vehicles	(6) Clothing and Apparel
TYPE II RETIRED	≤ £20	6.44	1.52	2.12	4.42	.20	.51
	£20-30	6.74	1.80	2.14	7.77	.49	.83
	£30-40	6.99	2.60	2.21	9.15	.73	1.01
	£40-50	6.95	3.01	3.00	11.93	.76	1.29
	£50-60	6.29	1.81	3.03	11.02	1.14	1.17
	£60-70	5.68	1.11	2.54	14.23	.81	1.25
	£70-90	6.03	2.93	2.41	15.23	1.34	1.04
	>£90	4.95	3.66	3.50	17.12	1.40	1.49
TYPE II UNOCCUPIED	≤ £20	4.19	1.18	1.40	3.21	.19	.36
	£20-30	4.75	1.86	1.73	5.21	.44	1.25
	£30-40	4.20	2.33	1.45	6.04	.45	1.25
	£40-60	5.85	2.35	2.04	7.43	1.00	.99
	>£60	6.80	3.91	3.30	14.17	1.75	2.06
TYPE III MANUAL	≤ £30	9.43	3.19	3.01	4.31	.36	.97
	£30-40	9.25	3.29	2.86	4.48	.67	1.25
	£40-50	8.52	3.42	2.77	5.97	.77	1.31
	£50-60	9.56	4.07	3.16	7.70	.97	1.84
	£60-70	10.09	4.51	3.22	8.17	1.08	2.39
	£70-80	10.55	5.25	3.64	7.66	1.34	2.55
	£80-90	11.14	6.58	3.80	7.33	1.61	2.46
	£90-100	10.35	5.50	3.25	9.17	1.51	2.61
	>£100	13.37	12.37	4.82	9.88	2.16	4.28
TYPE III NON-MANUAL	≤ £40	7.17	2.38	2.58	6.42	.40	1.45
	£40-50	7.75	1.87	2.65	9.70	.77	1.33
	£50-60	8.08	2.71	2.76	11.48	.99	1.55
	£60-70	9.41	2.56	3.75	14.47	1.30	1.84
	£70-80	9.75	2.97	3.48	13.98	1.38	2.12
	£80-90	8.77	3.08	3.53	19.46	1.44	2.36
	£90-100	10.88	3.93	4.17	19.04	1.85	3.27
	>£100	11.82	5.11	5.07	25.47	2.23	3.72
TYPE III SELF-EMPLOYED	≤ £30	6.11	1.44	2.08	4.90	.33	.85
	£30-40	10.65	2.29	3.34	7.98	.93	1.22
	£40-50	10.45	3.77	3.15	6.78	.86	3.18
	£50-60	11.14	5.62	3.75	12.69	1.07	2.38
	£60-70	10.13	5.43	4.71	12.30	1.31	2.00
	£70-80	7.52	3.32	2.27	47.01	1.08	1.76
	£80-90	14.11	4.82	4.41	14.96	2.15	1.76
	£90-100	17.14	5.06	5.16	19.72	2.45	3.16
	>£100	21.40	13.93	7.40	30.04	3.88	5.88
TYPE III RETIRED	≤ £30	8.65	2.14	2.36	5.03	.27	1.02
	£30-40	8.22	3.78	2.53	4.30	.50	1.35
	£40-50	9.82	3.53	2.39	4.42	.64	1.52
	£50-60	7.22	4.14	1.98	22.42	.72	1.97
	£60-70	9.72	4.93	3.07	6.43	.99	1.02
	£70-80	11.18	6.59	4.38	7.07	1.50	4.02
	>£80	14.59	6.63	6.53	14.85	1.67	3.74
TYPE III UNOCCUPIED	≤ £30	6.73	2.60	1.79	2.84	.19	.62
	£30-40	5.14	2.13	1.80	3.56	.52	1.19
	£40-60	10.31	4.58	3.01	5.10	.92	1.43
	>£60	11.06	7.77	3.29	21.05	1.38	2.59

diture as the government repurchases the services of its own
capital stock. This treatment of the public sector capital
stock as yielding both imputed income and imputed expenditure is adopted as a more realistic treatment than that
implicit in the national accounts.[11] Ownership of dwellings
reflects the ownership of housing by local authorities.
Substantial subsidies appear on the expenditure side of the
account reflecting rent controlled tenancies of local
authority houses.

The net receipts from changes in financial assets and
liabilities reflect the financial transactions of the public
sector in the year, including both redemption of existing
debt and new debt issues. Income from public corporations
includes the surpluses of public corporations which are
transferred to the central government.

On the expenditure side the major item is expenditures on
goods and services. Component expenditures on Public
Services do not appear, since we treat these in the model as
a single produced good purchased exclusively by the government. Thus expenditures on defence, education, health, highways, and other items do not separately appear and are not
separately identified in the expenditure account. In
addition, government purchases of market goods and services
(which are broken down and reported at producer prices in
Table 5.7) are reported as an expenditure item. In the
model, subsidies are analyzed in some detail as they result
in distortion of relative prices affecting the structure
both of employment by industry and consumer purchases of
products. Transfers include social security payments to
persons, a major component of which is old-age pensions.

TABLE 5.11

Public Sector Receipts and Expenditures, 1973

£ million

RECEIPTS

Taxes	£ million
Income Tax + Surtax	7271.0
Capital Gains Tax	304.0
Estate Duty	420.0
National Insurance and Related Contributions	3905.0
Corporate Tax	3224.0
Specific Excises	3691.0
VAT	2155.0
Car Tax	108.0
Motor Vehicle Licence Duties	518.0
Stamp Duty	205.0
Rates	2617.0
Protective Duties	429.0
Gambling Duties	184.0

Imputed Income	
Ownership of Dwellings	3735.0
Other Owned Capital Stock	3141.2

Other	
Net Receipts from Changes in Financial Assets and Liabilities	1980.0
Income from Public Corporations	1023.6
Other Business Income	100.0
Transfers from Abroad	63.0
TOTAL	35074.0

EXPENDITURES

Subsidies	5281.0
Transfers to Persons Abroad	6455.0
Expenditures on Public Services	11665.0
Market Commodities	8598.0
Debt Interest	2665.0
TOTAL	35074.0

Notes to tables are given in Appendix B.

5.10 Sources of Income by Sector and Treatment of Financial Transactions

Table 5.12 summarizes the sources of income by sector and our accommodation of financial transactions involving personal sector savings and interest on public sector debt. The interest on public sector debt is treated as all paid (directly and through intermediation) to the private sector even though some payments are in practice made abroad.

The £1145 million profit type return received by the external sector reflects all interest and dividends paid abroad. The £1697 million inward foreign investment is treated as all real investment expenditures by foreigners even though a portion of this is purchase of financial rather than real assets.

TABLE 5.12

Income Sources by Sector and Adjustments Accommodating
Financial Transactions (£mill, 1973)

	UK Personal Sector	UK Corporate Sector	Public Sector	External Sector	Total Income
Income Originating in UK					
Profit Type Return	7579.2	–	7999.8	1145.0	16724.0
Labour Income	42603.6	–	–	–	42603.6
Tax Revenues	6455.0	–	12887.3	410.0	19752.2
Interest on Public Sector Debt	2665.0	–	-2665.0	–	–
Income Originating Abroad					
Profit Type Return	–	1697.0		-1697.0	–
Transfers	–	–	63.0	-63.0	–
Personal Sector Net Savings					
(Transferred to government and corporate sectors)	-5367.0	3387.0	1980.0	–	–
Personal Direct Taxes	-7995.0				-7995.0
Expenditures	45940.8	5084.0	20265.1	-205.0	71084.9

Notes to tables are given in Appendix B.

Notes

1.   The UK national accounts are published annually in the
      Blue Book; National Income and Expenditure H.M.S.O.
      This is referred to henceforth as N.I.B.B.

2.   Input-Output tables for the UK are constructed from
      periodic industrial censuses. These tables are then
      updated by annual revisions using a method similar to
      the RAS technique outlined in Chapter 4. The tables
      used here are updated from the 1971 tables which them-
      selves are updated from the 1968 tables (UK Input-
      Output tables for 1968, HMSO, 1973). Since the publi-
      cation of the 1971 tables (the latest available at
      point of original data assembly), updated official
      tables to 1973 have appeared. Since we update the 1971
      table anyway for our consistent data set, we have not
      devoted the extra resources necessary to incorporate
      the published 1973 table.

3.   Household data both on expenditures by commodity and on
      sources of income by household are given in the annual
      Family Expenditure Survey [HMSO].

4.   Foreign trade data include both merchandise trade
      statistics and balance of payments data given in the
      CSO's annual Balance of Payments Pink Book.

5.   Taxation data are drawn both from the Annual Report of
      the Board of Customs and Excise and from the Inland
      Revenue Statistics. NIBB gives total collections by
      tax.

6.   The reason for this subtraction is discussed below.

7.   The self-employment income originating in any industry
      represents the total return to individual
      entrepreneurs. A calculation is made of the implicit
      wage which they would have received had they been
      employed at average earnings in that same industry,
      which is subtracted to yield a return to capital by
      residual method. The treatment of self-employment
      income is a well known problem facing national income
      accountants and the allocation procedure adopted in
      this study is one of the methods commonly followed. The

industrial concentration in agricultural, retail trade, and professional services reflects the industrial concentration of small business.

8. This may be thought of as the differential between lending and borrowing rates accruing to financial institutions as a charge for services arranged.

9. The National Accounts procedure is to take total valuations of owner occupied property for rating purposes at the last valuation and correct for price level changes since that date. A valuation was undertaken in 1973. Although these rateable values are intended to reflect the rent which the property would fetch on the open market, the resulting figure is approximately one third of that obtained by imputing a return to the current stock valuation of private sector dwellings after allowing for the relatively small portion of private sector housing which is rented rather than owner-occupied.

10. In work on the measurement of profit type return by industry in the US a similar, if somewhat less extreme, result is obtained (see Rosenberg [1969], Harberger [1966]). The picture is made more severe than it appears in the National Accounts both by the correction for the income from housing and by the inclusion of the imputed income on government-owned capital.

11. In the National Accounts the imputation made for the public sector is the value of estimated capital consumption in the public sector. The implicit real net rate of return on public sector capital is therefore zero.

CHAPTER 6

SPECIFYING VALUES FOR SUBSTITUTION ELASTICITIES

In this chapter we discuss some of the problems involved in
selecting elasticities of substitution for industry production functions and household demand functions. We discuss
difficulties in interpreting these parameters in light of
the empirical estimates we have been able to find, and outline the sources used in our choice of values for the model.
We also comment on the reliability of the estimates.

Elasticity values are critical parameters in determining
impacts of policy changes generated by the model, and careful discussion of their values is needed prior to presentation of results. We separately report and discuss elasticity
values we use for production functions, demand functions,
and foreign trade behaviour. In view of the extensions to
our basic variant model, we also summarize the elasticities
we use in modelling labour supply and savings behaviour.

6.1 Production Function Elasticities

Our model incorporates CES value added functions for each
industry. We therefore need to specify a separate value for
the elasticity of substitution between capital and labour
for each industry in the model.

Since the introduction of the CES function in the early
1960's, there has been a continuing debate as to whether the
elasticity of substitution for manufacturing industry is
approximately unity. If unity is a correct value, the more
complex CES form can be replaced by the simpler Cobb-Douglas
form which has unitary elasticity of substitution. This
debate has concentrated primarily on substitution elasticities for aggregate manufacturing rather than component
industries as specified in the model. This issue is nonetheless important in assessing our choice of values.

Early estimation of the elasticity of substitution in
manufacturing industry by Arrow, Chenery, Minhas, and Solow
(ACMS) (1961), involved a pooled cross country data set of
observations on output per man and wage rates for a number

of countries. The same production function was assumed to apply in all countries, and the first order condition from the industry cost minimization problem equating the marginal product of labour to the wage rate was used to estimate the elasticity of substitution. Their result was that the elasticity was below one, but for some of the industries they examined the difference between the estimated coefficient and unity was not significant at a 90% level. This was used as support for the position that a Cobb-Douglas production function is a reasonable specification of aggregate production functions.

Following ACMS, a number of econometric studies have estimated substitution elasticities for manufacturing industries (primarily in the US) by a number of methods and produced results with substantial variation.[1] Cross-section studies, many of which use statewide data, produce estimates which are close to unity, but time-series studies produce lower estimates typically differing from cross-section by a factor of around 2. Also, estimates of substitution elasticities appear to vary systematically with the choice of estimating equation. Using the marginal product of capital relationship produces lower estimates than using the marginal product of labour.

A number of explanations of these differences have been offered, such as lagged adjustment, technical change and problems in measurement of inputs, serial correlation in time series data, and cyclical variations in utilization rates. At present no single explanation is widely accepted. A recent attempt by Berndt [1976] to reconcile alternative elasticity estimates used six different functional forms, five alternate measures of capital prices, and two estimation methods. His main finding was that estimates of substitution elasticities "are extremely sensitive to differences in measurement and data construction", and he concurred with an earlier remark of Nerlove [1967] that "even slight variations in the period or concepts tend to produce drastically different estimates of the elasticity."

The added uncertainty in the reliability of the estimates that we use compared with estimates of aggregate substitution possibilities must be emphasized. We interpret the current consensus to be that the case for Cobb-Douglas functions being a reasonable approximation of production possibilities is not firm, and we have therefore considered alternative sets of elasticity estimates for UK industries generated using three different sets of procedures.

(a) Central tendency tables have been produced for elasticity estimates by industry. These have been constructed using a catalogue of industry estimates of substitution elasticities recently compiled by Caddy [1976]. They are compiled for all estimates in a given industry, and separately for cross-section and time-series estimates, and are shown in Table 6.1. A small number of estimates are rejected as being implausible; (due to a wrong sign, for instance), and the remainder are classified according to the industries used in the model. The majority of these estimates are for US industries, only a few are generated using UK data. For some of the industries in the model no estimates exist in the literature because of the problems of measurement of outputs (examples are financial services, government, and other service industries).

(b) A limited amount of time-series estimation has been undertaken for UK industries using both quarterly and annual data by industry from 1950 to 1974.[2] There are difficulties in arranging the data series on a consistent basis through time and the industries for which estimation is possible do not include all those entering the model. Regression coefficients obtained are also shown in Table 6.1.

(c) Ranges of identical values for all industries are considered in our sensitivity analyses reported on later, which represent high and low substitutability cases. The intention is to provide bounds on estimates of general equilibrium impacts obtained from the model.

These alternative procedures are used to select a central set of elasticity values around which sensitivity analysis is conducted. For industries not covered in the central tendency tables, elasticity values of 1.0 have been assumed (Cobb-Douglas). In the case of the two housing industries, lower values of 0.25 have been used; both of these industries are so overwhelmingly capital intensive that the values used for the substitution elasticities are not of as much consequence as at first sight might appear. The sensitivity analyses considered are reported in Table 6.2.

It is important to emphasize that these elasticity values represent technological relationships, and when alternative general equilibria are calculated for policy variations the adjustments between equilibria are assumed to be complete. An assumption of smooth substitutability between capital and labour services in any industry in the short run is clearly not appropriate. Much capital is industry specific and cannot be easily adapted for alternate uses and complete substitution only takes place in the longer run as capital depreciates and is not replaced. Some adjustments between equilibria may be relatively small and capable of being made quickly, others may require much longer periods of time.[3] The time scale for the model is left ill-defined in terms of a precise number of years. It is assumed that sufficient time elapses for all adjustments between equilibria to be complete and that the counterfactual equilibrium can be achieved under the alternative policy regime as a long-run equilibrium solution.

6.2 Demand Function Elasticities

On the demand side of the model, household demand functions derived from staged CES utility functions are used. These functions specify constant substitution elasticities between sub-groups from the list of commodities. As already described, a three level nesting structure is used for each household. The bottom level nests contain comparable domestically produced and imported goods between which a degree of substitutability is assumed consistent with import demand price elasticity estimates. In the intermediate nests are blocks of commodities between which various elasticities of substitution are assumed. A constant elasticity of substitution also prevails between commodity blocks. The classification of commodities into these blocks along with the elasticity values assumed are shown in Table 6.3.

TABLE 6.1

Central Tendency and Estimated Elasticities of Substitution by Industry

INDUSTRIES	CENTRAL TENDENCY VALUES[1] (figures given in parentheses are the number of estimates used, and their variance)			REGRESSION RESULTS (selected time series coefficient estimates)
	Overall	Cross Section	Time Series	
Agriculture and Fishing	.607 (29, .13)	.809 (17, .10)	.322 (12, .03)	0.763
Coal Mining	-	-	-	-
Other Mining and Quarrying	-	-	-	-
Food	.789 (58, .17)	.937 (14, .13)	.433 (17, .08)	-
Drink	.657 (30, .15)	.879 (17, .11)	.368 (13, .06)	0.764
Tobacco	.848 (12, .24)	1.309 (3, .24)	.694 (9, .13)	-
Mineral Oils	.827 (24, .17)	1.002 (13, .15)	.621 (11, .13)	-
Other Coal and Petroleum Products	-	-	-	-
Chemicals	.827 (42, .16)	1.009 (26, .11)	.531 (16, .12)	1.120
Metals	.806 (79, .16)	.967 (51, .09)	.511 (28, .14)	-
Mech. Engineering	.587 (35, .11)	.663 (21, .11)	.451 (14, .09)	-
Instr. Engineering	.893 (16, .14)	1.053 (10, .12)	.627 (6, .06)	-
Elec. Engineering	.750 (32, .13)	.811 (24, .11)	.568 (8, .17)	0.411
Shipbuilding	.808 (21, .35)	1.043 (14, .33)	.341 (7, .04)	-
Vehicles	.810 (25, .31)	1.040 (15, .33)	.471 (9, .08)	-
Textiles	.914 (67, .18)	1.093 (46, .11)	.520 (21, .11)	0.902

Clothing	1.106 (25, .17)	1.221 (20, .14)	.649 (5, .05)	0.148
Leather, Fur, etc.	.940 (50, .13)	1.058 (35, .09)	.664 (15, .08)	0.554
Timer, Furniture, etc.	.843 (76, .13)	.974 (56, .07)	.475 (20, .10)	0.058
Paper, Printing, and Publishing	.908 (65, .14)	1.057 (48, .08)	.489 (17, .08)	0.134
Manufacturing n.e.s.	.944 (76, .17)	1.067 (54, .11)	.641 (22, .196)	0.888
Construction	-	-	-	0.324
Gas, Electricity and Water	-	-	-	0.167
Transport	-	-	-	1.676
Communications	-	-	-	-
Retail Trade	-	-	-	-
Wholesale Trade	-	-	-	0.860
Banking and Insurance, etc.	-	-	-	-
Housing Services (Private)	-	-	-	-
Housing Services (Local Auth.)	-	-	-	-
Public Service	-	-	-	-
Professional Services	-	-	-	-
Other Services	-	-	-	-

1. Estimates are taken from Caddy [1976] and are classified according to the industries used in the model.

TABLE 6.2

'Central Case' and Sensitivity Analysis Values
for Production Function Elasticities

A.   Central Case Values

Overall Central Tendency Values, with 1.0 assumed for
industries with no value appearing in Table 6.1 (except
the 2 housing industries for which values of 0.25 are
assumed).

B.   Sensitivity Variations

1.   0.5 for all industries (0.25 for housing industries).

2.   1.5 for all industries (0.25 for housing industries).

The elasticities used are based on literature price elasticity estimates even though no econometric estimates of substitution elasticities for CES demand functions of the staged variety exist, and few (if any) demand function systems are separately estimated by household type. A set of indirect procedures has been used to obtain elasticity values which have some claim to plausibility. These procedures involve collection of central tendency estimates from a literature survey of (uncompensated) own price elasticities of demand (by product) of household sector demand functions. We then choose substitution elasticities for the various levels of nests to calibrate to these as point estimates of the demand functions of the model at the benchmark equilibrium. We do not calibrate to estimates of cross price elasticities and we use homothetic preference functions to generate demands so that all expenditure elasticities are unity. The latter feature could be relaxed through use of an LES variant of the CES functions but we have chosen not to do this as we concentrate on the relative price effects of taxes.

Our procedure of calibrating point estimates of own price elasticities at the benchmark equilibrium to estimates of substitution elasticities is illustrated most simply in the case of a single stage CES demand function. The N commodity demand functions derived from maximization of a single stage CES utility function subject to a household budget constraint are:

$$(6.1) \qquad X_i = \frac{a_i^{\sigma} I}{P_i^{\sigma} \cdot \sum_j a_j^{\sigma} P_j^{1-\sigma}} \qquad (i = 1, \ldots, N)$$

where I is household income, the a_i are weighting parameters, σ is the elasticity of substitution, and P_i is the commodity price of good i.

TABLE 6.3

'Central Case' Demand Function Categories and Elasticities
of Substitution within the Levels of Utility Function Nests

The same values are assumed to apply for all UK personal sector households.

A.   Bottom level 'nests':   These each contain a maximum of 2 commodities, the domestically produced good and the comparable import. For non-traded goods, only one good is in the nest and substitution is irrelevant. A substitution elasticity of 1.25 is assumed. (1.25 also assumed for the rest of the world.)

B.   Intermediate level 'blocks':   The 33 composite goods are arranged in the following blocks with the elasticity of substitution between elements within the blocks given in parentheses.

Block 1 (.5)

Agriculture and Fishing
Food
Drink
Tobacco

Block 2 (.75)

Coal
Gas, Electricity and Water
Mineral Oils
Other Coal and Petroleum Products

Block 3 (.7)

Other mining and
    Quarrying Products
Chemicals

Block 4 (1.0)

Metals
Mech. Engineering
Instr. Engineering
Shipbuilding
Vehicles

Block 5 (.45)

Textiles
Clothing
Leather, fur, etc.
Paper, Printing and Publishing
Manufacturing n.e.s.

Block 6 (.5)

Vehicles
Construction

Block 7 (.8)

Public Service
Professional Services
Other Services
Transport
Communications
Retail Trade
Wholesale Trade
Banking and Insurance, etc.

Block 8 (.5)

Housing Services
 (Private)
Housing Services
 (Local Auth.)

C. Top level elasticity of substitution between intermediate 'blocks': Value of 0.5 used in central case (see text for discussion).

Taking derivatives through the demand function yields

$$(6.2) \quad \frac{\partial X_i}{\partial P_i} = -\sigma \, a_i^{\sigma} \, I \, P_i^{-\sigma-1} \cdot (\Sigma a_j^{\sigma} \, P_j^{1-\sigma})^{-1} -$$

$$a_i^{\sigma} \, I \, P_i^{-\sigma} (\Sigma_j a_j^{\sigma} \, P_j^{1-\sigma})^{-2} \cdot (1-\sigma) a_i^{\sigma} \, P_i^{-\sigma},$$

which gives the expression for the uncompensated own price elasticity

$$(6.3) \quad \varepsilon_{ii} = -\sigma - \frac{a_i^{\sigma} \cdot (1-\sigma)}{P_i^{(\sigma-1)} \cdot \Sigma a_j^{\sigma} \, P_j^{(1-\sigma)}} .$$

This can be rewritten as

$$(6.4) \quad \varepsilon_{ii} = -\sigma - \eta_i(1-\sigma),$$

where η_i is the budget share of the ith good. This, in turn, can be arranged as

$$(6.5) \quad \varepsilon_{ii} = -\sigma(1-\eta_i) - \eta_i$$

which is simply the Slutsky equation for the CES form. The compensated own price elasticity for demand functions derived from maximizing a CES utility function is $-\sigma(1-\eta_i)$, and the income elasticity of demands is unity.

The (uncompensated) cross price elasticities can be shown to be

$$(6.6) \quad \frac{-a_k^{\sigma} \, (1-\sigma)}{P_k^{(\sigma-1)} \cdot \Sigma_j a_j^{\sigma} P_j^{(1-\sigma)}} = -\eta_j(1-\sigma) \qquad (i \neq k)$$

In those cases where budget shares are small, therefore, the uncompensated own and cross price elasticities are approximately given by

(6.7) $\varepsilon_{ii} \approx -\sigma;$ $\varepsilon_{ik} \approx 0.$

In the case of two level staged CES functions, an expression for the uncompensated own price elasticity at the benchmark equilibrium is obtained:

(6.8) $\varepsilon_{ii} = -\sigma_L - \eta_i^L(1-\sigma_L) - (1-\sigma_L)(1-\eta_k^T)(1-\sigma_T) \dfrac{a_i^{\sigma_L} P_i^{1-\sigma_L}}{\sum_j a_j^{\sigma_L} P_j^{(1-\sigma_L)}}$

where σ_L and σ_T are elasticities of substitution at the lower and upper levels respectively, η_i^L is the expenditure share on good i out of expenditures on the lower level nest of commodities, and η_k^T is the expenditure share on category k (containing all commodities in the lower level nest) out of total income. As with (6.7), in the case where the budget share η_i^L is small, since a_i is also small

(6.9) $\varepsilon_{ii} \approx -\sigma_L.$

Under these approximations the own price elasticity of a commodity or composite of commodities is determined primarily by the elasticity of substitution in the lowest level of nesting in which it appears. Similar but more complex expressions can be obtained from three level staged CES functions.

An important property of the demand functions derived from a single stage CES utility function is what Deaton [1974] refers to as "Pigou's Law". This is an approximate constant proportionality between income and own price elasticities for any demand functions derived from directly additive preferences (of which a single stage CES function is an example). Other restrictions are also imposed by additivity most notably the absence of inferiority and the unambiguous sign of compensated cross price elasticities. Our preference

functions are nested rather than single stage CES functions
and these restrictions apply only to demands for the implied
composite goods rather than for the individual goods. With
this structure the restrictions implied by direct additivity
will no longer hold exactly although for the parameter
values we use they nonetheless hold approximately, and they
still apply within nests.

The selection procedure used for substitution elasticities
is to utilize these expressions to generate values for elasticities of substitution from estimated (uncompensated) own
price elasticities by product. Central tendency estimates
have been obtained from literature estimates in a manner
similar to that adopted for production function
elasticities, and these values are reported in Table 6.4.
The majority of estimates reported in the literature are for
demand function systems for which price elasticity estimates
are only available as the point estimates at sample means.
For this reason, the central tendency figures are differentiated by estimating equation. Moreover, these estimates
relate to aggregate demand functions rather than household
demand functions, and imported commodities are not separately distinguished from domestically produced commodities.
Although individual studies exist for the UK, estimates for
other countries (chiefly the US and other European
countries) have been included to widen the sample. The
majority of estimates use time-series data and the stratification between time-series and cross-section estimates,
important on the production side, has not been made since
insufficient cross-section estimates exist.

The central case elasticity values have been derived from
the following procedure. The value for the substitution
elasticity between comparable domestically produced and
imported commodities is selected first on the basis of estimates of trade elasticities (import and export demand elasticities). We return to this issue in the next section but
note that a value of 1.25 is assumed. Given the fixed coefficient nature of intermediate use of imported products this
value is approximately consistent with the estimates of
aggregate price elasticities of demand for imports in the UK

reported in Stern, Francis and Schumacher (1976). This same value is assumed to apply for all the pairwise nests between imported and domestically produced goods and for all households.

Central case elasticities between components of blocks are derived from the overall central tendency price elasticities presented in Table 6.4. We base our selection of these values on the approximation that the own price elasticity of any commodity type (in composite form aggregated across domestically produced and imported goods) is given by the substitution elasticity within the intermediate block containing that commodity type. We group commodities into blocks primarily with an eye to similarity of commodity type but we also try to group commodities whose own price elasticities of demand in Table 6.4 are similar (in terms of the 'total' central tendency value). We then choose our elasticities of substitution within blocks as an approximate average over the values for own price elasticities in the 'total' column of Table 6.4. A top level elasticity value of 0.5 is assumed in our central case. This value was chosen on the following grounds. Firstly, it is consistent with the elasticity of demand for housing, an important commodity which occupies a complete category in our staged structure, and which is central to a number of important tax/subsidy distortions. Secondly, it reflects the intuition that substitution elasticities increase with the degree of disaggregation among commodities. Thirdly, in our endogenous labour supply variant, a value of 0.5 gives a plausible uncompensated labour supply elasticity. This is discussed further in Section 6.4.

We have also performed sensitivity analysis around our central case specification elasticity selections as described in Table 6.5. Results from these are reported in Chapter 7.

6.3 Trade Elasticities

We consider a central case analysis for our model in which a terms of trade neutralizing tax appears as part of our equal yield tax/subsidy replacement. Nonetheless, two implicit

TABLE 6.4

Central Tendency Values for Uncompensated Own Price Elasticities of Household Demand Functions

(All uncompensated price elasticity estimates; figures in parentheses refer to the number of studies included and the variance of estimate[1].)

Commodities	Linear Expenditure System Estimates	Log Linear Demand Estimates	Other	Total
Agriculture and Fishing	.334 (17, .03)	.420 (25, .05)	.562 (44, .08)	.468 (86, .07)
Coal	-	.321 (1, 0)	1.265 (2, .84)	.950 (3, .76)
Other Mining and Quarrying Products	.425 (1, 0)	.905 (3, .06)	.257 (2, .01)	.609 (6, .13)
Food	.353 (15, .03)	.580 (30, .19)	.476 (27, .08)	.494 (72, .13)
Drink	.617 (5, .07)	.780 (12, .25)	.464 (15, .06)	.607 (32, .16)
Tobacco	-	.611 (8, .15)	.431 (11, .04)	.507 (19, .10)
Mineral Oils	.425 (1, 0)	.905 (3, .07)	.257 (2, .01)	.609 (6, .13)
Other Coal and Petroleum Products	1.283 (2, .01)	1.404 (3, 180)	1.978 (3, 1.41)	1.589 (8, .90)
Chemicals	.685 (1, 0)	.890 (1, 0)	.680 (3, .07)	.724 (5, .05)
Metals	-	1.522 (19, .42)	.989 (18, .40)	1.083 (51, .48)
Mech. Engineering	-	1.296 (16, .61)	1.068 (15, .43)	1.005 (45, .48)
Instr. Engineering	.606 (14, .15)	1.099 (17, .57)	1.240 (11, .54)	.972 (42, .49)
Elec. Engineering	-	1.388 (19, .377)	1.049 (17, .410)	1.060 (50, .44)
Shipbuilding	-	-	-	-
Vehicles	.606 (14, .15)	1.137 (19, .55)	1.099 (18, .40)	.985 (51, .44)

Clothing	.277 (16, .03)	.491 (26, .16)	.564 (19, .15)	.458 (61, .18)
Timber, Furniture, etc.	.570 (14, .09)	1.258 (19, .23)	.974 (20, .39)	.969 (53, .33)
Paper, Printing, and Publishing	.191 (1, 0)	.343 (5, .02)	.416 (5, .02)	.362 (11, .02)
Manufacturing n.e.s.	.578 (14, .02)	.527 (7, .11)	.626 (17, .12)	.592 (38, .09)
Construction	-	-	-	-
Gas, Electricity and Water	1.203 (1, 0)	.921 (9, .02)	.369 (10, .01)	.659 (20, .10)
Transport	.761 (4, .23)	1.027 (14, .26)	.994 (10, .16)	.977 (28, .23)
Communications	-	-	-	-
Retail Trade	-	-	-	-
Wholesale Trade	-	-	-	-
Banking and Insurance	-	.559 (3, .02)	.894 (1, 0)	.642 (4, .04)
Housing Services (Private)	.461 (15, .11)	.550 (29, .45)	.434 (9, .09)	.505 (53, .29)
Housing Services (Local Auth.)	-	-	-	-
Public Service	-	-	-	-
Professional Services / Other Services	.488 (7, .08)	1.09 (27, .56)	.946 (16, .39)	.961 (50, .48)

1. References for literature estimates used appear in the bibliography.

Table 6.5

Sensitivity Analyses of Demand Function Elasticities

	Bottom Level	Intermediate Levels							Top Level
		Block 1	Block 2	Block 3	Block 4	Block 5	Block 6	Block 7	
A. Central Case									
	1.25 (1.25)	.5	.75	.7	1.0	.45	.5	.8	.5
B. Bottom Level Variations (Substitution between UK produced and foreign products)									
	1.0 (1.25)	.5	.75	.7	1.0	.45	.5	.8	.5
	3.0 (1.25)	.5	.75	.7	1.0	.45	.5	.8	.5
C. Top Level Variations (Substitution between leisure and other goods)									
	1.25 (1.25)	.5	.75	.7	1.0	.45	.5	.8	.3
	1.25 (1.25)	.5	.75	.7	1.0	.45	.5	.8	1.0

trade elasticities we set as part of our elasticity value
selection are important for our results. In our model the UK
trades with the rest of the world, with all international
markets clearing. As stated in Chapter 2, products produced
in the UK and the rest of the world are treated as qualitatively different while being substitutes in demand. This
implies that substitution elasticities between domestic and
foreign goods in the UK can be chosen to calibrate to estimates of import price elasticities in the UK, while comparable substitution elasticities in the rest of the world
can be chosen to calibrate to estimates of UK export price
elasticities.

The most complete set of estimates of trade elasticities
is the recent compendium compiled by Stern, Francis and
Schumacher (SFS) (1976). They briefly summarize the results
of approximately 150 empirical studies from the period 1960-
1975 which estimate trade elasticiites by product and by
trading area. They report the main finding of each study and
produce central tendency tables from which they extract best
guess estimates. They suggest that there is little basis on
which to produce best guess estimates on a more detailed
product classification than single digit SITC categories,
and they also stress the small sample size for estimates for
countries other than the US. Their uncompensated price elasticity estimates for the UK are -0.65 for import demand and
-0.48 for export demand.

The estimates for both import and export price elasticities summarized in SFS strike many people as surprisingly low. Crudely averaging across all countries, numbers
in the range of -1 are obtained with lower estimates for the
UK. There has been extensive discussion of bias in estimates
based on time series data following Orcutt's well known
paper (1950), and further papers by Kemp (1962) and Kakwani
(1972) have provided arguments as to why trade elasticities
might be biased towards -1. Some authors argue for and use
substantially higher trade elasticities based on so-called
'tariff elasticities'. Balassa and Kreinin (1967), for instance, in their empirical work on Kennedy Round tariff
cuts, use significantly higher elasticities in absolute

value. Some recent literature has suggested that the problems of bias first raised by Orcutt may not be as serious as once supposed and estimates in the range reported by SFS, remain both widely accepted and widely used.

In our central case we chose values for bottom level substitution elasticities of 1.25 for both the UK and the rest of the world in final demand functions. The same value is considered to apply for all households and all commodity categories. Given the fixed coefficient nature of intermediate UK production in our model, this value for the final demand functions implies a price elasticity for total UK imports approximately consistent with the central tendency UK import price elasticity reported by SFS. The export price elasticity which the UK faces implied by these values is higher than that suggested by the SFS values for the UK alone but is approximately consistent with an average over the major OECD countries included.

6.4   Elasticity Values and the Labour/Leisure Choice

As has already been mentioned, one purpose of introducing a three level nesting structure into the household utility functions is to allow for a labour/leisure choice of households to be incorporated as one of a number of model extensions to our basic variant. The distortion of the choice between working (labour) and not working (leisure) through the tax system has occupied the attention of many public finance economists in recent years. One of the features of the model is its capability of analysing the distortionary effects of taxes on labour supply through changes in prices of all other goods relative to leisure.

From a formal point of view, the incorporation of a labour/leisure choice into the model is straightforward. The labour endowment of each household is increased and leisure enters the utility function; there is thus a demand function for leisure which depends, as with other commodities, on income and all prices. The principal difficulty with this extension is in determining realistic numerical values for demand function parameters.

The procedure followed is to consider one additional category in the utility function nesting structure containing
leisure only. Endowments of labour for each household are
increased by a factor of 1/4 reflecting an ability to work a
50-hour week while currently working 40 hours. Household
incomes are determined by the sale of all endowments and
leisure is repurchased. In the modified benchmark equilibrium data set, expenditures on leisure are given by 1/5 of
"expanded" labour income and this information is used to
select distribution parameters in the household demand functions through application of the replication requirement.
The use of 40 and 50 hours in this way is clearly an approximation; the maximum potential work week is ill-defined and
may be larger than 50 hours for some households and less for
others. In addition, a 40-hour week may be an underestimate
of the current labour supply for household groups with large
numbers of secondary workers.[4] For the retired and non-
employed household groups no labour leisure choice is considered, even though small amounts of work are performed by
these groups.

The value for the top level elasticity of substitution
between categories is chosen by reference to the econometric
literature on labour supply wage rate elasticities. The
relationship between this elasticity of substitution and the
uncompensated labour supply elasticity is derived as
follows. Leisure and labour are linked by the relationship

$$(6.10) \quad L + H = T$$

where T is allocable time, H is the quantity of labour supplied, and L is the quantity of leisure consumed. This
implies that

$$(6.11) \quad \frac{\partial H}{\partial P_L} = - \frac{\partial L}{\partial P_L} ,$$

where P_L is the net of tax wage. The uncompensated elasticity of labour supply is given by

$$(6.12) \quad \varepsilon_S = \frac{\partial H}{\partial P_L} \cdot \frac{P_L}{H} ,$$

and the corresponding uncompensted elasticity of leisure demand is

$$(6.13) \qquad \varepsilon_D = \frac{\partial H}{\partial P_L} \cdot \frac{P_L}{L} \, .$$

It follows that

$$(6.14) \qquad \varepsilon_S = -\varepsilon_D \, (\tfrac{L}{H}) \, .$$

The expression for ε_D can be derived from the expression for the demand for leisure, which in the single stage CES case is given by

$$(6.15) \qquad \varepsilon_D = (1-\sigma)(1-\eta_L) - \frac{A}{I} \, ,$$

where A is non-labour income, I is "expanded" income, including the imputed income from leisure, and η_L is the expenditure share on leisure.

For values (approximately consistent with those implied by our data for households in aggregate) of $\frac{A}{I} = 0.25$, $\eta_L = .15$, and $\sigma = .5$, the implied uncompensated labour supply elasticity is -0.04. The same value for σ of 0.5 is assumed in all cases for each household group. This magnitude of the implied uncompensated labour supply elasticity is somewhat larger algebraically than the econometric literature suggests for working males. Stern (1976) suggests a range of -.10 to -.20, and quotes a similar suggestion due to Douglas (1934). Lewis (1975) offers -.15 as widely agreed to be "in the ballpark" (p.29). However, the evidence suggests strong positive uncompensated elasticities for secondary workers. Given these considerations, our implied uncompensated labour supply elasticity seems plausible.

6.5   Elasticities and Savings Decisions

As an alternative extension to our basic variant model we also consider cases where household savings are endogenous and vary with the anticipated real rate of return on capital. In this case we also consider an additional category in the household utility functions, but representing the anticipated future consumption stream from current savings instead of leisure. This formulation involves a reorganization of our benchmark data set in much the same way as our labour/leisure extension. All savings are made by households rather than by a corporate consumer and involve purchases of newly produced capital goods; all financial intermediation is assumed to be disintermediated. Income of the corporate consumer is transferred back to households. In Chapter 9 we present the algebra of our formulation.

In this case we specify the top level elasticity of substitution to calibrate to an implied elasticity of savings with respect to the real net of tax rate of return on savings. We use an approximation result that for the CES case, one plus the savings elasticity equals the substitution elasticity between current and anticipated future consumption. A similar result is derived by Feldstein [1978b] and the same point is made by Bailey [1962].[5] This reduces the problem of choice of top level substitution elasticity in this case to agreement on the elasticity of savings with respect to the real net of tax rate of return.

For many years the conventional wisdom was that savings are largely interest inelastic; a study frequently cited in support of this view was that by Wright (1969). In the last couple of years this view has been sharply challenged; first by Boskin (1978) who uses long time series for the US to produce an elasticity estimate of 0.4 and more recently by Summers (1980) who uses a lifecycle framework to produce an elasticity of 2.0. Summers' estimate calibrates to the pure substitution effect consistent with Boskin but has a large wealth effect from the recapitalization of human wealth as rates of return change. Summers' estimate thus involves a large difference between the compensated and uncompensated elasticities. We do not capture the lifecycle effects of Summers' approach and thus we place most emphasis on a top level substitution elasticity (derived from the Boskin estimate) of 1.4. We also use substitution values of 1.0 and 3.0 as sensitivity analyses to approximately calibrate to the positions of Wright and Summers.

6.6 Elasticities in the Public Good Model Variant

A further extension to the basic model variant considered in Chapter 9 involves public goods treated as arguments in individual household utility functions. We assume a rule to be followed by government in deciding upon the level of public provision that the sum of marginal rates of substitution between a composite of private goods and the single public good equal the corresponding marginal rate of transformation. Government revenues then have to be sufficient to finance the endogenously determined level of public good provision.

The key elasticity in this formulation is the elasticity of substitution in the CES preference functions between private and public goods. In this formulation we enter public goods as an additional argument of household utility functions at the top level of the nesting structure, in the same way as additional arguments enter in the savings and labour supply extensions.

We use a value of 0.5 as the substitution elasticity in the top level of nesting, which implies an uncompensated elasticity of demand with respect to the 'personal price' of public goods of -0.5 if the private expenditure shares are small. The literature which is relevant to appraising the realism of this is that on estimation of so-called 'median voter' models. In this literature levels of provision of public goods in local jurisdictions are assumed to be determined by the preferences of the median voter (ranked by income), and if preferences are identical over a large number of jurisdictions the demand for public goods can be estimated.

The -0.5 value appears to be in the neighbourhood of the range of estimates generated by these studies. Bergstrom and Goodman [1973] estimate tax share (price) elasticities in the study of 826 municipalities in the US with 1960 populations between 10,000 and 150,000 located in 10 states. For general municipal expenditures (excluding education and welfare) elasticities by state range from -0.01 to -0.50, for expenditures on police from -0.13 to -0.76, and for expenditures on parks and recreation from +0.25 to -0.81.

Pommerehne and Schneider [1978] estimate tax share elasticities in their study of 110 Swiss municipalities at -0.17 to -0.72, depending on the classification of municipalities and estimating equation.

Notes

1. The discussion here draws heavily on the summary pre-
    sented by Berndt [1976] in his attempt to reconcile
    alternative estimates of elasticities of substitution
    in aggregate production functions.

2. A quarterly series on production indices by industry is
    used, published on an occasional basis in Economic
    Trends, annual series appear in the National Income and
    Expenditure Blue Book. Monthly data on the money hourly
    wage rate and man hours (by industry) are given in the
    Department of Employment Gazette, and annual data in
    the British Labour Statistics Yearbook. Retail price
    indices were used to construct a measure of real wages
    by industry. Where monthly data are available, the
    middle month of each quarter was used.

3. Given depreciation rates on the housing stock of a
    little over 1% per year (the approximate magnitudes
    assumed in the UK National Accounts capital stock
    data), removal of subsidies to local authority housing
    and tax preferences to owner occupied housing could
    result in adjustments which may take 30 years or more
    to complete in a long-run sense.

4. Housewives' services are not treated as yielding labour
    income either in the model or in the national accounts
    data used to estimate model parameter values. If this
    treatment is changed, 40 hours will be a more substan-
    tial underestimate.

5. We return to this in the discussion of intertemporal
    utility maximization in Chapter 9.

PART II

EMPIRICAL ANALYSIS OF THE UK TAX SUBSIDY SYSTEM
USING THE GENERAL EQUILIBRIUM MODEL

Introduction

In this part of the monograph we report our findings on the
allocative and redistributive effects of the UK tax/subsidy
system using the model described in preceding chapters. We
simulate a number of counterfactual equilibria for the economy under alternative policies from those associated with
the 1973 benchmark equilibrium. We compare counterfactual
and the benchmark equilibria to arrive at our evaluation of
the impacts of the tax/subsidy system.

In these comparisons we concentrate on various summary
indices. In our welfare analysis we stress Hicksian compensating and equivalent variations. The compensating variation
(CV) for a single household is the sum of money that would
need to be taken away from a household so as to restore its
original utility level prevailing before the change. The
Hicksian equivalent variation (EV) is the sum of money which
would need to be given to a household to increase its welfare to a level equivalent to that which it would have en-
joyed had some proposed policy change been enacted. The
compensating variation is a measure at the new equilibrium
prices; the equivalent variation is measured at the pre-
change prices. These definitions imply that a positive
equivalent or compensating variation indicates a welfare
gain from moving to the counterfactual equilibrium from the
benchmark. As Kay [1980] points out, in a sequence of
wise comparisons between alternative counterfactual equilibria and the same benchmark equilibrium, the sequence of
comparisons using EV's uses the same price data, since the
EV is based on original benchmark prices. This is not so
with CV's.

To construct an economy-wide measure of aggregate welfare
change, we take the algebraic sum of compensating and equivalent variations across households for each of the measures.
This aggregation procedure is subject to a number of objec-
tions which are well known in the applied welfare literature; one notable difficulty involves the paradox which has

been stressed by Boadway (1974). The widespread use of algebraic sums in cost-benefit analysis suggests that many applied welfare economists accept this as an appropriate criterion for measuring welfare gain or loss.[1]

In addition to our welfare calculations, we analyze distributional impacts of tax changes. We construct measures of alternative income distributions using Gini coefficients and other summary statistics and use these to evaluate changes in a number of distributions. Detailed movements in particular prices and quantities are examined to assess the extent to which various industries or products are impacted by the tax/subsidy system. We summarize the main conclusions from these results at the end of each chapter.

We examine three different types of counterfactual equilibria. In Chapter 7 we take a single experiment which we examine in detail; we have termed this our central case analysis. This case involves the removal of all major industry and commodity tax/subsidy distortions in the UK with a yield preserving broadly based 'neutral' sales tax as a replacement. We take up the issue of the distorting effects of the tax system on savings and labour supply in Chapter 9.

Chapter 8 begins by investigating the distorting effects of various components of the tax/subsidy system in order to provide an overview of tax structure. We consider cases in which alternative portions of the tax system are removed and we break the tax/subsidy system down into a number of model equivalent and legal forms and analyze each in turn. This allows us to rank portions of the tax system in terms of their distorting and distributional impact and also to assess the extent of their interdependence. In addition, we carry out a number of experiments which examine the response which might be expected from radical changes in tax structure. We evaluate the effect on redistribution of major changes in the personal income tax; the extent of redistribution which can be achieved through significant tax induced changes in relative consumer prices; and possible effects of tax induced industrial restructuring programmes.

In Chapter 9 we present results from a number of extensions to our basic variant model. We examine the distortions involved with taxation and saving, and taxation and labour supply. We also examine the interaction between taxation and inflation. We modify our treatment of public sector expenditures and examine an alternative solution concept for our model by including public goods in household preferences. We analyze the impact of transfers upon our measures of cost of tax/subsidy distortions. Lastly, we analyze a particular tax reform case to illustrate the ability of our procedures to analyze realistic policy proposals. We examine the tax changes introduced in the UK in April 1973, and use our model to simulate an equilibrium corresponding to a pre-1973 tax system. This is an analysis in reverse of the case examined earlier by Whalley (1973, 1975) using a simpler model.

CHAPTER 7

DETAILED ANALYSIS OF CENTRAL CASE MODEL EXPERIMENT
INVOLVING REMOVAL OF NON-SAVINGS/NON-LEISURE
TAX/SUBSIDY DISTORTION

7.1 Introduction

This chapter presents results from our analysis of the
static industry and commodity distortions in the UK
tax/subsidy system using 1973 data. Distortions of labour
supply, savings decisions, those attributable to a non-
indexed tax system, and analysis involving public goods are
all left until Chapter 9. In this chapter, we concentrate on
one central counterfactual experiment from the model and
explore the results in detail.

The characteristics of this central case are as follows:

1. Fixed factor static formulation. Aggregate factor sup-
    plies are fixed; household savings do not vary with the
    rate of return on capital. A single period static equi-
    librium is assumed in the presence of alternative
    policy regimes.

2. Equal yield tax replacement of all existing taxes and
    subsidies. All existing taxes and subsidies are abol-
    ished and replaced by a non-distorting yield preserving
    single rate sales tax.[1] The size of the public sector
    is preserved in real terms. The replacement follows
    Musgrave's (1959) concept of "differential incidence".

3. Terms of trade neutralizing surtax/subsidy. Because of
    the nature of the tax system and the trade elasticities
    used, terms of trade effects accompany tax changes in
    the model. UK trade elasticities are low, and since
    high effective tax rates apply to the production and
    sale of exports in the model, the tax system produces a
    terms of trade gain to the economy. Without a terms of
    trade neutralizing tax we find that the welfare gains
    to the UK are smaller than they would be with such a
    tax. Given that we wish to estimate the national costs
    to the UK of tax/subsidy distortions, it seems natural
    that the replacement policy regime incorporates an

additional tax on exports to neutralize any movement in
the terms of trade associated with the tax change so as
to segment these effects.

4. External and government sectors satisfy budget balance.
    Equilibrium conditions hold in the replacement policy
    regime and all sectors (including government and the
    external sector) are in balance. For government, finan-
    cial transactions occurring in benchmark data (such as
    debt issues) are incorporated through equivalent real
    transactions (a real resource transfer from the private
    to the public sector). For the external sector, inward
    and outward investment, dividend flows, and transfers
    enter as real transactions.

5. Elasticities. The set of elasticities used corresponds
    to central case values described in Chapter 6. We per-
    form some sensitivity analysis around these values and
    report the corresponding additional cases below.

Section 7.2 discusses the aggregate welfare cost estimates. In Section 7.3 we analyze detailed household imports,
while Section 7.4 examines price and quantity movements.
Other aspects of the central case experiment are discussed
in Section 7.5.

7.2. Aggregate Welfare Analysis of the Central Case

In Table 7.1 we present the aggregate welfare impacts from
our central case analysis. We report the sum of Hicksian
compensating and equivalent variations across all the agents
in the UK economy giving us a measure of the welfare gain to
the economy from removal of all non-savings/non-leisure
distortions in the tax/subsidy system. These gains are
£5.3 billion (using 1973 data) for the sum of compensating
variations and £5.0 billion for the sum of equivalent variations. As fractions of NNP and net tax revenues these are 7
$\frac{1}{2}$ % and 26% respectively.

These numbers represent one of our most significant
results. On the basis of this finding and later sensitivity
analyses, we emphasize a range for the annual welfare cost
of the tax/subsidy system in the UK of between 6% and 9% of

TABLE 7.1

Aggregate Welfare Impacts of Central Case Analysis
(1973 prices)

(Abolition of UK Tax/Subsidy system and replacement by yield preserving broadly-based sales tax
plus terms of trade neutralizing tax.)

A.	Sum of Compensating Variations[1] across all UK agents (ΣCV)	£ 5.3 bill
B.	Sum of Equivalent Variations[1] across all UK agents (ΣEV)	£ 5.0 bill
C.	1973 GNP at factor cost in data used in model	£69.8 bill
D.	Taxes less subsidies consolidated across all levels of government in 1973	£19.8 bill
E.	ΣCV as % of 1973 GNP	7.59%
F.	ΣCV as % of Net Revenues	26.23%

1. This involves an algebraic (unweighted) sum.
    See the discussion in the text.

NNP at factor cost. This is substantially larger than might
be suggested on the basis of simple projections of previous
Harberger type calculations of welfare costs of selected tax
distortions (which we summarize later) for various economies
over the last 15 to 20 years. Harberger calculates the loss
in productive efficiency due to capital taxes in the US in
the region of .4% to .6% of GNP using data for the 1950s. It
has been common to argue that this represents one of the
major distortions in the tax system and therefore the combined costs of distortions will be relatively small. While
there has been some recent literature producing larger loss
estimates in the case of savings (such as Summers [1981]),
on which we comment later, a common view among public
finance economists is that the static annual welfare cost of
tax/subsidy distortions is small. This is not the conclusion
suggested by the numbers reported in Table 7.1.

It is also important to emphasize that we report a recurring annual flow loss. As a result of the tax system the
economy is annually foregoing a welfare equivalent of around
7 $\frac{1}{2}$ % of NNP. In 1973 prices this works out at approximately
£250 per household or £650 per household in 1980 prices. As
a fraction of net revenues collected, the welfare loss is
even larger. Table 7.1 suggests that in the process of collecting net revenues (taxes less subsidies) of a little
under 30% of NNP in 1973, the government inflicted a welfare
cost on the economy equal to approximately $\frac{1}{4}$ of the net
revenues collected. We have not calculated the marginal
welfare loss associated with an extra pound of revenues
raised. Because tax distortion losses in partial equilibrium
analysis increase with the square of the tax rate, however,
it seems likely that an extra pound of revenue raised would
have a social cost considerably larger than 25p.

Our results contrast with magnitudes which have been estimated in calculations of welfare gains or losses resulting
from customs unions and other international trade policy
changes where distortions impact on relatively small portions of economic activity. A good example is provided by
the calculations of welfare gains from the formation of the
EEC and subsequent British entry. Scitovsky (1957) calcu-

lates static annual welfare gains from the formation of the
EEC as 1/20th of one percent of GNP. Miller and Spencer
(1977) also calculate small welfare effects to be involved
with British entry into the EEC. In our central case
results, in Table 7.1 we find the welfare effects of policy
changes affecting the whole economy, rather than just the
external sector, to be much larger.

In Table 7.2 we report results from a tax change similar
to that in Table 7.1 but with the substantial redistribution
implicit in the central case removed. In the central case we
abolish the income tax along with other taxes, and as a
result there is a significant redistribution against low
income groups. Because the large income effect could have an
impact on our welfare loss estimate due to the aggregation
of our welfare measure across households, we attempt to
correct for this. We have taken the same tax replacements in
the central case in Table 7.1, but have left the income tax
in place and removed only the distortions within the income
tax along with the removal of other tax/subsidy distortions.
This produces a modified central case which incorporates a
broadly based income tax along with the yield preserving
broadly based sales tax. In this case the redistributive
effects of the tax change are quite different than in the
central case, and we explore these differences in a later
section on detailed household impacts. This income effect
has a significant impact however on our aggregate welfare
estimates. The sum of compensating variations falls from
£5.3 billion to £4.6 billion, and the sum of equivalent
variations from £5.0 billion to £4.9 billion. We interpret
these results as indicating some sensitivity in our calculation of welfare loss to aggregation over households, reducing the estimate of 7.5% of NNP to the region of 6% of NNP.
This is also confirmation of the importance of income
effects in calculation of welfare costs of taxes.

Sensitivity analysis results are continued in Table 7.3.
In this set of experiments we have varied some of the elasticity values from our central case specification. In each
instance we have performed the same tax change analysis but
with different elasticities both in the model calibration

TABLE 7.2

Welfare Effects of Removal of Distortions in UK Taxes and
Subsidies as in Table 7.1, but Leaving the Income Tax
in Place as a Broadly Based Tax
(1973 prices)

	Central Case Specification as in Table 7.1	Central Case Specification but with broadly based income tax left in place
A. Welfare Measures	£ billion	£ billion
(i) Sum of compensating variations	5.3	4.6
(ii) Sum of equivalent variations	5.0	4.9

TABLE 7.3

Sensitivity Analysis of Aggregate Welfare Gains from Removal
of Tax/Subsidy Distortions (Table 7.1) to Changes in
Substitution Elasticities in Demand and Production Functions
(1973 prices)

		Sum of Equivalent Variations (£ billion)	Sum of Compensating Variations (£ billion)
1.	Central Case Elasticity Values (Table 7.1)[1]	5.0	5.3
2.	'Top Level' Substitution Elasticities in all household demand functions set at 0.3	4.3	4.6
3.	'Top Level' Substitution Elasticities in all household demand functions set at 1.0	5.8	6.2
4.	'Bottom Level' Substitution Elasticities in all household demand functions set at 1.0	4.9	5.1
5.	'Bottom Level' Substitution Elasticities in all household demand functions set at 3.0	4.8	5.3
6.	All Production Function Elasticities set at 0.5	4.2	4.6
7.	All Production Function Elasticities set at 1.5	5.8	6.1

1. All variations reported in (2) - (7) are single variations on
   the central case specification in Table 7.1 with only the change
   listed included. Changes are not cumulative across the various
   cases.

and in the counterfactual experiment. We report the sum of
compensating and equivalent variations in each case. Under
the elasticity variations the sum of compensating variations
ranges   from £4.6 billion to £6.2 billion. Once   again   we
interpret these as providing some indication of sensitivity
of the central case results while remaining within the range
that we emphasize. More variation occurs with changes in the
top level elasticity of substitution in demand than with
other elasticity values.

   In Table 7.4 we report the impact on the aggregate welfare
measure of a reallocation of capital between industries in
the benchmark data set. As we mentioned earlier, a feature
of the benchmark data on capital service use by industry is
that a large portion of the total capital services in the
economy are concentrated in service industries (particularly
housing, utilities, and government services). This industrial concentration is more pronounced in national accounts
flow data than in capital stock statistics. In producing
Table 7.4 we have taken aggregate capital income in our
benchmark data and reallocated it among industry groups
using 1973 National Accounts capital stock data as a guide.
This results in a reallocation of capital in favour of manufacturing industry. One effect is to reduce the effective
tax rate on capital income. We repeat our calibration procedures and consider the same abolition of distortions as in
our central case. The sum of compensating variations falls
from £5.3 billion to £4.6 billion, and the sum of equivalent
variations from £5.0 billion to £4.3 billion.   As with the
earlier sensitivity calculations, we interpret these as
lying within the range which we emphasize. We have not explored the extent to which our various sensitivity analyses
compound. Thus, an experiment involving removal of all distortions leaving the income tax in place, using low elasticity values, and reallocating capital services in the
benchmark could well produce a loss estimate outside the
range we stress.

TABLE 7.4

Impact of Capital Reallocation[1] in Benchmark Data
Set on Central Case Results in Table 7.1
(1973 prices)

	Central Case as in Table 7.1	Effects of Same Abolition of Distortions but after capital reallocation in benchmark data
A. <u>Welfare Measures</u>	£ billion	£ billion
(i) Sum of compensating variations	5.3	4.6
(ii) Sum of equivalent variations	5.0	4.3
B. <u>Functional Share Impacts</u>		
Ratio of capital to labour return in new equilibrium (old equilibrium values in parentheses)	0.423(0.392)	.455(0.392)

1. This is described more fully in the text.

TABLE 7.5

Impact on Central Case Results (Table 7.1) of not
including terms of trade neutralizing tax
(1973 prices)

	Central Case Result (Table 7.1)	Central Case Specification excluding terms of trade neutralizing tax
	£ billion	£ billion
A. Welfare Measures		
(i) Sum of compensating variations	5.3	1.7
(ii) Sum of equivalent variations	5.0	1.6
B. Terms of Trade		
Ratio of Export to Import prices (Benchmark Equilibrium Value equals 1.0)	1.0	0.76
C. Rate of Terms of Trade Surtax on Exports	37.1%	0.0%

Table 7.5 highlights the importance of the terms of trade
neutralizing tax which we consider along with the other
elements of our central case. Were we not to allow this
additional tax to be present, the sum of compensating variations for the economy would not be £5.3 billion as in Table
7.1 but only £1.7 billion. A further feature of this calculation is that the endogenously determined terms of trade
neutralizing tax on exports in the Table 7.1 results is
37.1%. This may seem to be quite unrealistic, particularly
if one argues that the UK can be represented as a small open
price-taking economy. This is a reflection of the trade
elasticities we use. We have used values based on literature
estimates of trade elasticities for the UK which themselves
strike some people as implausibly small, but which are
reconfirmed in repeated studies. (Broadway and Treddenick
[1977] independently produce similar strong terms of trade
effects in calculations on tax and tariff distortions they
have performed with Canadian data.) Changing these trade
elasticities would change the strength of the terms of trade
effect and affect the level of the terms of trade neutralizing tax. In alternative cases that we have examined with
the terms of trade neutralizing tax there is relatively
little impact on the aggregate welfare measures from such an
exercise.[3]

7.3   Detailed Impacts on Household Groups for the Central Case Analysis

In Table 7.6 we present the welfare gains from the removal
of distorting taxes and subsidies for various groups drawn
from the 100 household types which we consider in the model.
Aggregate gains are decomposed by household composition, by
occupation of the household head, and by size of household
gross income.

The household composition breakdown reveals that single
households (comprising 19 percent of all households) lose
relative to the other households. In a large proportion of
these households, the head of the household is retired. On
average such households face lower average income tax rates
than others, and the abolition of the personal income tax
will thus leave them relatively worse off.

When the aggregate gains are distributed according to the occupational status of the household head, non-manual employees and the self-employed gain relative to other groups. This is true whether the gains are measured as a proportion of disposable income or in absolute terms. These two groups gain for different reasons. Non-manual households gain because they face the highest average tax rates of all occupational groups. The self-employed gain because they receive a larger proportion of the income from capital than any other group. As the net price of capital increases relative to the price of labour between equilibria, their gross income increases proportionately more than for any other occupational group.

When households are ranked by their gross incomes in the benchmark, the most dramatic redistributive effects of the tax/subsidy system become apparent. High income households are better off by 20-25% while low income groups are worse off by a similar percentage. The top seven deciles gain because of the large efficiency gain associated with the change. The sharp redistribution between the tails of the distribution results from three features: (i) the higher average tax rates for the rich, (ii) the greater importance of capital income in higher income households, (iii) the large budget share of the poor on heavily subsidized local authority housing. Low income groups lose sharply in the central case, and more than 50% of the total gain from the economy goes to the top 10% of households.

We report the compensating variation by household, and estimate the gain per household from abolition of all distortions as £250 per year using 1973 data. The large gains of the top income households can be seen in Table 7.6 with the top 10% of households realizing gains per capita in the region of £1500 per year (around $\frac{1}{4}$ of their disposable income).

These results suggest significant redistributive effects from the tax/subsidy system. They contrast with tax incidence calculations using shifting assumptions such as by Case, Leonard, and Musgrave [1967], and Pechman and Okner [1974] for the US, and for Canada by Gillespie [1970], as

TABLE 7.6

Welfare Gains by Alternative Household Groupings from the Replacement of Distorting Taxes and Subsidies in t
Central Case (as specified in Table 7.1) (1973 prices)

		Compensating Variation Calculated Using New Equilibrium Prices	Equivalent Variation Calculated Using Benchmark Equilibrium Prices
		£ bill	£ bill
1. Sum over all U.K. Households		5.3	5.0
2. Distribution of Gains by Household			
(a) Single Households	(19% of households)	0.2	0.3
Married + 1 child	(43% of households)	2.7	2.5
Married 1 + children	(38% of households)	2.4	2.2
(b) Manual	(42% of households)	1.6	1.5
Non-manual	(24% of households)	2.8	2.5
Self-employed	(7% of households)	0.6	0.6
Retired	(23% of households)	0.2	0.3
Unoccupied	(4% of households)	0.1	0.1
(c) Households Ranked by Size of Gross Income in Benchmark			
0- 10%	(6% of households)	-0.2	-0.2
10- 20%	(12% of households)	-0.4	-0.3
20- 30%	(11% of households)	-0.1	-0.1
30- 40%	(8% of households)	0.1	0.1
40- 50%	(11% of households)	0.1	0.1
50- 60%	(11% of households)	0.1	0.1
60- 70%	(10% of households)	0.6	0.6
70- 80%	(10% of households)	0.7	0.6
80- 90%	(11% of households)	1.1	1.1
90-100%	(10% of households)	3.2	3.0

Ratio of Compensating Variation to Disposable Income in the New Equilibrium	Ratio of Equivalent Variation to Disposable Income in the Benchmark Equilibrium	Compensating Variation per Household £/year	Equivalent Variation per Household £/year
0.08	0.10	265	250
0.03	0.05	48	60
0.10	0.12	323	299
0.08	0.09	328	303
0.06	0.07	189	174
0.14	0.16	580	432
0.10	0.12	455	426
0.02	0.04	45	60
0.07	0.09	145	142
-0.26	-0.20	-196	-140
-0.15	-0.13	-165	-129
-0.03	-0.13	-58	-47
0.03	0.03	54	51
0.02	0.02	58	53
0.03	0.03	89	80
0.08	0.08	255	227
0.09	0.10	361	325
0.12	0.13	561	513
0.21	0.26	1590	1474

well as the annual series of incidence calculations for the
UK in Economic Trends. All of these tend to show a pattern
of average tax rates by income range which is closer to
uniform. The difference in results here suggests that the
commonly shifting assumptions may be misleading if tax incidence is evaluated in a general equilibrium context.

In Table 7.7 we report the distribution of welfare gains
by household with the broadly based income tax left in place
(the same case as in Table 7.2). Here, the tax change produces a distribution of welfare gains by group which is less
extreme than in Table 7.6. Instead of receiving a gain of
£3.2 billion as in Table 7.6, the top 10% of households gain
around £1.5 billion. Interestingly, the bottom group still
lose, as a result of the abolition of local authority housing subsidies.

In Table 7.8 welfare gains and losses for each household
are reported for the removal of distorting taxes and subsidies. We also report the fractions of households in each
of the various cells in the data set. We report the gross of
tax annual incomes of households in the benchmark data set,
along with their net of tax incomes. We also report the
equivalent and compensating variations by household. The
equivalent variation is reported as a ratio of the benchmark
gross income.

In proportional terms welfare gains can be seen to be
large for a small number of the groups. However, these comprise only a small fraction of the total households. Those
areas of the income distribution where a large portion of
the total population is concentrated receive relatively
small welfare gains and losses.

The importance of the average personal tax rate in determining whether a given household group gains or loses, can
be clearly seen. The highest average tax rate associated
with a household which experiences a welfare loss is 7.1%
(for household number 34). The lowest tax rate associated
with a household who experiences a welfare gain is 5%. Only
5 households with average tax rates less than 7.1% experience a welfare gain, and all these are self-employed households, which have higher relative endowments of capital

TABLE 7.7

Distribution of Welfare Gains with Broadly Based Income Tax

Left in Place in Tax Replacement (as in Table 7.2)

(1973 prices)

Households Ranked by Size of Gross Income in Benchmark	Compensating Variation	Compensating Variation per Household	Equivalent Variation	Equivalent Variation per Household
	£ billion	£/year	£ billion	£/year
0-10% (6% of households)	-0.06	-51	-0.05	-42
10-20% (12% of households)	0.06	24	0.06	23
20-30% (11% of households)	0.20	94	0.20	97
30-40% (8% of households)	0.17	105	0.18	111
40-50% (11% of households)	0.31	142	0.32	149
50-60% (11% of households)	0.33	182	0.34	191
60-70% (10% of households)	0.58	235	0.61	249
70-80% (10% of households)	0.60	306	0.64	327
80-90% (11% of households)	0.89	417	0.96	452
90-100% (10% of households)	1.48	732	1.63	807

TABLE 7.8

Welfare Gains and Losses by Household from Replacing all U.K. Taxes and Subsidies
(As Specified in Table 7.1)
(1973 prices)

Household Type	F.E.S. Gross Weekly Incomes £	Percentage of Households in Each Group	Gross of Tax Annual Income by Household in Benchmark Data Set £/yr.	Net of Tax Annual Income by Household in Benchmark Data Set £/yr.	Equivalent Variation per Household £/yr.	Compensating Variation per Household £/yr.	Average Personal Tax Rate in Benchmark	Ratio of Equivalent Variation to Benchmark Gross Income
1 Type I Manual	<20	2.3	966.5	934.2	-126.8	-163.2	3.3	-13.1
2	20-30	1.3	1386.8	1219.5	17.1	20.3	12.0	1.2
3	30-40	.9	1969.0	1657.1	142.2	165.0	15.8	7.2
4	>40	.5	2587.7	2126.0	421.3	451.7	17.8	16.2
5 Type I Non-manual	20	.6	934.7	899.2	-75.0	-92.1	3.7	-8.0
6	20-30	.9	1411.2	1231.7	48.0	56.0	12.7	3.4
7	30-40	1.1	1900.9	1606.5	233.5	255.3	15.4	12.2
8	40-50	.4	2451.2	2046.6	334.1	365.8	16.5	13.6
9	50-60	.3	3138.5	2599.2	367.4	413.6	17.1	11.7
10	60-70	.2	3572.6	2701.6	765.9	835.4	24.3	21.4
11	>70	.2	6097.0	4066.7	2007.3	2177.2	33.2	32.9
12 Type I Self-employed	<20	.3	981.5	923.8	-13.2	-15.6	5.8	-1.3
13	20-40	.2	2327.7	2197.2	103.6	115.7	5.6	4.4
14	>40	.2	4657.8	3920.1	1015.5	1054.8	15.8	21.8
15 Type I Retired	<10	3.6	654.5	652.9	-156.3	-225.7	.2	-23.8
16	10-20	6.1	935.7	918.6	-116.8	-150.2	1.8	-12.4
17	20-30	.5	1897.5	1719.4	129.4	148.5	9.3	6.8
18	30-40	.3	2750.0	2393.9	366.0	410.0	12.9	13.3
19	40-50	.2	3552.9	2462.2	1126.9	1268.8	30.6	31.7
20	>50	.2	6108.6	2919.3	3226.3	3630.7	52.2	52.8
21 Type I Unoccupied	<10	.3	445.9	445.9	-50.9	-62.3	.0	11.4
22	10-20	1.1	862.1	851.8	-144.3	-190.5	1.1	-16.7
23	20-30	.3	1243.2	1195.3	-93.5	-115.0	3.8	-7.5

#	Group	Range							
24	Type II Manual	>30	.2	3794.0	2412.4	1311.3	1498.9	36.4	34.5
25		<20	.5	1462.4	1440.1	-105.8	-123.9	1.5	-7.2
26		20-30	2.3	1613.0	1518.8	-96.2	-116.5	5.8	-5.9
27		30-40	3.8	2039.6	1820.6	39.1	45.3	10.7	1.9
28		40-50	4.4	2566.7	2238.3	288.6	124.2	12.7	4.1
29		50-60	3.3	3086.1	2631.9	405.8	322.8	14.7	9.3
30		60-70	2.0	3619.6	3065.4	548.4	-446.6	15.3	11.2
31		70-80	1.1	4193.3	3464.0	825.6	605.4	17.3	13.0
32		80-90	.6	4747.1	3853.3	1196.8	880.9	18.8	17.3
33		>90	.2	5509.6	4231.8		-1272.6	23.1	21.7
34	Type II Non-manual	<30	.5	1490.3	1384.5	-7.6	-8.9	7.1	-.5
35		30-40	.9	2031.9	1836.3	85.3	95.6	9.6	4.2
36		40-50	1.5	2664.4	2371.2	206.0	226.6	11.0	7.7
37		50-60	2.1	3191.7	2744.8	283.7	317.2	14.0	8.8
38		60-70	1.5	3690.6	3163.3	426.8	464.3	14.2	11.5
39		70-80	1.4	3209.6	3585.5	635.6	687.5	16.8	14.7
40		80-90	.7	4804.7	4025.5	736.5	786.6	16.2	15.3
41		90-100	.5	5266.4	4294.2	910.7	969.9	18.4	17.2
42		>100	1.3	8963.9	6574.6	2178.9	2374.8	26.6	24.3
43	Type II Self-employed	<20	.2	1076.0	1076.0	-71.2	-83.6	.0	-6.6
44		20-30	.4	1754.5	1628.9	138.3	150.7	7.1	7.8
45		30-40	.5	2333.0	2190.8	48.0	54.7	6.0	2.0
46		40-50	.3	3010.9	2779.4	227.4	248.8	7.6	7.5
47		50-60	.4	3638.4	3376.2	328.5	-352.6	7.2	9.0
48		60-70	.2	4345.5	3932.6	459.0	498.4	9.5	10.5
49		70-90	.2	5081.8	4619.2	470.1	513.5	9.1	9.2
50		>90	.4	10154.6	8262.1	2182.1	2338.3	18.6	21.4
51	Type II Retired	<20	4.5	1173.9	1169.4	-163.7	-208.4	.3	-13.9
52		20-30	2.6	1789.5	1737.7	-84.1	-100.2	2.8	-4.7
53		30-40	1.0	2436.9	2240.0	66.8	77.1	8.0	2.7
54		40-50	.6	3022.8	2664.4	215.5	246.9	11.8	7.1
55		50-60	.4	3831.6	3060.1	704.7	791.7	20.1	18.3
56		60-70	.2	4750.6	3653.7	1048.2	1180.3	23.0	22.0
57		70-90	.2	5742.2	4260.9	1431.4	1598.5	25.7	24.9
58		>90	.2	9856.2	3737.3	6690.1	7142.7	62.0	67.8

TABLE 7.8 (cont'd.)

	Household Type	F.E.S. Gross Weekly Incomes £	Percentage of Households in Each Group	Gross of Tax Annual Income by Household in Benchmark Data Set £/yr.	Net of Tax Annual Income by Household in Benchmark Data Set £/yr.	Equivalent Variation per Household £/yr.	Compensating Variation per Household £/yr.	Average Personal Tax Rate in Benchmark	Ratio of Equivalent Variation to Benchmark Gross Income
59	Type II Unoccupied	<20	.5	959.3	959.3	-106.4	-130.4	.0	-11.0
60		20-30	.3	1484.0	1456.1	-37.4	-42.6	1.8	-2.5
61		30-40	.2	2253.6	2069.6	110.9	125.7	8.1	4.9
62		40-60	.2	3197.6	2736.5	402.3	452.1	14.4	12.5
63		>60	.2	6119.5	4264.4	2093.4	2253.8	30.3	34.2
64	Type III Manual	<30	.9	1903.2	1863.6	-225.4	-279.1	2.0	-11.8
65		30-40	2.7	2144.0	2031.8	-137.1	-164.8	5.2	-6.3
66		40-50	4.0	2601.6	2354.7	4.7	5.3	9.4	.1
67		50-60	4.0	3127.1	2784.8	111.9	127.8	10.9	3.5
68		60-70	3.0	3664.5	3217.2	177.0	202.2	12.2	4.8
69		70-80	2.0	4218.1	3669.3	316.5	353.9	13.0	7.5
70		80-90	1.3	4857.5	4209.2	476.2	520.7	13.3	9.8
71		90-100	.8	5354.5	4569.8	611.3	665.5	14.6	11.4
72		>100	1.4	6648.7	5594.7	1066.4	-1114.7	15.8	16.0
73	Type III Non-manual	<40	.4	1971.8	1860.7	-33.1	-37.9	5.6	-1.6
74		40-50	1.1	2668.2	2425.3	45.8	52.4	9.1	1.7
75		50-60	1.6	3192.7	2862.4	157.8	177.2	10.3	4.9
76		60-70	1.5	3761.2	3303.8	255.3	286.1	12.1	6.7
77		70-80	1.3	4309.2	3730.4	396.1	438.4	13.4	9.1
78		80-90	.9	4795.2	4089.4	486.9	540.6	14.7	10.1
79		90-100	.7	5409.8	4579.9	609.2	672.3	15.3	11.2
80		>100	2.1	7983.0	6332.6	1504.7	1628.0	20.6	18.8
81	Type III Self-employed	<30	.3	1646.2	1593.4	-88.8	-107.0	3.2	-5.3
82		30-40	.7	2437.7	2365.9	-40.3	-46.3	2.9	-1.6
83		40-50	.6						
84		50-60	.5	3667.8	3484.3	93.3	103.9	5.0	2.5
85		60-70	.3	4252.6	3967.7	368.4	391.9	6.6	8.6

86	.3	4884.5	4562.4	108.8	123.7	6.5	2.2
87	.1	5358.2	4854.9	529.5	571.1	9.3	9.8
88	.3	6205.3	5654.4	543.9	593.3	8.8	8.7
89	.6	9874.0	8428.2	1738.3	1844.9	14.6	17.6
90	.4	1794.3	1770.6	-216.3	-270.6	1.3	-12.0
Type III Retired							
91	.3	2304.5	2209.4	-6.8	-7.8	4.1	-.2
92	.3	2890.2	2603.8	78.9	91.3	9.9	2.7
93	.1	3427.0	3085.2	109.2	126.0	9.9	3.1
94	.3	4338.9	3516.6	330.4	360.8	10.7	8.3
95	.2	4532.2	3927.4	581.5	626.4	13.3	12.8
96	.2	6785.1	5539.6	1272.2	1365.9	18.3	18.7
97	.2	1555.0	1555.0	-185.7	-226.0	.0	-11.9
Type III Unoccupied							
98	.2	1693.1	1693.1	-114.0	-130.3	7.3	-6.7
99		3090.5	2864.3	150.8	166.0		4.8
100		5841.6	4818.4	933.8	1032.2	17.5	15.9

than other households. The occasional very high average
personal tax rates (such as 52.2% for household number 20,
and 62% for household number 58) result from capital gains
and estate tax liabilities being attributed to these groups.
(See Chapters 3 and 5).

In Table 7.9 we report the impact of the same tax change
as in Table 7.1 on the household income distribution using a
number of different measures of income. Panel A reports
changes in the distribution of gross and disposable incomes,
including transfers, between the two equilibria. The cumulative percentages indicate that the Lorenz curves of distributions of disposable income do not cross. All measures
reported in the lower half of Part A of the table move in
the direction of greater inequality. The coefficient of
variation, which tends to emphasize movements in the upper
tail of the distribution, changes substantially, reflecting
the relatively high income tax liability faced by the upper
tail.

The Gini coefficient changes by about 30 points out of
1000 between equilibria. This may seem a small change, but
the Gini coefficient is generally recognized to be insensitive to changes in the tails of the distribution. This
change mostly reflects the abolition of the personal income
tax. When gross of tax distributions are compared, the Gini
does not significantly change.

We also report changes in the size distribution of incomes
excluding transfers, and including transfers and an imputed
social wage. While the level of concentration changes in
both benchmark and counterfactual situations with the different income concepts which are considered, the same overall view of the redistributive impact of the tax system
remains. The impact of transfers on the distribution of
incomes can be easily discerned by comparing Panel B with
Panel A. Both the Gini coefficient and the mean to median
ratio move further when transfers are excluded from the
definition of income, than when the personal income tax is
excluded. The per household imputation of publicly provided
services makes the distribution of income more equal (as
Panel C reveals). This imputation is crude, and if more data

on the distribution of benefits of individual public expenditures were available it is quite possible that higher
imputations would accrue to higher income groups. The equality improvement revealed in Panel C would then be less significant.

In Table 7.10 we present alternative distributional calculations for the central case. We report household incomes
adjusted for the compensating and equivalent variations for
each household. We have taken the benchmark income distribution and augmented the incomes of households by the equivalent variations, and reduced new incomes by compensating
variations. These measures capture redistribution through
the tax/subsidy system not only directly through income
changes, but also indirectly through changes in relative
prices. The larger change in the Gini coefficient compared
to that reported in Table 7.9 suggests that significant
'extra' redistribution occurs through the tax system because
of its impact on relative prices in favour of the lower
income groups. Much of this 'extra' redistribution occurs
through subsidies to local authority housing.

7.4 Price and Quantity Adjustments Associated with the Central Case

Besides welfare impacts in aggregate and by household, we
also examine the price and quantity adjustments which would
be involved with a removal of industry and commodity
tax/subsidy distortions. In Table 7.11 we report summary
statistics of changes in outputs and changes in capital and
labour use by industry.

A notable feature of the output effects is the reduction
in the quantity of housing services, confirming the preferential treatment of housing which is suggested by the summary tax rates presented in Chapter 3. In addition, there is
a substantial increase in output of manufacturing, suggesting that manufacturing industry is heavily taxed under the
existing tax system. Particularly pronounced is the expansion in use of capital services in manufacturing, and the
reduction in use of capital by housing and primary production.

TABLE 7.9

Central Case Replacement

Income Distribution Impacts of the 1973 U.K. Tax Subsidy System

(as in Table 7.1)

A. Household Incomes Including Transfers

Share of Income Received by Groups of Households Ranked by Gross of Tax Income Per Household	Gross of Tax Incomes		Net of Tax Incomes	
	Benchmark	New Equilibrium	Benchmark	New Equilibrium
top 10%	24.6	24.8	24.3	24.8
top 25%	40.7	40.8	37.7	40.8
top 50%	74.1	74.0	72.8	74.0
top 70%	88.3	87.8	87.7	87.8
top 80%	94.0	93.9	93.1	93.9
top 90%	98.6	98.6	98.5	98.6
Gini coefficient	.329	.328	.299	.328
Mean to median ratio	1.146	1.157	1.145	1.157
Coefficient of variation	.631	.634	.564	.634

B. Household Incomes Excluding Transfers

Share of Income Received by
Groups of Households Ranked
by Gross of Tax Income Per
Household

	Gross of Tax Incomes		Net of Tax Incomes	
	Benchmark	New Equilibrium	Benchmark	New Equilibrium
top 10%	27.0	27.2	25.4	27.2
top 25%	44.1	44.3	41.6	44.3
top 50%	78.8	79.1	77.6	79.1
top 70%	93.4	93.4	92.8	93.4
top 80%	97.8	97.7	97.5	97.7
top 90%	99.4	99.4	99.3	99.4
Gini coefficient	.405	.406	.385	.406
mean to median ratio	1.101	1.091	1.059	1.091

TABLE 7.9 (cont'd.)

C. Household Incomes Including Transfers and an 'Imputed Social Wage'[1]

Share of Income Received by Groups of Households Ranked by Gross of Tax Income Per Household	Gross of Tax Incomes		Net of Tax Incomes	
	Benchmark	New Equilibrium	Benchmark	New Equilibrium
top 10%	20.5	20.5	18.8	20.5
top 25%	34.9	35.1	32.2	35.1
top 50%	67.5	67.4	66.2	67.4
top 70%	82.8	82.7	82.6	82.7
top 80%	90.1	90.0	89.2	90.0
top 90%	97.4	96.7	96.4	96.7
Gini coefficient	.233	.232	.203	.232
mean to median ratio	1.105	1.109	1.079	1.109

1. This imputation gives households an equal per capita amount calculated as the value of public goods at producer prices divided by the number of households. This is a crude imputation and a more satisfactory procedure could be followed if public goods appeared in individual preference functions.

This same broad picture reoccurs in Table 7.12 where we present sub-aggregate price and quantity adjustments between the benchmark equilibrium and the new equilibrium characterizing the central case. This table reveals a movement of capital services out of Primary Production and Housing into Manufacturing and industrial non-manufacturing. One explanation for this is in the relative size of capital income tax rates in our benchmark data. The increase in total output of these sectors, however, is also partly accounted for by the commodity pattern of output taxes, which are concentrated on manufacturing. The expansion in manufacturing contributes to the outcome in primary production. The industries in this group - Agriculture and Mining - have traditionally been favoured by the subsidy system (see Chapter 3). The reason that the total output of this group increases is that intermediate demands by the manufacturing sector have increased.

This intermediate production link is absent in the case of housing. The decrease in output of housing occurs because the owner-occupied personal income tax break has been abolished, as has the subsidy to Local Authority Housing. The elimination of these features, together with the rise in price of capital services stemming from the abolition of other taxes discriminatory against income from capital, leads to a strong decrease in the total (and final) output of this commodity group.

The price movements reported for producer prices involve a combination of changes in taxes and indirect changes in prices. The price of primary products rises sharply because of the elimination of subsidies. In addition, the producer prices of non-manufacturing commodities fall sharply. At the consumer level there are larger changes in prices involved because of the abolition of subsidy elements. The consumer price of housing rises sharply by 60% because of the abolition of tax preferences on owner-occupied housing and subsidies on Local Authority Housing.

Table 7.13 presents detailed industry and product price adjustments from removal of the tax/subsidy distortions in the central case. The changes in capital use by industry are

TABLE 7.10

Alternative Distributional Calculations of Impacts of Replacing the
1973 Tax/Subsidy System by a Yield-Preserving Sales Tax:
CV and EV Adjusted Incomes

(1)

(Table 7.1)

Share of Benchmark Income Accruing to Groups in Households Ranked by Gross Incomes per Household	Benchmark Equilibrium Size Distribution of Net of Tax Household Incomes Including Transfers
top 5%	15.7
top 10%	24.3
top 25%	37.7
top 50%	72.8
top 70%	87.7
top 80%	93.1
top 90%	98.5
Gini Coefficient	.299
Mean to Median Ratio	1.145
Coefficient of Variation	.564
Atkinson's ε = 0.5	.053
Measure	
ε = 1.0	.107
ε = 2.0	.220

1. With valuation of incomes at new equilibrium prices.

(2)	(3)	(4)
(EV Augmentation)	(CV Diminution)	(Table 7.1)
Benchmark Equilibrium Size Distribution of Net of Tax Household Incomes Including Transfers plus the Household Equivalent Variation	New Equilibrium Size Distribution of Net of Tax Household Incomes Including Transfers[1] minus the Household Compensating Variation	New Equilibrium Size Distribution of Net of Tax Household Incomes Including Transfers
15.1	21.0	17.7
25.5	19.8	24.8
48.4	39.6	40.8
72.8	68.9	74.0
88.4	84.1	87.8
94.1	91.1	93.9
97.3	94.2	98.6
.350	.276	.328
1.200	1.080	1.157
.675	.521	.634
.097	.044	.089
.188	.088	.173
.352	.180	.323

TABLE 7.11

Industry Reallocation of Production and Employment under Central Case
Replacement of 1973 U.K. Tax Subsidy System (as in Table 7.1)
(£ million, 1973 prices)

Aggregated Industry Groups (Index numbers of disaggregated industries given in parentheses)		Capital Use			
		Bench-mark	New Equil-ibrium	Change	Bench-mark Capital Tax
Primary Production (1-3)	Benchmark Prices New Prices	498.2 680.8	491.6 559.4	-106.6 -121.4	-50.2 -57.1
Manufactur-ing (4-21)	Benchmark Prices New Prices	1085.1 1234.9	1956.3 2226.4	871.2 991.5	1634.4 1861.2
Construction, Utilities, Communica-tions, Trade and Finance (22-28)	Benchmark Prices New Prices	2407.1 2739.4	3196.6 3637.9	789.5 898.5	1425.7 1622.6
Government and Services (31-33)	Benchmark Prices New Prices	3934.0 4477.1	4549.2 5177.3	615.2 700.2	600.9 683.8
Housing (28-29)	Benchmark Prices New Prices	8697.0 9900.0	6531.2 7432.8	-2167.8 -2467.2	1276.1 1452.3

Labour Use				Total Output		
Bench-mark	New Equil-ibrium	Change	Bench-mark Labour Tax	Bench-mark	New Equil-ibrium	Change
1691.6	1734.9	43.3	148.4	5250.9	5290.9	40.0
1773.5	2828.8	45.3	155.6	5885.4	5922.3	36.9
13704.0	13484.4	-219.6	1268.4	58268.9	62794.8	4525.9
14366.7	14136.5	-230.2	1329.7	59215.6	63678.4	4462.8
14642.2	14806.1	163.9	1221.5	37925.8	41545.1	3619.3
15350.3	15522.1	171.8	1280.6	36640.8	39891.9	3251.1
12275.3	12337.9	62.6	1135.9	22005.9	23369.4	1363.5
2868.9	12534.6	65.7	1190.9	20789.5	22069.5	1280.0
290.6	241.4	-49.2	17.6	10226.4	7856.2	-2370.2
304.6	253.1	-51.5	18.5	10204.5	7685.9	-2518.6

TABLE 7.12

Sub-Aggregate Price and Quantity Adjustments Between
Benchmark Equilibrium and New Equilibrium; Central
Case Replacement (as in Table 7.1)

Industry and Product Grouping (Index Numbers of Dis-aggregated Industries given in parentheses)	Fisher Quantity and Price Indices (Benchmark Equilibrium = 100)				
	Total Output	Inter-mediate Output	Final Output	Producer Price	Consumer Price
Primary Production (1-3)	100.3	103.1	96.6	112.5	140.2
Manufacturing (4-21)	107.4	106.8	107.9	100.8	98.9
Construction, Utilities, Communications, Trade, Finance (22-28)	108.8	107.6	109.5	94.7	112.3
Government and Services (31-33)	106.3	109.7	105.3	94.9	105.1
Housing (28-29)	75.2	-	75.2	98.4	163.3

heavily concentrated in high tax areas coinciding with the
tax rates reported in Chapter 5. The large expansion of
capital in manufacturing industry reported earlier is confirmed, but for certain manufacturing industries where tax
rates measured in effective terms turn out to be high there
is an even more dramatic increase. The large reductions in
capital use reflect the abolition of subsidies. This is the
case with Coal Mining and Metals which receive subsidies
through their preferential treatment as nationalized industries.

The changes in labour use by industry are small because
the tax differentials on labour use across industries in the
economy are small. Most of the changes reflect the direct
impact of increases in output. The sharp increases in labour
use in the Drink and Tobacco industries, for instance, reflect the increase in output in those industries. A similar
feature occurs in the case of Professional Services.

Movements in total output vary from 46 percent of the
benchmark (Local Authority Housing), and 72 percent (Coal
Mining), to 172 percent (Tobacco) and 164 percent (Drink).
The large reduction in Local Authority Housing service output can be traced to the abolition of subsidies. The effect
on private housing is principally due to the elimination of
its preferential personal income tax treatment. The increase
in outputs of Drink, Tobacco, and Petrol reflect the abolition of excises. Although producer prices vary substantially, from 70 percent of benchmark value (Wholesale Trade)
to 124 percent (Coal Mining), consumer prices are far more
volatile. They range from 34.6 percent of the benchmark
value (Tobacco) to 594.3 percent (Local Authority Housing),
and generally correspond to output changes.

When examined at the level of complete industry detail,
the most striking deviations from the summary figures in
Tables 7.11 and 7.12 are the responses for the excise items
- drink and tobacco. Because the tax rates on these items
are so large, the abolition of these taxes induces large
quantity responses, and the tax abolitions also produce
large changes in consumer prices. Consumer prices of excisable items fall to approximately 40% of their levels prevailing in the benchmark equilibrium.

TABLE 7.13

Detailed Industry and Product Price Adjustments from Central Case
Replacement
(All benchmark values = 100)

Industry and Product Classification in the Model	Capital Use by Industry	Labour Use by Industry
1. Agriculture (Inc. For. and Fish)	97.3	102.9
2. Coal Mining	22.7	103.1
3. Other Mining and Quarrying	166.6	84.6
4. Food	168.4	94.9
5. Drink	245.0	130.1
6. Tobacco	324.5	142.7
7. Mineral Oils	235.2	91.0
8. Other Coal/Petroleum Products	158.0	86.6
9. Chemicals	150.9	91.0
10. Metals	92.9	101.2
11. Mechanical Engineering	220.7	96.6
12. Instrumental Engineering	324.1	33.2
13. Electrical Engineering	220.7	91.7
14. Shipbuilding	177.5	93.7
15. Vehicles	266.4	100.6
16. Textiles	172.6	98.7
17. Clothing and Footwear	313.1	99.3
18. Leather, Leather Goods and Fur	253.0	91.1
19. Timber Furniture Etc.	168.8	99.8
20. Paper Printing and Publishing	162.3	101.6
21. Manufacturing NES	172.4	95.7
22. Construction	124.6	101.9
23. Gas, Electricity and Water	85.5	107.3
24. Transport	43.7	110.6
25. Communications	54.6	105.7
26. Retail Trade	171.7	101.4
27. Wholesale Trade	442.6	90.4
28. Banking Insurance and Finance	141.3	95.9
29. Housing Services (Private)	96.7	95.6
30. Housing Services (Loc. Auth.)	45.7	46.2
31. Public Service	112.9	95.8
32. Professional Services	107.5	110.7
33. Other Services	152.5	105.5

Total Output of Product	Final Output of Product	Producer Price of Product	Consumer Price of Product
101.2	98.2	111.9	138.7
95.2	82.2	123.8	154.4
103.3	106.8	94.5	108.4
104.1	104.2	106.3	131.6
163.8	166.6	85.0	44.9
182.4	186.6	100.5	34.6
115.4	127.4	123.0	46.3
98.5	97.7	100.5	123.0
102.8	100.4	100.2	115.5
100.3	90.4	108.0	134.6
104.6	103.9	96.3	120.0
98.1	97.5	101.6	126.6
104.1	103.1	98.2	122.4
95.5	93.4	104.4	130.2
107.6	108.0	97.4	96.5
106.9	104.2	102.4	114.9
115.0	115.5	98.3	112.5
107.5	103.8	102.9	115.5
106.1	104.0	108.9	122.6
109.8	103.4	100.7	121.2
105.9	105.1	98.8	111.3
104.6	104.0	97.6	121.7
99.6	93.4	109.3	136.3
104.5	96.0	104.9	130.8
101.3	90.0	113.3	141.1
115.5	119.8	91.5	102.8
128.6	133.5	80.5	90.4
111.9	112.4	90.1	107.4
95.6	95.6	94.6	117.9
45.7	45.7	106.7	594.3
101.5	101.5	95.2	106.1
110.3	111.4	95.9	108.4
115.1	121.2	92.6	96.9

In Table 7.14 we report our sensitivity analyses of price and quantity adjustments in the central case to variations in production side parameters. This table indicates that if the production function elasticities are low, the inability to substitute between factors changes the impact of the abolition of taxes and quantity adjustments are smaller. There is a smaller increase in the output of manufacturing, and a smaller reduction in the output of housing industries. Contrasted with this is a larger response in relative prices; consumer prices of primary products rise more and consumer prices of housing services fall more than in the central case. If production function elasticities are increased to 1.5 in all industries, quantity and price adjustments are changed relative to the central case. Quantity responses are larger and price responses are smaller. Output of primary production increases (rather than falls) relative to the benchmark, and the output of manufacturing industry increases more relative to the central case specification. A sharp change also occurs for the adjustment in functional share of income.

Table 7.15 reports our sensitivity analyses of price and quantity adjustments to demand side parameters. If all top level demand function elasticities are set equal to 0.3, this implies a limited ability to substitute between categories on the demand side, and there is less response in quantities for our central case analysis. The output of manufacturing increases by smaller amounts in this case compared to the central case. This contrasts with top level demand function elasticities set equal to 1.0, where there is a more pronounced increase for manufacturing products. There is also a difference on the price side. With a relative inability to adjust between quantities, the price responses are larger. With demand function elasticities set at 0.3, the increase in consumer price of housing is 75% as against 45% if all top level demand function elasticities are equal to 1.0. Here again, the direction of change in capital's share of product alters as the elasticity of sub-

TABLE 7.14

Sensitivity Analysis of Price and Quantity Adjustments
in Central Case Results (Table 7.1) to Production
Side Parameters

(Fisher Price and Quantity Indices; Benchmark = 100)

	Central Case Specifi- cation (Table 7.1)	All Production Function Elasticities equal 0.5	All Production Function Elasticities equal 1.5
Total Output by Sector			
Primary Production	100.3	99.4	101.8
Manufacturing	107.4	106.1	109.1
Construction, Utilities, Communications, Trade and Finance	108.8	106.9	110.9
Government and Services	106.3	103.6	108.9
Housing	75.2	79.6	72.8
Consumer Price Index by Industry			
Primary Production	112.5	114.4	110.6
Manufacturing	100.8	102.8	99.0
Construction, Utilities, Communications, Trade and Finance	94.7	98.0	92.1
Government and Services	94.9	96.5	93.4
Housing	98.4	88.2	106.0
Ratio of Income Accruing to Capital to Income Accruing to Labour	105.0	92.1	115.5

TABLE 7.15

Sensitivity Analysis of Price and Quantity Adjustments
in Central Case Results (Table 7.1) to Demand
Side Parameters

(Fisher Price and Quantity Indices; Benchmark = 100)

	Central Case Specification (Table 7.1)	All 'top level' Demand Function Elasticities set equal to 0.3	All 'top level' Demand Function Elasticities set equal to 1.0
Final Demands for UK Products			
Primary Products	96.6	92.6	103.6
Manufacturing	107.9	106.9	108.8
Construction, Utilities, Communications, Trade and Finance	109.5	106.9	114.2
Government and Services	105.3	105.1	106.6
Housing	75.2	82.1	62.3
U.K. Consumer Prices			
Primary Products	140.2	141.4	138.6
Manufacturing	98.9	98.9	98.6
Construction, Utilities, Communications, Trade and Finance	112.3	113.5	110.8
Government and Services	105.1	106.3	103.3
Housing	163.3	175.1	145.5
Ratio of Income Accruing to Capital to Income Accruing to Labour	105.0	109.7	97.2

stitution is increased. This can be traced to the preferential tax treatment of capital-intensive industries. When
these preferences are abolished consumer prices of these
goods and services increases. The high elasticity of substitution in demand implies a correspondingly substantial
decrease in demand for these products. This leads to a
decline in the derived demand for capital services which
must relocate in alternative, relatively labour intensive,
industries. Thus, the price of capital services must decline
in order for the factor markets to clear.

Additional support for this interpretation can be found in
the first panel of results by sector, which reports variations in final demand as the top level elasticity of substitution is changed. In particular, the demand for private
Housing Services decreases to 62.3% of its benchmark value
when the elasticity of substitution is set at unity. The
decrease is so marked that the final demands for all other
goods and services increase from their benchmark values. The
second panel of sectoral results report consumer price
changes. In general, these are relatively insensitive to
variations in the elasticity of substitution.

7.5 Additional Analyses in the Central Case

In this section we report some additional tables of results
which do not fit naturally into one of the three categories
discussed so far.

In Table 7.16 we report the national accounting measures
corresponding to the benchmark and new counterfactual equilibrium situations. Because two sets of equilibrium prices
are involved, it is possible for us to compute national
accounts aggregates for each equilibrium using the prices
prevailing in each equilibrium, giving us four sets of estimates. We report personal sector expenditures, net business
investment expenditures, real (non-transfer) government
expenditures, final imports, total imports, exports, and net
final expenditures in the UK. The last figure can be thought
of as comparable to a value of net national income.

TABLE 7.16

National Accounting Measures Corresponding to Central Case

(Table 7.1) Valuation at Producer Prices (Factor Cost)

	Benchmark equil- ibrium at Benchmark Prices	New equil- ibrium at Benchmark Prices	Benchmark equil- ibrium at New Prices	New equil- ibrium at New Prices
	£ bill.	£ bill.	£ bill.	£ bill.
Personal Sector Expenditures[1]	44.3	46.9	44.7	46.5
Net Business Investment Expenditures[2]	4.6	4.5	5.0	4.8
Real (non-transfer) Government Expenditures	19.6	19.6	18.9	18.9
Final Imports by the U.K.	3.7	3.0	5.3	4.2
Total U.K. Imports[3]	16.0	16.3	22.6	22.8
U.K. Exports[3]	15.8	15.8	15.8	15.7
Total Net U.K. Final Expenditures (Intermediate Imports excluded)	69.3	71.9	69.3	71.0
% Change in Total Final Expenditures at Benchmark Prices		+ 3.7%		
% Change in Total Final Expenditures at New Prices		+ 2.5%		

1. Includes residential construction net of depreciation.

2. This differs substantially from National Accounts Investment Expenditures because of the exclusion of both depreciation and personal sector non-financial capital acquisition (mainly residential construction).

3. These numbers in the benchmark case are slightly less than the value of goods and services given as National Accounts imports and exports because of adjustments to service items; a major item is the exclusion of military pay to personnel stationed abroad.

We report these numbers partly because they reflect changes in our accounting scheme compared to conventional national accounts. One important feature is the size of investment expenditures which are smaller in our accounts relative to national accounts because of the exclusion of both depreciation and personal sector residential construction. In addition, the size of government expenditures is larger than in the national accounts because of the inclusion of the imputed income to government and the imputed expenditure on government owned capital stock.

In Table 7.17 we report the functional distribution impacts from our central case analysis. When we abolish all tax/subsidy distortions, the net of tax return to capital increases relative to the net of tax return to labour. This indicates that capital bears a heavier tax burden than labour.

TABLE 7.17

Functional Distribution Impacts of the Central Case

(Table 7.1)

	Benchmark Equilibrium	New Equilibrium[1]
Net of factor tax return to capital (£ bill.)	16.72	19.03
Net of factor tax return to labour (£ bill.)	42.60	45.03
Capital taxes (£ bill.)	4.89	0.0
Labour taxes (£ bill.)	3.79	0.0
Ratio of net of tax returns $(\frac{K}{L})$	0.392	0.423
Ratio of gross of tax returns $(\frac{K}{L})$	0.465	0.423

1. The return to both factors rises in monetary terms because the yield preserving tax is a sales tax. In real terms both factors are not better off.

TABLE 7.18

Decomposition of the Distributional Impacts of Central Case
Analysis of Removal of Tax/Subsidy Distortions (Table 7.1)
into Price Effects and Tax Effects

Distribution of Household Incomes Including Transfers

A. General Equilibrium Calculation of Removal of All Tax/Subsidy Distortions in Table 7.1

Groups of households ranked by income per household	Gross of Tax Incomes		Net of Tax Incomes	
	Benchmark	New Equilibrium	Benchmark	New Equilibrium
top 10%	24.6	24.8	24.3	24.8
top 25%	40.7	40.8	37.4	40.8
top 50%	74.1	74.0	72.8	74.0
top 70%	88.3	87.8	87.7	87.8
top 80%	94.0	93.9	93.1	93.9
top 90%	98.6	98.6	98.5	98.6
Gini coefficient	.329	.328	.299	.328

B. Effects of Price Changes Alone with No Tax Change

Groups of households ranked by income per household	Gross of Tax Incomes		Net of Tax Incomes	
	Benchmark	New Equilibrium	Benchmark	New Equilibrium
top 10%	24.6	24.8	24.3	24.3
top 25%	40.7	40.8	37.7	37.7
top 50%	74.1	74.0	72.8	72.6
top 70%	88.3	87.8	87.7	87.5
top 80%	94.0	93.9	93.1	92.6
top 90%	98.6	98.6	98.5	97.8
Gini coefficient	.329	.328	.299	.297

C. Effects of Tax Changes Alone with No Price Change

Groups of households ranked by income per household	Gross of Tax Incomes		Net of Tax Incomes	
	Benchmark	New Equilibrium	Benchmark	New Equilibrium
top 10%	24.6	24.6	24.3	24.6
top 25%	40.7	40.7	37.7	40.7
top 50%	74.1	74.1	72.8	74.1
top 70%	88.3	88.3	87.7	88.3
top 80%	94.0	94.0	93.1	94.0
top 90%	98.6	98.6	98.5	98.6
Gini coefficient	.329	.329	.299	.329

In Table 7.18 we report results from a set of fixed price calculations which we use to assess whether or not the general equilibrium nature of our model which incorporates price endogeneity substantially changes the analysis of distributional impact of the tax system. In Part B we examine the price changes which are associated with our central case experiment but assume that no tax change results. In this case the size distribution of gross of tax incomes in the new equilibrium is almost the same as the size distribution of gross of tax incomes in the benchmark. In Part C we examine the effects of redistribution from changes in the tax system, assuming fixed prices. In this case the change in the size distribution of incomes is exactly that which is implied by our benchmark equilibrium calculation of the difference between gross and net income. Thus, the importance of price endogeneity for income distribution calculations of tax impacts seems somewhat secondary compared to the direct impact of changes in taxes on the income distribution. In this analysis the direct effects dominate the indirect effects produced by price endogeneity. However, we have shown in Table 7.10 the importance of price endogeneity when impacts on welfare, rather than income, are examined.

7.6 Summary of Main Findings in Chapter 7

In this section we present a summary of the main findings from the results which we report in this chapter.

1. The overall view presented of the UK tax/subsidy system is that the annual welfare costs of its distorting effects are significant, and marked redistribution occurs. This contrasts with an often asserted view that no significant redistribution occurs through the tax/subsidy system (save for direct transfers), and that welfare costs of distortions are small. This latter view leads to a policy prescription of attempts at further and increased redistributive taxation since costs are small. Our model findings suggest the opposite policy orientation of more concern with efficiency and less with redistribution in tax reform.

2. We emphasize an aggregate estimate of the static annual welfare loss from non-savings/non-leisure distortions produced from tax/subsidy policies in the UK of 6% to 9% of NNP at factor cost per year. This is an annual recurring loss which is larger than might be expected from an extrapolation of some of the currently available estimates of distortionary costs in the public finance literature.

3. We estimate the distributional impact of the tax/subsidy system to be relatively marked in terms of welfare gain or loss as a fraction of household disposable income. The abolition of all taxes and subsidies with replacement by a yield preserving general sales tax makes the top 10% of households some 26% better off and the bottom 10% some 20% worse off. The impact on the Gini coefficient of size distribution of incomes is much smaller changing by around 30 points out of 1000.

4. The impact of relative factor price changes induced through the tax system on the distribution of income appears to be relatively small. The additional characteristic of price endogeneity which our model incorporates has only a small secondary effect on estimates of the income distribution impact of tax changes. The direct effects of tax changes themselves on the income

distribution appear more significant than secondary effects induced by price changes. However, these income distribution effects exclude welfare effects from changes in relative consumer prices.

5. The tax system substantially protects the housing industry. Removal of tax/subsidy distortions shows a sharp reduction in the provision of housing services. Equally, the tax system penalizes manufacturing industry which we show as being relatively heavily taxed.

6. Removal of tax/subsidy distortions involves larger adjustments in consumer prices than in producer prices. This is because of the removal of subsidies and distorting taxes on consumer choice.

7. While qualifying our findings because of the choice of model and parameter values along with less than wholly satisfactory data, our sensitivity analyses suggest that most of the findings reported above are reasonably robust within ranges of parameter values. We would however reiterate that all of the calculations we make are heavily dependent upon the assumed values for elasticities and tax rate parameters, the assumptions implicit in our model, and the characterization of each tax in model equivalent form.

In the next chapter we expand on these findings by examining the structure of the tax system in more detail, stressing the various components of the tax system, the way they interlink, and their relative importance in assessing distributional and efficiency impacts of taxes and subsidies.

Notes

1. An alternative approach is to replace existing taxes by
    an optimal tax rather than a broadly based sales tax.
    An optimal commodity tax is that which minimizes the
    deadweight loss from the tax, given administrative
    constraints, such as an inability to tax leisure. In
    the fixed factor supply central case variants used in
    this chapter, a uniform rate sales tax is also an opti-
    mal tax. In Chapter 9 where we consider the model
    variant incorporating tax distortions of labour supply,
    optimal taxes will differ from the uniform tax on all
    goods, including leisure, which we use as our substi-
    tute tax.

2. With trade elasticities of 3.0 there is little impact
    on the aggregate welfare effects from the abolition of
    central case distortions.

CHAPTER 8

ANALYSIS OF STRUCTURAL CHARACTERISTICS OF
THE TAX/SUBSIDY SYSTEM

8.1 Introduction

In this chapter we present results from a number of counterfactual experiments designed to analyze structural features
of the tax/subsidy system. We consider various partitions of
the whole set of UK taxes and subsidies, and provide indications as to which components of the tax system are more
important in terms of their distributive and allocative
impacts. We examine the separate producer and consumer price
distortions in the tax and subsidy system, together with
some of the more narrowly defined 'legal' components of the
tax system. A number of specific policy options are also
considered: changes in personal tax progressivity, restructuring consumer prices to redistribute income, industry aid,
and altering the balance between direct and indirect taxation. One application of this analysis is in indicating
possible directions for future tax reform in the UK.

8.2 Model-Type Taxes and Legal Tax Instruments

In Table 8.1 we present the results of cases which
separately analyze the producer and consumer price distortions implicit in the tax/subsidy system. We report our
central case analysis from Table 7.1 and two further cases
where we separately abolish the distortions of consumer and
producer prices with the same tax replacement as in our
central case. All other characteristics of our central case,
including the elasticity values used and the terms of trade
neutralization, are unchanged.

The main taxes included as producer price distorting are
the corporate and property taxes, while those classified as
consumer price distorting are excise taxes and local authority housing subsidies. Other components of the tax system,
such as the value added tax, the income tax, and national
insurance, are included but generate milder distortions. As
with our central case we continue to exclude tax distortions
of savings and labour supply from our calculations.

The most striking finding from this table is that tax induced distortions of consumer prices dominate distortions of producer prices in terms of aggregate welfare impacts. This confirms the suggestion made in Chapter 7 that the major distorting effects of the tax system occur through the sub-system of indirect taxes and subsidies which distort consumer prices, rather than through the sub-system of direct taxes. A further implication of this, also stressed in Chapter 7, is that reform of the tax system along the lines suggested by the Meade Committee Report, which focuses on direct taxes, misses a substantial portion of the poten- tial gains from removal of distortions.

In the second part of Table 8.1 we report the distribution of welfare gains in three cases. Interestingly, the per capita gains from removal of producer and consumer price distortions are different from the case where all distor- tions are abolished. Low income groups lose as a result of the abolition of consumer price distortions, while top in- come groups gain. The most significant feature explaining this result is that groups at the lower end of the income distribution tend to lose as a result of the abolition of local authority housing subsidies.

A number of cases appear where the additivity of the sepa- rate measures of producer and consumer price distortion removal into the total measure for all distortion removal breaks down for individual income ranges. For instance, for manual worker households the sum of the equivalent varia- tions for consumer price distortions abolition is over £2 billion, and for producer price distortions abolition £150 million, whereas if all distortions are abolished the gain is £1.4 billion. This suggests that in a number of ways the separate distortions of consumer and producer prices tend to be offsetting. While this does not show up in the aggregate, it shows up clearly in the sub-aggregates for the various groups.

In the third part of Table 8.1 we present the aggregate distributional statistics from the separate abolition of these distortions. Interestingly, the abolition of neither set of distortions significantly changes the size distri-

TABLE 8.1

Effects of Removal of U.K. Tax Subsidy System Separately Analyzed by Distortions of Consumer and Producer Prices
(Fixed Factor, Central Case Specification: Standard Replacement as in Table 7.1.)
(1973 prices)

1. Aggregate Welfare Gain

	All Abolished	Producer Price Distortions Abolished	Consumer Price Distortions Abolished
Sum of Compensating Variations (CV)	£5.3 billion	£1.8 billion	£3.2 billion
Sum of Equivalent Variations (EV)	£5.0 billion	£1.6 billion	£3.8 billion

2. Distribution of Welfare Gains

	Total £ million/year EV	CV	Per Household £/Year EV	CV	Total £ million/year EV	CV	Per Household £/Year EV	CV	Total £ million/Year EV	CV	Per Household £/Year EV	CV
Single	260.5	209.9	60.7	48.9	268.5	299.3	62.6	69.8	75.7	54.2	17.7	12.6
Married + 1*	2531.3	2729.8	299.6	323.1	769.5	858.3	91.1	101.6	1548.5	1303.2	183.3	154.3
Other	2207.7	2385.3	303.9	328.4	593.8	664.9	81.8	91.5	2203.0	1859.0	303.3	255.9
Manual	1476.6	1598.3	174.7	189.1	156.7	189.8	18.5	22.5	2110.2	1800.5	249.7	213.5
Non Manual	2538.3	2769.4	532.3	580.8	313.0	353.0	65.6	74.0	1454.1	1208.8	304.9	253.5
Self Employed	589.1	628.5	426.6	455.1	502.9	548.4	364.2	397.2	239.2	195.2	173.2	141.2
Retired	274.6	205.8	60.3	45.2	543.0	603.2	119.3	132.5	-3.0	-10.3	-0.7	-2.3
Unoccupied	120.9	122.9	142.7	145.0	116.2	128.1	137.1	151.1	26.8	22.1	31.6	26.1

Households Ranked by Gross Income	Total £ million/year EV	CV	Per Household £/Year EV	CV	Total £ million/year EV	CV	Per Household £/Year EV	CV	Total £ million/Year EV	CV	Per Household £/Year EV	CV
0 - 10%	-157.2	-220.3	-140.0	-196.3	8.0	9.0	7.1	8.0	-39.4	-40.4	-35.1	-36.0
10 - 20%	-347.3	-443.1	-129.2	-164.8	113.4	128.7	42.2	47.9	1.1	0.1	0.4	0.1
20 - 30%	-97.3	-119.6	-46.9	-57.7	107.4	120.6	50.3	56.5	118.8	103.1	57.3	49.7
30 - 40%	81.1	87.1	50.7	54.5	21.3	25.0	13.8	16.2	239.4	205.0	149.7	128.1
40 - 50%	116.2	125.2	53.4	57.6	95.7	107.6	44.0	49.5	311.0	268.5	143.0	123.4
50 - 60%	142.3	158.7	79.9	89.0	112.1	128.2	49.9	57.0	262.8	225.8	147.5	126.7
60 - 70%	561.1	629.5	227.4	255.2	108.0	120.8	54.8	61.3	588.9	502.1	238.7	203.5
70 - 80%	630.6	701.0	324.7	361.0	179.7	202.1	91.1	102.4	530.1	448.4	272.9	230.9
80 - 90%	1092.3	1192.9	513.5	560.7	209.2	234.8	98.3	110.4	815.1	681.7	383.1	320.4
90 - 100%	2977.7	3213.5	1473.6	1590.2	677.1	745.8	335.1	369.0	999.5	822.2	494.6	406.9

3. Aggregate Distribution Statistics

	Benchmark	All Abolished	Producer Distortions Abolished	Consumer Distortions Abolished
Gini	0.299	0.328	0.299	0.300
Mean to Median Ratio	1.145	1.157	1.121	1.111
Coefficient of Variation	0.564	0.634	0.578	0.560
Atkinson's Measure:				
$\epsilon = 0.5$	0.053	0.089	0.057	0.052
$\epsilon = 1.0$	0.107	0.173	0.111	0.103
$\epsilon = 2.0$	0.220	0.323	0.219	0.204
Cumulative Distribution of Disposable (Net of Tax) Incomes (Households ranked by Disposable Income):				
Top 10%	24.3	24.8	23.2	22.6
25%	37.7	40.8	39.3	37.7
50%	72.8	74.0	70.6	71.6
70%	87.7	87.8	88.2	86.9
80%	93.1	93.9	94.1	92.8
90%	98.5	98.6	97.8	98.3

*"Married + 1" refers to a married couple with no children or one child.

bution of net of tax incomes. In both cases the Gini coefficient is approximately equal to that which applies in the benchmark. This suggests that little income redistribution occurs through the change in relative prices from either of these two portions of the tax system, although in the case of consumer price distortions this comparison is misleading in that these statistics do not reflect changes in consumer prices, and the only distributional effect is the change in factor rewards. In later tables we show that the excise taxes and local authority housing subsidies involve substantial differential impacts in welfare effects across households.

In Table 8.2 we report aggregate welfare gains from piecewise abolitions of components of the tax system, along with information on the gainers and losers in the total population. We have grouped taxes by their model equivalent form, and within that classification by components of the more narrowly defined 'legal' structure. The most striking conclusion in terms of aggregate effects is the dominance of the effects from the abolition of indirect taxes and subsidies. The removal of excisable items within the indirect tax/subsidy group yields a welfare gain in the region of £1 billion and, along with the distorting effects of other commodity taxes and subsidies, gives a total welfare cost of £3.5 billion. Gains from removing excises and local authority housing subsidies are the dominant portion of the total group effect of £3.5 billion.

Gains from removal of factor tax distortions total £1.5 billion. These are accounted for exclusively by distortions in the capital tax system. This reflects the fact that limited industrial discrimination exists within the system of labour taxes (National Insurance Contributions). Within the capital tax system, effects are shared between corporate taxes and rates, with the corporate tax being dominant. Interestingly, the abolition of rates alone results in a loss for the economy since the rating system has distortions of capital use by industry which tend to offset the distortions occurring with the corporate tax.

TABLE 8.2

Aggregate Welfare Gains and Proportion of Gainers from the
Removal of Distortions Associated with Particular Taxes or Tax
Groups   (Fixed Factor, Central Case Specification; Standard
Replacement as in Table 7.1)   (1973 prices)

	Sum of Equivalent Variations £ billion	Sum of Compensating Variations £ billion
1. Factor Taxes		
All	1.5	1.7
Capital	1.5	1.6
Corporate	1.1	1.1
Rates	-0.4	-0.4
Labour	0.0	0.0
2. Indirect Taxes and Subsidies		
All	3.5	3.2
Excises	1.1	1.0
3. Direct Taxes		
Income Tax	0.2	0.3
4. Subsidies		
All	2.3	2.2
Nationalized Industry	0.3	0.3
Local Authority Housing	1.9	1.9

Gains of Gainers £ million		Losses of Losers £ million		Proportion of Gaining Households in Population
Valuation at Pre-Tax Change Prices	Valuation at Post-Tax Change Prices	Valuation at Pre-Tax Change Prices	Valuation at Post-Tax Change Prices	%
1548.1	1725.6	-28.3	-28.2	80.1
1668.8	1797.2	-191.3	-186.9	59.2
1126.5	1091.5	-6.5	-8.5	94.0
324.5	337.6	-704.1	-733.0	32.0
214.9	220.4	-208.8	-223.9	58.3
3752.1	3462.2	-263.5	-269.1	77.3
1177.5	1120.4	-71.5	-72.5	84.4
1587.0	1861.5	-1338.3	-1524.0	36.1
2566.7	2408.6	-217.1	-210.3	72.8
338.7	319.9	-29.7	-30.5	87.4
2130.2	2035.0	-182.1	-183.6	72.1

A broad overview of the distorting effects of the entire tax/subsidy system (ignoring for now labour supply and savings distortions) is that distorting losses are concentrated in three specific areas. Local authority housing subsidies, the corporate tax and excises all provide significant distortionary losses. These are of approximately comparable size with local authority housing subsidies providing the largest distorting loss. Because local authority housing is quantity-constrained, our calculations (which incorporate no such constraints) may misestimate the welfare cost of this distortion. It is not clear whether this omission leads to a downward or upward bias of our estimate. In addition, our formulation misses some components of welfare cost associated with local authority housing policy, in particular labour immobility.

In the second portion of Table 8.2 we report the gains of gainers, the losses of losers and the proportion of the population which gains or loses as a result of any particular tax abolition. For some taxes gains of the gainers are close to being the total gain for the economy. For other tax changes this is not so. With the abolition of the income tax, for instance, gains of the gainers and losses of the losers are in absolute value almost the same, with only 36% of households gaining from the tax aboliton. In contrast, an abolition of the excise tax system involves gross gains which are close to the total gain with approximately 85% of households gaining. A striking feature of this table is the large proportion of people who gain as a result of the abolition of factor taxes and in particular the abolition of corporate taxes.

In Table 8.3 we present our results on the distribution of welfare gains associated with the abolition of selected taxes or groups of taxes. The abolition of rates generates gains which are heavily concentrated in the tails of the income distribution. This is because capital is the factor which gains from the removal of the tax and the capital intensity of incomes of households is highest for the bottom and top income groups. As already noted, our bottom income group includes a large number of retired households who are

significant recipients of capital income, including the
imputed income from owner-occupied housing. All groups gain
from the removal of corporate taxes. With the abolition of
both capital taxes (corporate taxes and rates) the top income group gains even more than the sum of the two separate
cases would suggest. There is a sharper increase in the
price of capital because of the compounding of the two
taxes. In the case of the abolition of labour taxes, little
impact occurs across income groups.

The abolition of consumer taxes also leads to interesting
results. Excise taxes contain items which are bought heavily
both by low and high income groups. Tobacco tends to be
heavily purchased by low income groups, whereas gasoline
tends to be heavily purchased by high income groups. The net
effect is that the top income groups are gainers from the
abolition of excise taxes, although in proportional terms
households in the middle of the income distribution gain
most. The loss to low income groups through excise tax abolition may be a reflection of suspected under-reporting by
low income groups of alcohol and tobacco purchases. If these
purchases represented a higher proportion of low income
budgets in the model, low income groups might gain from the
excise abolition. However, it should also be remembered that
the bottom two deciles comprise most of the 'retired' and
'unoccupied' households, and these groups may not make large
purchases of excisable items. This conjecture is supported
by the results reported on gains by occupational type. With
the abolition of local authority housing subsidies the large
gainers are in the top income range, with losers being concentrated in the bottom range. The size of the gain to the
top income group is noteworthy in this case, approximately
one half the gain from the abolition of the income tax. In
the case of the abolition of the income tax, as would be
expected, there are sharp redistributive effects across the
various income ranges.

In most cases, distributional results across occupational
and family types are broadly consistent with prior expectations about the relationships between sources of income
and other household characteristics. Only the manual group

TABLE 8.3

Distribution of Welfare Gains Associated with the Abolition of Selected Particular Taxes or Tax Groups
(1973 prices)

1. Abolition of Producer Taxes

Distribution of Welfare Gains

Households ranked by Gross income Benchmark	Abolition of Rates				Abolition of Corporate Taxes				Abolition of Capital Taxes[1]				Abolition of Labour Taxes[1]			
	Aggregate £million/year		Av. Household £/year		Aggregate £million/year		Av. Household £/year		Aggregate £million/year		Av. Household £/year		Aggregate £million/year		Av. Household £/year	
	EV²	CV²	EV	CV	EV	CV	EV	CV	EV	CV	EV	CV	EV	CV	EV	CV
0 - 10%	0.1	0.1	0.1	0.1	13.9	13.8	12.4	12.3	13.0	14.0	11.5	12.4	1.1	1.0	1.0	0.9
10 - 20%	51.1	53.0	19.0	19.7	106.6	107.6	39.6	40.0	154.2	167.0	57.4	62.1	-22.2	-23.6	-8.3	-8.8
20 - 30%	1.0	0.9	0.5	0.4	106.0	105.5	49.6	49.4	109.3	117.8	51.2	55.2	6.6	6.6	3.1	3.1
30 - 40%	-47.8	-49.9	-31.1	-32.4	23.8	23.2	15.5	15.1	-8.5	-6.9	-5.5	-4.5	24.6	25.5	16.0	16.6
40 - 50%	-64.2	-67.1	-29.5	-30.8	94.3	92.0	43.4	42.3	61.2	68.3	28.2	31.4	27.7	28.5	12.7	13.1
50 - 60%	-73.6	-76.6	-32.7	-34.1	56.8	52.8	25.3	23.5	96.2	108.7	42.8	48.4	-0.1	-1.4	-0.0	-0.6
60 - 70%	-82.7	86.2	-42.0	43.8	85.3	81.7	43.3	41.5	56.5	63.4	28.7	32.2	33.2	34.0	16.8	17.2
70 - 80%	-62.5	-70.2	-34.2	-35.6	105.4	100.6	53.4	51.0	151.3	167.6	76.7	84.9	1.5	0.2	0.7	0.1
80 - 90%	-112.5	-116.9	-52.9	-54.9	107.2	100.5	50.4	47.3	147.2	165.1	69.2	77.6	18.3	17.4	8.6	1.2
90 - 100%	16.4	17.5	8.1	8.6	420.7	405.3	208.2	200.6	697.2	745.3	345.0	368.8	-84.6	-91.8	-41.9	-45.7
Occupation Type																
Manual	-448.7	-508.8	-57.8	-60.2	63.4	48.6	7.5	5.7	-54.2	-27.7	-6.4	-3.3	121.2	122.7	14.3	14.5
Non-Manual	-204.3	-212.5	-42.9	-44.6	90.9	79.2	19.1	16.6	204.3	228.3	42.9	47.9	26.8	24.0	5.6	5.0
Self-Employed	104.3	108.6	75.5	78.7	420.1	418.2	304.3	298.5	542.0	570.1	392.5	412.9	-42.9	-45.4	-31.1	-32.9
Retired	180.6	187.7	39.7	41.2	449.9	448.3	98.8	98.5	658.8	704.6	144.7	154.8	-89.8	-94.9	-19.7	-20.9
Unoccupied	28.4	29.6	33.5	34.9	95.6	94.7	112.8	111.8	126.6	134.9	149.4	159.2	-9.3	-9.9	-11.0	-11.7
Family Type																
Single	62.9	65.2	14.7	15.2	213.8	213.8	49.9	49.9	293.5	316.2	68.4	73.7	-18.6	-20.1	-4.3	-4.7
Married + 1	-101.8	-105.9	-12.1	-12.5	522.2	507.5	61.8	60.1	739.1	801.6	87.5	94.9	-28.6	-34.2	-3.4	-4.1
Other	-340.7	-354.7	-46.9	-48.8	384.0	361.8	52.9	49.8	444.8	492.4	61.2	67.8	53.4	50.7	7.3	7.0

2. Abolition of Consumer Taxes and Subsidies
Distribution of Welfare Gains

Households ranked by gross income benchmark	Abolition of Excises				Abolition of Local Authority House Subsidies				Abolition of Income Taxes			
	Aggregate £ million/year		Av. Household £/year		Aggregate £ million/year		Av. Household £/year		Aggregate £ million/year		Av. Household £/year	
	EV	CV	EV	CV	EV	CV	EV	CV	EV	CV	EV	CV
0 - 10%	-9.1	-9.3	-8.1	-8.3	-48.3	-52.3	-43.0	-46.6	-98.0	-112.5	-87.3	-100.2
10 - 20%	-3.8	-4.7	-1.4	-1.8	-71.1	-71.1	-26.4	-26.4	-392.5	-378.2	-122.5	-140.7
20 - 30%	79.8	76.5	37.4	35.8	-6.1	-7.2	-2.9	-3.3	-247.7	-284.2	-119.4	-137.5
30 - 40%	94.8	90.1	61.6	58.6	79.8	76.8	51.9	49.9	-56.9	-63.8	-35.5	-39.9
40 - 50%	161.3	153.6	74.1	70.6	70.1	67.6	32.2	31.1	-156.8	-177.7	-72.1	-81.7
50 - 60%	145.7	138.7	64.8	61.7	196.7	190.7	87.5	84.8	-171.9	-193.5	-96.4	-108.6
60 - 70%	120.2	115.1	61.0	58.4	244.3	234.1	124.0	118.8	12.1	20.8	4.9	8.4
70 - 80%	136.6	130.1	69.2	65.9	304.6	293.0	154.4	148.5	26.7	38.1	13.8	19.6
80 - 90%	171.8	163.4	80.7	76.8	497.2	473.9	233.7	222.7	155.7	189.0	73.2	88.9
90 - 100%	208.8	194.5	103.3	96.3	680.9	645.9	336.9	319.6	1114.8	1299.6	551.7	643.1
Occupational Type												
Manual	826.7	781.4	97.8	92.5	741.2	722.8	87.7	85.5	-99.7	-88.1	-11.8	-10.4
Non-Manual	143.8	138.8	30.1	29.1	1202.8	1135.4	252.2	238.1	737.6	869.4	154.7	182.3
Self-Employed	102.6	98.9	74.3	71.6	112.4	104.7	81.4	75.8	-191.2	-218.7	-138.5	-158.4
Retired	16.1	13.0	3.5	2.9	-96.8	-99.5	021.4	-21.9	-184.0	-209.2	-40.4	-46.0
Unoccupied	16.8	15.9	19.8	18.8	-11.5	-12.0	-13.5	-14.2	-14.0	-15.9	-16.5	-18.7

continued on page 242

Family Type												
Single	-0.5	-3.4	-0.1	-0.8	-0.0	-8.7	-0.0	-2.0	-18.3	-18.7	-4.3	-4.4
Married + 1	418.3	399.3	-49.5	47.3	852.9	-810.7	101.0	96.0	406.5	489.8	48.1	58.0
Other	688.1	652.1	94.7	89.8	1095.2	1049.4	150.8	144.5	-139.5	-133.5	-19.2	-18.4

[1] Capital taxes include the Corporation tax, Rates, and Nationalized Industry Capital Subsidies. Labour taxes comprise National Insurance, and Regional Employment Premiums. See Chapter 5 for details.

[2] EV = Equivalent Variation, CV = Compensating Variation.

loses when capital taxes are abolished, and only manual and non-manual occupational types gain from the abolition of labour taxes. When consumer taxes and subsidies are considered, the manual group is once again the largest gainer from the abolition of excises, while the retired and unoccupied groups lose from the abolition of local authority housing subsidies. When the personal income tax is abolished, the non-manual group is the only gainer.

When the distribution of welfare gains by family type is considered for each tax abolition, results are once more consistent with prior expectations. Single households, comprising a large proportion of retired persons, gain from the abolition of rates at the expense of other groups. All groups gain from the abolition of corporate and capital taxes. Welfare effects associated with the abolition of labour taxes are small, and little weight should be placed upon the estimates of their distributional impact.

When consumer taxes are considered, the single person households lose as a result of the abolition of excises and the abolition of local authority housing subsidies. On the other hand, childless married couples or married couples with only one child, gain from the abolition of the personal income tax at the expense of other groups. Since this group is likely to contain a larger proportion of multiple worker households than others, this outcome is to be expected.

In Table 8.4 we report the effect of removing distortions within the personal income tax. We examine three separate cases: an elimination of the tax break to owner occupied housing, an elimination of the tax break to leisure implicit in the distortion of the labour leisure choice, and total elimination of the income tax in the presence of the labour leisure choice. The latter two cases involve our model variant with endogenous labour supply behaviour. Considered separately, the elimination of neither of the specific distortions leads to a substantial welfare gain.

Our results are broadly consistent with those obtained by Harberger (1964) indicating small welfare impacts of labour supply distortions. The welfare gain from the elimination of the income tax as a whole is greater than the sum of the

TABLE 8.4

Welfare Effects of Distortions in the Personal Income Tax with a
Labour Leisure Choice Incorporated   (Standard Replacement with
Sales Tax Applying to Imputed Leisure Purchases)   (1973 prices)

Elimination of Owner-
Occupied Tax Break

Aggregate Welfare Gains

Sum of Equivalent Variations (ΣEV)   £185.1 million
Sum of Compensating Variations (ΣCV)   £160.2 million

Distribution of Welfare Gains

Household Percentiles Ranked by Benchmark Gross Income	Aggregate £ million/year		Av. Household £/year	
	EV	CV	EV	CV
0 - 10	20.3	19.5	20.2	19.3
10 - 20	75.0	71.6	25.3	24.1
20 - 30	27.9	26.5	14.6	13.9
30 - 40	17.9	16.6	9.2	8.6
40 - 50	43.0	40.7	22.6	21.4
50 - 60	4.9	3.0	2.6	1.6
60 - 70	41.5	37.7	17.6	15.9
70 - 80	8.5	5.3	4.2	2.7
80 - 90	17.8	14.6	10.2	8.3
90 - 100	-71.7	-75.3	-31.7	-33.3
Occupation Type				
Manual	334.3	314.2	39.6	37.2
Non-Manual	-71.4	-75.1	16.2	17.1
Self-Employed	-63.9	-62.2	45.3	44.1
Retired	17.7	15.9	3.9	3.5
Unoccupied	29.9	1.4	37.3	1.7
Family Types				
Single	12.6	11.2	2.9	2.6
Married + 1	14.5	5.9	1.7	0.7
Other	158.1	143.0	21.6	19.7

Elimination of Leisure Tax Break	Elimination of Income Tax
£398.7 million £373.5 million	£630.3 million £707.0 million

Aggregate £ million/year		Av. Household £/year		Aggregate £ million/year		Av. Household £/year	
EV	CV	EV	CV	EV	CV	EV	CV
38.4	35.5	38.1	35.2	-73.1	-81.1	-72.6	-80.5
183.2	169.4	61.7	57.0	-299.7	-332.0	-100.9	-111.8
108.5	100.2	56.9	52.5	-176.8	-195.4	92.6	-102.4
12.5	11.8	6.5	6.1	-93.4	-102.5	-48.2	-52.9
-6.8	-5.8	-3.6	-3.0	-99.8	-109.4	-52.5	-57.6
39.0	36.2	20.6	19.1	-117.7	-128.3	-62.0	-67.6
-25.7	-22.8	-10.9	-9.6	7.2	10.3	3.0	4.4
4.7	5.2	2.4	2.6	50.1	57.8	25.0	28.9
-34.3	-30.6	-19.6	-17.5	170.7	190.5	97.5	108.8
79.1	74.5	35.0	33.0	1262.8	1397.0	558.9	618.3
-170.2	-152.8	-20.1	-18.1	-113.7	-116.9	-13.4	-13.8
-81.9	-73.0	-17.2	-15.3	793.0	879.1	166.3	184.4
187.5	172.0	135.8	124.5	-80.7	-88.8	-58.5	-64.3
388.2	358.1	85.3	78.7	8.4	7.9	1.9	1.7
75.2	69.2	88.7	81.6	23.3	25.6	27.5	30.2
197.2	182.1	46.0	42.5	84.1	92.1	19.6	21.5
194.4	182.1	23.0	21.6	591.6	656.6	70.0	77.7
7.1	9.3	1.0	1.3	-45.3	-41.7	-6.3	-5.7

gains from its two major distortions considered separately. This result occurs because of income effects - the elimination of the tax puts more real income in the hands of those households who have preferences which lead to expenditures associated with minor distortions elsewhere in the tax/subsidy system; this transfer is from households whose expenditures are concentrated in areas where distortions are severe.

The owner occupied tax break has an associated redistributive impact. The top income group is the major loser as a result of this elimination, with other groups gaining. While we show that housing is a major source of distortion in public sector activity, our results are sharply differentiated between owner occupied and local authority housing. The ad valorem subsidy rate to local authority housing that we use is much larger than the income tax break to owner occupiers.

The importance of the tax distortion of labour supply varies with the marginal tax rates which the various household groups face. When households are divided into income groups, intermediate income households tend to lose at the expense of low and high groups. This is because the replacement 'neutral' tax also applies to leisure. The amount of leisure each household is assumed to consume is equal to 25% of the amount of labour sold. Households with higher labour incomes will therefore have a higher imputed expenditure on leisure, and will suffer more directly from the elimination of the leisure tax break. In addition the amount of labour supplied to industries will increase, and this drives down the price of labour relative to the price of capital. Households whose incomes are relatively capital intensive will therefore gain.

The conclusion from the first set of tables in this chapter is thus that non-labour supply, non-savings distortions in the tax/subsidy system are heavily concentrated in three components of the entire system. Local authority housing subsidies, excises, and the corporate tax (in that order) account for the major portion of the total distorting losses. We also note that the distortions in the tax/subsidy

system are not additive. In some cases distortions within
the tax system offset one another and have compounding effects which are not apparent from casual inspection. Redistributive impacts are also somewhat deceptive, the sharp
redistribution in favour of the top income group as a result
of the elimination of subsidies to local authority housing
being a striking example.

8.3 The Relationship of Results in 8.2 to Other Studies of
Tax Subsidy Distortions

In Table 8.5 we present a list of other studies offering
estimates of the welfare costs of tax-subsidy distortions,
covering the period to 1981. We begin with the complete
labour supply distortion studies of Harberger and Browning.
Traditionally the welfare costs of these distortions have
been thought to be small based on the intuition that labour
supply elasticities themselves are small. Thus, Harberger's
early calculation suggests a welfare cost of only 0.2% of
GNP, only 2 $\frac{1}{2}$ % of tax revenues. More recent literature has,
however, suggested that somewhat larger estimates may be
more defensible. Browning includes not only income taxes,
but also sales, excise, and social security taxes, in examining the total tax distortion of labour supply. He also
importantly highlights the higher marginal welfare cost
calculation of incremental deadweight losses from raising an
extra dollar of revenues through an already distortionary
tax.   Other work by Hausman in ed. J. Pechman "How Taxes
Affect Economic Behavior", Brookings, 1980, and others has
argued that higher (compensated) labour supply elasticities
than previously thought may be in order, increasing these
welfare cost estimates further.

A further area of work on tax distortions is the analysis
of interindustry distortions of capital use. Here the focus
is on the distorting effects of the combinations of corporate, property, and personal income taxes on the industrial
allocation of capital. The corporate sector of the economy
has to pay the corporate tax, while personal income taxes
give preferences to housing which, in turn, are partially
offset through the property tax. The combination of these

TABLE 8.5

Summary of Calculations of the Welfare Costs[a] of Tax-Subsidy Distortions

Description of calculation	Annual welfare cost as % of:		Marginal welfare cost per $ of tax collections
	GNP	Tax collections	
Labour supply distortions			
Harberger (1964)... Consumer surplus calculation using U.S. data for 1961--income tax distortions only	0.2	2.4% of income tax collections	
Browning (1976).... Consumer surplus calculation similar to Harberger (1974) U.S. data--labour distortions through income, sales, excise, and social security taxes.	0.9	4.5% of income, sales, excise, and social security tax collections	
Marginal welfare cost from income tax distortions of labour supply--consumer surplus measure for 1974 U.S. data			14-16¢
Interindustry distortions of capital use (corporate, property and personal income taxes)			
Harberger (1964)... Welfare loss calculation--corporate tax only--U.S. data for 1953-1955	0.3	5.0% of corporate tax collections	
Welfare loss calculation--depletion provisions only--U.S. data for 1953-1955	0.1-0.3	2.5-5.0% of corporate tax collections	
Harberger (1966)... Welfare loss calculation--corporate, property, and personal income tax--U.S. data for 1953-1959	0.4-0.6	4.1-7.0% of capital tax collections	

Shoven............	Recalculation of Harberger's 1966 calculation using static general equilibrium model of U.S. economy--product loss measure	0.35	3.6% of capital tax collections
Ballentine.........	Calculation of intersectoral and intertemporal welfare loss due to the U.S. corporate tax	1.6-2.3	40.0-57.9% of corporate tax collections
Fullerton, King, Shoven, and Whalley	Dynamic sequence of general equilibrium--model of U.S. economy and tax system using 1973 data--removal of corporate tax distortion only	1.1	29.8% of corporate income tax collections
Savings distortions (income taxes only)			
Hall; Mieszkowski..	Computation of change in consumption per capita in balanced growth using stylized U.S. data	1-1.5	10.0-15.0% of income tax collections
Fullerton, Shoven, and Whalley........	Dynamic sequence of general equilibria--model benchmarked to 1973 U.S. data	0.5	4.7% of income tax collections
Summers............	Empirical life-cycle model of U.S. economy	10.0	exceeds income tax collections
Home ownership			
Laidler............	Consumer surplus calculation using 1960 U.S. data	0.1	1.3% of income tax collections
Excise (drink, tobacco, gasoline)			
Browning (1976)....	Marginal welfare cost from excise distortions--consumer surplus measure using 1974 U.S. data		

TABLE 8.5 (Cont'd.)

| | Annual welfare cost as % of: | | Marginal welfare cost per $ of tax collections |
Description of calculation	GNP	Tax collections	
Other studies			
Boskin............	Differential tax treatment of market and nonmarket economy (homeowner plus labour supply distortions)--consumer surplus calculations using 1972 U.S. data	1.7-3.4	5.8-11.6% of total net taxes	
Browning (1979)....	Tax preferences in U.S. income tax (home-owner plus others)--consumer surplus calculation for 1974 U.S. data	0.6	6.7% of income tax collections	13¢
Nonqualified distortions			
	Tax treatment of human capital formation			
	Distortions of retirement decisions through social security			
	Displacement of private sector capital accumulation through anticipated social security benefits			
	Distortions implicit in overground/under-ground economy			
Other issues	Discounting of static gains into present value terms: Feldstein argues that for the United States rate of time preference is below the labour force growth rate in efficiency units and that the discounted present value of any recurring loss is unbounded			

Administrative costs: For the United States administrative costs of IRS run at around 0.5% of taxes collected; Musgrave and Musgrave conjecture government administration plus private compliance costs are around 2-2.5% of revenues; Sandford for the United Kingdom suggests that the ratio of private to government costs is in the range 4-7:1

[a]Some of these studies measure only the incentive effects of taxation or effects on output, and thus tend to underestimate the total welfare cost.

taxes distorts the interindustry allocation of capital in
the economy.

Work in this area largely follows Harberger's approach. A
number of points should be made about the calculations shown
in Table 8.5. The four studies listed under the heading
"Interindustry distortions..." calculate distortions only in
terms of effects on the productive efficiency of the economy
(the loss in potential production caused by the taxes in
question), whereas the final study also includes the additional loss from distortions of consumer choice.

The first calculation by Harberger is a welfare loss calculation for the corporate tax only. He suggests that 0.3
per cent of US GNP is involved. Harberger has also analysed
depletion allowances within the US corporate tax which give
preferences to extractive industries, and suggests that
another 0.1 to 0.3 per cent of GNP is involved. In a later
paper, Harberger analyses the combined effects of the US
corporate, property, and personal income taxes and calculates a production loss of 0.4 to 0.6 per cent of GNP.
Shoven's recalculation of the Harberger estimate does not
substantially change the earlier figures.

Ballentine produces a combined intersectoral and intertemporal welfare loss estimate of 1.6 to 2.3 per cent of GNP
for the United States, while we produce a 2.1 per cent welfare loss from UK corporate and property tax distortions.
The tax rates involved for the United Kingdom are more
sharply differentiated than in the US case. In both studies,
the welfare losses from consumer distortions, as well as
producer distortions, are included. The Ballentine calculation suggests that about half of the revenues collected
through the corporate tax are "lost" through the distortions
produced.

Fullerton, King, Shoven and Whalley analyse the removal of
consumer and producer distortions associated with corporate
and personal tax integration in the US, and also include
some calculations of the effects of intertemporal distortions of the corporate tax. Based on US data for 1973, their
results suggest that the welfare loss from distortions in
the corporate tax are in the region of 1 per cent of GNP.

Approximately 30 per cent of corporate income tax collections are "lost". The last three studies referred to thus suggest very clearly that on efficiency grounds distortions of interindustry use of capital are more important as a tax reform target than are distortions of labour supply.

In analyzing tax distortion of savings Summers' work suggests that the distorting loss to the US economy may be as high as 10 per cent of GNP on an annualized equivalent basis. The Fullerton, Shoven, and Whalley estimates are not as large; welfare costs are smaller, but still more significant than distortions of labour supply.

For home-ownership distortions - an area that public finance economists have long been interested in for possible tax reform - the most widely quoted welfare loss estimate is by Laidler; 0.1 per cent of GNP for the United States, using 1960 data.

Excise taxes typically involve high tax rates and, therefore, large distortions. A problem with a simple interpretation of the distortions is the suggestion that a removal of a distortion that results in sharp increases in consumption of drink and tobacco would represent a beneficial change for the economy. Browning stresses the importance of excise tax distortions with his estimate that the marginal welfare cost in the United States per dollar of additional tax collection amounts to 26 cents.

Two other studies listed in Table 8.5 are not included under the heading of individual distortions. Boskin looks at the differential tax treatment of the market and the non-market economy, focussing heavily on homeowner and labour supply distortions. His loss estimate from these distortions (using 1972 US data) is 1.7 to 3.4 per cent of GNP (5 to 11 per cent of total taxes collected). Browning in a study of tax preferences in the US income tax (which includes homeowner preferences), suggests that 0.6 per cent of GNP is lost through a misallocation of resources. A marginal welfare cost estimate of 13 cents on the dollar is involved.

In Table 8.5, we also list some further distortions of the tax system which (to our knowledge) are not quantified. A potentially important distortion arises with the tax treat-

ment of human capital formation. Distortions within the
social security system, especially of retirement decisions
and displacement of private sector capital accumulation by
anticipated social security benefits, are stressed by
Feldstein. Welfare cost estimates are not, however, included
in the literature. One last distortion arises through the
operation of the underground economy. There have been recent
suggestions that the total value of underground activity in
the US may be as large as 30% of GNP. Since the underground
economy is untaxed, a large tax distortion operates.

Most of the welfare cost estimates in Table 8.5 refer to
static annual loses imposed by the tax system. This raises
the important question of discounting the flow of these
annual losses. Feldstein (1979) has argued that in the
United States the rate of time preference is below the
labour force growth rate in efficiency units; therefore, the
discounted present value of any recurring loss in the economy is unbounded. This conclusion suggests that if the tax
system imposes an annual recurring loss, the discounted
present value of the loss may be more important than may
appear if the flow loss alone is calculated.

The final item in Table 8.5 allows us to compare efficency
loss estimates with administrative costs for the tax system.
For the United States, the administrative costs of the
Internal Revenue Service are about 0.5 per cent of total
taxes collected. Musgrave and Musgrave conjecture that the
total sum of government administration, plus private compliance costs, is about 2 to 2.5 per cent of revenues. It
appears, then, that the welfare costs of taxes are much
larger than the administrative costs, although the combined
costs inflicted on society through distorting taxes should
be increased somewhat to reflect administration.

8.4 Increasing Personal Tax Progressivity
In Table 8.6, we report the efficiency and distributional
effects of a major increase in personal tax progressivity.
We examine two cases, one in which we simply set marginal
income tax rates equal to the average income tax rates implied by our benchmark data, and the other in which we

increase personal income tax payments by 50%, and then
equate marginal rates to average rates. In the latter case a
yield preserving broadly based subsidy applies. In case 1,
there is an aggregate welfare gain, resulting from the
decrease in the average of the marginal rates applying to
the owner occupier tax break and the labour leisure tax
break. In case 2, the average of the marginal rates has
increased relative to the benchmark, and there is an
aggregate welfare loss.

When the distribution of welfare changes is examined, the
case 1 pattern reflects the changes in marginal rates. Since
average rates do not change, no direct redistributive effects result. Instead, the major impacts occur from the
change in marginal rates on the value of tax deductions for
imputed income on homeownership and leisure repurchased.
Intermediate groups, whose average rate falls below the
assigned benchmark marginal rate of 30%, lose. Better off
households, whose average rate exceeds the assigned marginal
rate of 30%, gain. In case 2, we find considerable redistribution of income from the increase in personal progressivity. The Gini coefficient moves by 10 points in 1000 and
the coefficient of variation moves by 19 points in 1000.

8.5 Restructuring Consumer Prices in Order to Redistribute Income

In Table 8.7 we present the welfare and distributional effects of attempts to redistribute income through specific
methods rather than broadly based redistribution. This assumes that the government adopts particular kinds of public
sector tax and subsidy policies in order to change the relative consumer prices as a way of indirectly redistributing
income to various household groups in the economy.

We begin by analyzing the already discussed case of abolishing local authority housing subsidies. It is possible to
argue that this subsidy is desirable since it is strongly
redistributive to the poor. Abolishing local authority housing subsidies involves a welfare gain to the economy of
approximately £2 billion, along with a sharp move in the
size distribution of welfare-augmented income. The Gini
coefficient, calculated from benchmark and EV-augmented

TABLE 8.6

The Efficiency and Distributional Effects of a Major Increase in
Personal Tax Progressivity   (1973 prices)

Case 1
Marginal Income Tax Rates Set Equal
to Average Income Tax
Rates

1. Aggregate Measures of Welfare Gains

	Summation of CVs	£206.2 million
	Summation of EVs	£223.9 million

2. Distribution of Welfare Gains

Household Percentile, Ranked by Benchmark Gross Income, Augmented to include the Imputed Income from Leisure	Aggregate £ million/year		Av. Household £/year	
	EV	CV	EV	CV
0 - 10	16.9	16.4	16.9	16.2
10 - 20	75.4	72.6	25.4	24.5
20 - 30	19.7	18.8	10.3	9.9
30 - 40	-25.6	-25.1	-13.2	-12.9
40 - 50	-29.4	-28.9	-15.5	-15.2
50 - 60	-47.84	-46.9	-25.2	-24.8
60 - 70	-22.8	-23.4	-9.7	-9.9
70 - 80	-15.2	-16.3	-7.6	-8.1
80 - 90	34.2	31.4	19.5	17.9
90 - 100	218.5	207.6	96.7	91.9

3. Measures of Inequality

	Case 1
	Net Income
Gini (Benchmark[1] = .319)	.230
Coefficient of Variation (Benchmark = .593)	.599
Atkinson's Measure ε	
0.5 (Benchmark = .059)	.063
1.0 (" = .120)	.128
2.0 (" = .244)	.262

[1]All Benchmark values refer to the distribution of
disposable income.

Case 2
50% Increase in Personal Income Tax
Payments, with Marginal Rates Set Equal
to New Average Rates; Yield Preserving
Non-Distortionary Subsidies

£281.2 million
£248.0 million

Aggregate £ million/year		Av. Household £/year	
EV	CV	EV	CV
75.9	67.5	75.4	67.0
320.9	285.2	108.1	96.1
147.6	130.9	77.3	68.6
14.6	11.9	7.6	6.2
11.6	8.9	6.1	4.7
4.6	6.2	2.3	3.3
-56.1	-53.7	-23.7	-22.7
-73.6	69.5	-36.7	-34.7
-81.9	-76.7	-46.8	-43.8
-602.7	-579.6	-266.7	-256.5

Case 2
Net Income
.309
.574
.069
.140
.283

TABLE 8.7

Welfare and Distributional Effects of Redistribution from
Specific Commodity Price Changes

(1)
Abolition of Local Authority Housing Subsidies
(Standard Replacement as in Table 7.1)
(1973 prices)

Aggregate Welfare Gains

Sum of Equivalent Variations (EV)   £1.9 billion
Sum of Compensating Variations (CV)   £1.9 billion

Gini (Benchmark = .299)   .313[1]

Relative Price Change[2]
(Benchmark = 100)   365

Relative Quantity Change
(Benchmark = 100)   53

Distribution of Welfare Gains

Household Percentiles Ranked by Benchmark Gross Income	EV	CV
0 - 10	-50.4	-54.6
10 - 20	-68.9	-68.8
20 - 30	36.9	33.7
30 - 40	36.8	35.7
40 - 50	68.5	66.0
50 - 60	214.5	207.8
60 - 70	221.2	212.2
70 - 80	335.4	322.7
80 - 90	456.1	434.6
90 - 100	698.1	661.9

[1]This Gini coefficient measures the concentration in the
vector of EV augmented incomes; see Chapter 7.

[2]Relative price changes are defined according to the
normalization rule between price vectors given in
Chapter 7.

(2)
Elimination of Owner-Occupied Income Tax Break
Plus 50% Tax on Consumption of Private Housing
Services; Yield Preserving Subsidy on Food

Aggregate Welfare Gains

Sum of Equivalent Variations (EV)   -£1.8 billion
Sum of Compensating Variations (CV) -£1.8 billion

Gini (Benchmark = .299)   .285[1]

Relative Price Change[2]
(Benchmark = 100)   Private Housing   183
                           Food   31
Relative Quantity Change
(Benchmark = 100)   Private Housing   73
                           Food   177

Distribution of Welfare Gains

Household Percentiles Ranked by Benchmark Gross Income	EV	CV
0 - 10	41.2	34.3
10 - 20	9.9	2.4
20 - 30	-46.7	-49.4
20 - 40	1.0	5.7
40 - 50	-2.0	-12.2
50 - 60	-80.1	-84.2
60 - 70	-164.8	-165.4
70 - 80	-239.3	-235.9
80 - 90	-398.4	-393.3
90 - 100	-939.5	-932.3

benchmark incomes, moves from approximately 0.3 to 0.313, half of the change in the Gini coefficient which is involved for a replacement of the whole tax/subsidy system by a 'neutral' tax, including the redistributive impact of the entire income tax. Use of EV-augmented incomes allows the Gini coefficient to capture the distributive effect of relative consumer price changes. The redistribution in favour of the top 10% of the income distribution is pronounced in this case. The top 50% of the income distribution gains £1.9 billion. Also noteworthy are the relative price effects. The relative consumer price of local authority housing increases by a factor of 300%. The provision of local authority housing services drops to almost 50% of the benchmark quantity.

In the second part of Table 8.7 we examine a case where there is an elimination of the owner-occupied income tax break, a 50% surtax on the consumption of owner-occupied housing services accompanied by a yield preserving subsidy on food. This is designed to produce an increase in the price of owner-occupied housing services - housing services purchased by higher income groups - along with a redistributive subsidy in favour of low income groups. In this case there is a welfare loss of £1.8 billion, and a redistributive impact in terms of welfare-augmented income which also is about one half the effect of the whole tax system - a move in the Gini coefficient of about 15 points out of 1000. The redistributive impact against the top income group is substantial with a loss of £800 million. This is a larger loss than that which local authority housing subsidies cause them. Once again, the relative price and quantity movements in this case are large.

The conclusion from these two calculations is that compared with the redistribution which the tax system actually produces, a significant amount of redistribution towards low income groups through specific (relative price alteration) methods rather than broadly based (income redistributive) methods seems to be possible. The welfare cost of these methods however, is probably too large to merit their widespread use.

In addition, the amount of redistribution which the tax system actually produces is relatively modest and may not be the appropriate criterion from which to evaluate specific egalitarianism in the UK. The effect of transfers, for example, is much more dramatic. A fixed price calculation, inferred from Table 7.8, Chapter 7, suggests their removal would move the Gini by 78 points in 1,000.

8.6 Industrial Policies and the Tax System

Over the last 10 to 15 years there has been substantial discussion and debate in the UK about the possibility of using the tax system to bring about major structural change in the economy. From time to time, the tax system has been advocated as the appropriate policy instrument for fostering the growth of UK manufacturing industry. For example, this was the thinking behind the introduction of selective employment tax in the UK in the mid-1960s.

In Table 8.8 we present the results of cases designed to examine the effects of the introduction of alternative kinds of tax preferences and subsidies to manufacturing industry. In case 1 we consider the effect of a self-financing subsidy to manufacturing. We impose a 50% output subsidy on all manufacturing goods and a replacement yield preserving non-distorting tax. The impact of this is to increase the output of manufacturing industries by 21% and to increase capital and labour use in those industries sharply. Surprisingly, the welfare cost of this policy is relatively modest at only £0.6 billion.

An alternative policy is to remove factor market distortions by using a labour use tax in manufacturing to offset the distortions in the capital tax system. This results in all industries facing the same factor price ratio, but the factor tax system has a distorting effect on output prices. This produces a situation where productive efficiency in the economy is restored but does so at a cost of increased distortions in goods markets. This is a classic example of a second-best problem; one distortion has been removed, but at the cost of worsening an existing distortion. There is a large welfare cost of this policy of £1.2 billion, and

TABLE 8.8

Industry Reallocation Via the Tax System

(1973 prices)

	Case 1	Case 2
	Subsidy to Manufacturing	Offsetting Labour Use Tax on Manufacturing
	A 50% Output Subsidy on the Consumer Prices of all U.K. Manufacturers; Yield Preserving Non-Distortionary Tax	Tax on Labour Use by Manufacturing Industries Set Equal to Tax on Capital Use, by Industry; Yield Preserving Non-Distortionary Subsidy
1. Aggregate Welfare Gains		
Sum of Equivalent Variations (ΣEV)	£661.5 million	-£1233.8 million
Sum of Compensating Variagions (ΣCV)	£542.6 million	-£1081.6 million
2. Index of Change in Manufacturing Industry	(Benchmark = 100)	(Benchmark = 100)
Output	121.4	82.3
Capital Use	123.9	134.3
Labour Use	112.4	79.7

associated with that a significant reduction in the output of manufacturing industry.

8.7 The Effects of Changing the Balance Between Direct and Indirect Taxation

In this section we consider the effects of changing the balance of taxation between direct and indirect taxes. In the years since the election of the Thatcher government, budgets have reflected the philosophy of changing the balance of taxation more heavily in favour of indirect taxes with a reduction in direct taxes. Indeed, over the years, the balance of taxation between direct and indirect taxes in the UK has been a source of major debate. At various times it has been suggested that the balance between direct and indirect taxation can be used as an anti-inflation device. In fact what has happened in the UK over a period of 10 years or so is that, with inflation and the absence of complete indexation in the income tax, the ratio of total taxes collected through the direct tax system has increased only to be sharply reversed by the Thatcher government. The changes which have recently been undertaken, moving taxation more heavily in favour of indirect taxes, can be thought of as a return to the historical composition of the tax system. The balance between the two taxes has substantial impact on the distribution of income and this is what we seek to show in the cases which we consider.

In Table 8.9, we first consider a case where all indirect tax rates are increased by 25%; importantly subsidies to local authority housing are left unchanged. This is accompanied by a yield preserving reduction in average personal income tax rates. Because the major distortions in the tax system are concentrated in the indirect taxes, this is a welfare losing proposition because the distortions in the indirect tax system are worsened. This welfare loss is accompanied by a redistribution against the low income groups because of the reduction in the income taxes. Thus a change which involves increasing indirect taxes proportionally is not a desirable change on either redistributive or efficiency grounds. This case differs from the proposals

TABLE 8.9

The Effects of Changing the Balance of Direct and Indirect Taxation
(1973 prices)

(1)	(2)
Indirect Taxes Increased by 25%; Yield Preserving Reduction in Average Personal Income Tax Rates	Indirect Taxes Decreased to 75%; Yield Preserving Increase in Average Personal Income Tax Rates

Aggregate Welfare Gains

	(1)	(2)
Sum of Equivalent Variations (ΣEV)	EV -£246.4 million	EV £116.9 million
Sum of Compensating Variations (ΣCV)	CV -£250.5 million	CV £100.9 million

Gini Coefficient
(Benchmark = .299)

	(Income)	(EV Augmented Benchmark Income)
(1)	.304	.302
(2)	.296	.296

Distribution of Welfare Gains

Household Percentile Ranked by Benchmark Gross Income	EV	CV	EV	CV
	£ million/year		£ million/year	
0 - 10	-10.5	-10.6	4.8	4.7
10 - 20	-37.3	-37.9	24.0	23.4
20 - 30	-37.8	-38.7	34.7	33.6
30 - 40	-30.2	-30.9	30.3	29.0
40 - 50	-53.9	-55.1	49.9	47.8
50 - 60	-50.5	-51.5	23.5	21.8
60 - 70	-45.8	-46.7	25.2	22.8
70 - 80	-41.6	-42.4	12.9	10.7
80 - 90	-41.0	-41.6	11.1	8.4
90 - 100	-102.1	-104.8	-99.6	-101.3

implemented in the Thatcher budgets since the excise taxes were not scaled proportionally in the tax changes enacted.

In column 2 of Table 8.9 we consider the converse case where indirect taxes are decreased to 75% of the rates associated with the benchmark equilibrium situation. A yield preserving increase in average personal income tax rates accompanies the change. This is a welfare improving measure because the distortions in the indirect tax system are weakened and there is an improvement in the distribution of income. Thus in terms of existing tax rates, changes which reduce the relative importance of indirect taxes are both redistributively and allocatively desirable. In interpreting these results, it should be remembered that the model we are using for these experiments does not accommodate intertemporal distortions. These would tend to rise with an increasing relative importance of direct taxes.

8.8 Summary of Findings of Chapter 8

The main points from results in Chapter 8 may be summarized as follows:

1. Major distortions in the tax/subsidy system (ignoring savings and labour supply) are concentrated in three areas; the corporate tax, local authority housing subsidies, and excise taxes. Of these, local authority housing subsidies appear to be the largest source of loss (although these estimates need careful qualifications), but the other two are also highly significant. Effects of tax distortions are largely additive (separate welfare losses from each can be added). In one notable case involving distortions within the capital tax system between the corporate taxes and rates this is not true.

2. Our estimates of tax distortions appear to be roughly consistent with previous literature estimates, where available, on an individual tax by tax basis. The total involved is in the region of 6% to 9% of GNP, as suggested in Chapter 7.

3. We find sharp redistributive effects associated with individual components of the tax system. This is espec-

ially the case with local authority housing subsidies. One striking feature is that the abolition of local authority housing subsidies gives a gain to the top income group which is one half of the total gain they would receive by the complete abolition of the progressive income tax.

4. The trade-off that we calculate between redistribution and efficiency in the income tax when we incorporate tax distortions of labour supply seems to involve only mild efficiency costs. This trade-off appears milder than is implicitly suggested by much of the analytical optimal income tax literature.

5. We find that significant redistribution through specific forms of egalitarianism in the tax/subsidy system is possible, and perhaps more effective than would be anticipated on the basis of casual examination of expenditure shares. Where these policies are heavily concentrated on items which are purchased intensively by particular income groups such as local authority housing, owner-occupied housing and food, large welfare costs also appear to be involved.

6. The welfare costs associated with existing tax preferences in favour of manufacturing appear to be relatively small.

7. The structure of the existing tax/subsidy system is such that major welfare gains are achieved through the removal of distortions in the indirect tax system. Changes in the ratio of direct and indirect taxes which move in favour of direct taxes tend to be both redistributively and allocatively desirable.

Notes

1. We discuss the small aggregate welfare gain from the
    elimination of the labour leisure distortion more fully
    in Chapter 9.
2. Larger welfare costs from the income tax distortion of
    the labour leisure choice have been reported by
    Browning (1976) (6.6% of income tax collections).
3. Musgrave (1969), for example, speculates that the over-
    all excess burden might be about 2% of tax collections.
    Musgrave and Musgrave (1973) suggest a range of 2.5%-4%
    for the US. Our estimates are about 20-25% of UK tax
    collections.

CHAPTER 9

FURTHER ANALYSIS OF TAX/SUBSIDY DISTORTIONS

9.1 Introduction

In this chapter we consider additional features of public
sector activity in the UK by extending our basic variant
model in a number of directions. We analyze both the tax
distortion of the labour-leisure choice and the distortion
of savings. We also evaluate the distorting effects of the
tax system through its interaction with inflation. We next
consider the income effects associated with the transfer
mechanism on the expenditure side of government activity and
briefly discuss some stylized calculations associated with
welfare reform. We also examine an alternative solution
concept for our model in which the level of provision of
public services is endogenously determined as part of the
optimizing procedure. Finally a particular tax reform experiment associated with the changes introduced in the UK is
reported, in order to demonstrate the applicability of our
approach to more practical situations where explicit tax
reform proposals are being considered.

9.2 Tax Distortions and Labour Supply

Our central case analysis in Chapter 7 assumes the supply of
factors is fixed as changes occur in taxes and subsidies. In
this section we use a factor supply model in which labour
supply depends on taxes.

We consider households to have utility functions which are
defined not only over the commodities in the model, but also
over consumption of leisure. We augment the labour endowment
of households so that households repurchase a portion of
their labour endowment in the form of leisure, with their
purchase decision following directly from utility maximization. The price of leisure is taken to be the net of tax
wage rate. The slope of the budget constraint which households face in terms of leisure and goods is therefore affected by the tax system. With an abolition of tax distortions,
the price of leisure to households increases and they substitute out of leisure into other goods, in effect increasing their labour supply by cutting their consumption of
leisure.

In the relevant model extension, households have a fixed endowment of augmented labour and in the modified benchmark equilibrium we expand the expenditure matrix of households to incorporate the purchases of leisure. We adopt elasticities in the nested CES utility function defined over the expenditures on leisure and other goods, and use this expanded version of the model to examine the effects of an abolition of tax/subsidy distortions.

To augment the endowment of labour of households we consider a fractional increase in the labour endowment which corresponds to a stylized situation of a longer potential work week for households. We consider a factor of 5/4 by which we multiply the labour endowment of households from the fixed factor case to represent a potential work week of 50 hours in contrast to an actual work week of 40 hours. The additional labour income created in this way is matched by a corresponding expenditure on leisure which appears in the expenditure matrix of households. This expenditure is then used in our replication procedures to generate parameter values for the model.

To select an elasticity value for the labour supply decision of households, we survey the econometric literature and other studies on labour supply and choose a central case elasticity estimate. We then calibrate the substitution elasticity in our utility functions to that parameter. We have earlier discussed this literature and suggested the range of -0.1 - 0.2 for prime age males. When combined with the higher elasticities generally found for secondary workers, this suggests an overall uncompensated elasticity close to zero. We incorporate this along with the fractional increase of the labour endowment to give a value for the elasticity of substitution between the broad categories of goods including leisure. Leisure appears as one of the nine major categories between which there is a constant elasticity of substitution.

Having expanded the labour endowment in this way and recalculated the set of parameters which characterize the model, we then proceed to make different tax replacements in the presence of labour supply endogeneity. In Table 9.1 we report results which give some indication of the impact of labour supply endogeneity upon our calculation of tax/subsidy distortion welfare losses. We consider a number of cases where we abolish the distortion of labour supply and allow the government to tax leisure, even though this is administratively infeasible. We have performed this experiment using values of the elasticity of substitution between goods and leisure of 0.5 and 1.0. (A substitution elasticity of 0.5 corresponds in our specification to an uncompensated labour supply elasticity of about zero). We also calculate the cost of all distortions in the tax system including the distortion of the labour supply.

Table 9.1 indicates that small welfare loss values are associated with labour supply tax distortions. Our calculations are approximately consistent with the estimates reported in Musgrave and Musgrave (1973, 1976), which also suggest small welfare loss associated with labour supply distortions.

9.3 Tax Distortion of Savings

In our central case analysis we include savings by household, but savings do not respond to changes in the expected real rate of return on assets. Household savings are a resource transfer by households to a mutual fund which then makes decisions upon the acquisition of different kinds of capital goods. However the size of this transfer, is independent of rates of return on capital. This simple modelling of the savings process is similar to that in a number of other general equilibrium models, but as we have stressed earlier, removes any savings endogeneity from our calculations.

In this section we report on some calculations of welfare losses from tax distortions which incorporate a simplified form of savings endogeneity. To incorporate endogenous savings behaviour of households we modify household utility functions and remove the financial intermediation implicit in the construction of an investment mutual fund. This follows a procedure used by Fullerton, Shoven and Whalley (1983) in their analysis of intertemporal tax distortions in

TABLE 9.1

Analysis of Model Extension Incorporating Endogenous Labour Supply Decisions of Households
(1973 prices)

	Basic Variant Central Case with Fixed Factor Supplies (Table 7.1)	Equal Yield Abolition of all tax/subsidy distortions; goods-leisure substitution elasticity = 0.5	Equal Yield Abolition of all tax/subsidy distortions; goods-leisure substitution elasticity = 1.0	Equal Yield Abolition of labour supply distortion in income tax; goods-leisure substitution elasticity = 0.5
A. Aggregate Welfare Impacts				
sum of CVs	£5.3 billion	£5.6 billion	£5.8 billion	£0.3 billion
sum of EVs	£5.0 billion	£5.4 billion	£5.6 billion	£0.3 billion
B. Percentage change in total labour supply	0.0	2.1	3.4	3.2
C. Percentage change in net of tax wage rate[1]	-4.1	-5.7	-6.7	-2.7

[1]UK factor prices are normalized to sum to 2.0 in the new equilibrium. The reported percentage change in the wage rate is calculated relative to unity.

the US although we do not perform the same sequenced equilibrium analysis here.

We consider savings in any period as reflecting a decision to acquire a stream of consumption in the future. A decision by any household to save implies a decision to purchase an annuity with an associated anticipated income stream based upon the flow of capital services which will be yielded period by period from the stock of the asset which is acquired. Expectations are formed on the future price of capital services which determine expected income in future periods. We model savings decisions using myopic expectations. Current period rental prices on capital are assumed to dictate the expected real rate of return on capital in future periods. This treatment is related to the endogenous household savings formulation of utility maximizing behaviour in Patinkin [1965], Leviatian [1966], and Archibald and Lipsey [1958].

If the economy is on a balanced growth path, myopic expectations are equivalent to perfect foresight since the rental price of capital will not change as the economy moves along its balanced growth path. Under an assumption of balanced growth we are therefore able to consider the behaviour of the economy in terms of an equivalent single period equilibrium problem, which motivates the formulation we adopt. If the economy grows at the rate of growth of the labour force, we are able to consider the effect of savings distortions in terms of an equivalent one period general equilibrium model and evaluate them through a comparison between balanced growth paths. What we miss in this analysis is the transition between steady states reflected in the more complete treatment in Fullerton, Shoven and Whalley.[1] There are also difficulties with the interpretation of welfare comparisons between equilibria, which require an income correction for changes in expected future income accruing to current period savers.

The one period general equilibrium model includes decisions by households on the allocation of current income to current consumption and expected future consumption. The utility from expected future consumption reflects the anticipated consumption stream which households expect to receive tomorrow on the basis of savings decisions made today. If we consider a no-tax regime, we can conceive of a household maximizing a utility function subject to a single period budget constraint:

(1)   max $U(C_O, C_F)$
       sto $I = P_O C_O + P_S S$

where

C_O represents current consumption,

C_F represents the stream of incremental consumption anticipated in the future in all periods, due to current period savings.

I is the income of the household,

P_O is the price of the current consumption,

P_S is the acquisition price of the capital asset which will yield the anticipated consumption stream, and

S is the quantity of the stock of the newly produced capital good acquired in the period.

Current period savings $P_S S$ equal the discounted present value of the consumption stream from savings. A uniform consumption stream is assumed in order to reduce the utility maximization problem to a two period problem defined over current and all future consumption from income spent today. We note that the arguments of the utility function do not all appear in the household budget constraint, and in order to complete this utility maximization problem we have to make some assumption on the expected future consumption stream which acquisition of a unit of currently produced capital good yields. This involves the specification:

(2) $P_{C_F} C_F = P_K \gamma S$

where

P_{C_F} represents the anticipated price of consumption in future periods,

γ represents the ratio of the capital service flow for a unit of the capital good stock acquired today, and

P_K represents the anticipated rental price on capital in the future periods.

The term $P_K \gamma S$ can be thought of as the value of capital income which is anticipated will be received in all future periods, per unit of capital goods bought today. The term $P_{C_F} C_F$ represents the anticipated value of consumption in each period in the future flowing from savings today. Using (2) we substitute into the budget constraint in (1) yielding:

$$(3) \quad \max \ U(C_O, C_F)$$
$$\text{sto} \ I = P_O \ C_O + \frac{P_S P_{C_F} \cdot C_F}{P_K \gamma}$$

This utility maximization problem can be solved for C_O and C_F for each household, and using equation (2) we are able to generate a derived demand for capital goods (savings) by the household. This formulation can be implemented in terms of the CES utility functions which we have in our model. This incorporates our nesting and the other model complexities stemming from the tax distortions we consider.

Formulation (1)-(3) differs from the more traditional intertemporal utility maximization used in Blinder [1974], Summers [1981], and elsewhere of a constant elasticity of marginal utility function with utility each period discounted at the subjective intertemporal discount rate. In life cycle models this formulation provides the convenient solution of a constant rate of growth of consumption through the lifetime. Once the interest rate and the lifetime budget constraint is given, the consumption plan over the lifetime is determined and current period savings can be calculated by residual from current period income.

We use a CES form for the utility function in (1) as the top level of a nesting structure, with subnests containing elements of current consumption as in the basic variant model. Unlike an iso-elastic form this can be used in our code without major modification. More importantly, the iso-elastic form cannot be used to generate a set of demand functions in a general equilibrium model of the type used here which satisfy Walras' Law, since Walras Law is only satisfied if either current consumption or savings is determined by residual. The CES form implies a subjective discount rate at the benchmark equilibrium once calibration is complete, but unlike the iso-elastic forms used in life cycle models the discount rate is not constant.

In a regime in which taxes operate we modify equation (2) to take account of the anticipated taxes which will prevail as a result of the tax distortion of savings. The classic analysis of the distortion of savings under the income tax stresses 'double' taxation, since savings must be made out of net of tax income in the current period with the interest income on savings then further taxed. This treatment assumes an absence of inflation since the marginal tax rate applies to the real and not nominal return to capital. We maintain this assumption in this section but relax it later where we consider the intertemporal distorting effects of a non-indexed tax system. We capture this simplified formulation through a modification of (2) which we write as:

(4) $P_{C_F} [(1 + t_{C_F})]C_F = P_K(1-t^I) \cdot \gamma \cdot S$

where

t^I represents the income tax rate which is anticipated will prevail in future periods, and

t_{C_F} is the anticipated tax on future consumption.

t_{C_F} can be interpreted as the anticipated future sales tax rate on consumption expenditures. Substituting equation (4)

into the budget constraint in problem (1) yields a with-tax
maximization problem for households:

(5)   max $U(C_O, C_F)$

   sto $I = P_O(1+t_{C_O})C_O + \dfrac{P_S P_{C_F}(1+t_{C_F}) \cdot S}{P_K(1-t^I)\gamma}$

where t_{C_O} is the sales tax rate on current consumption
expenditures. The term $(1+t_{C_F})/[(1+t_{C_O})(1-t^I)]$ can be
thought of as the tax discriminant on future consumption.
The effect of the income tax on future consumption decisions
is to distort the slope of the budget constraint of the
household which would prevail in a no-tax regime. If current
and future consumption are taxed at exactly the same rate,
the intertemporal distortion is given by a term $1/(1-t^I)$.
The substitution effect from this tax discriminant against
future consumption results in more consumption today than
would otherwise occur.

   In order to implement this analysis within our model, we
change our benchmark equilibrium data set to transfer all
savings to households and remove the imputation implicit in
the construction of the investment mutual fund. Our data
makes allowance for the fraction of savings which feeds
through pension funds on which capital income accrues tax
free. We also incorporate the tax preferences to home-
ownership in the intertemporal calculation. We choose a
value for the elasticity of substitution in the expanded
utility function incorporating the additional argument, C_F.
This elasticity is chosen to calibrate to literature estimates of this elasticity. If we interpret the utility function in (1) [or in (5)] as a simple CES utility function
between current and future consumption, then the value of
the elasticity of substitution between C_O and C_F can be
chosen to calibrate to a point estimate of the implied elasticity of savings with respect to the real net of tax rate
of return. We use Boskin's (1978) result that long-run time
series analysis for the US produces a value of the elasticity of financial savings with respect to the real net of

tax rate of return in the region of 0.4.

As suggested in Chapter 6, this value of 0.4 can be thought of as corresponding to a value of the elasticity of substitution between current and future consumption of approximately 1.4. The argument for this can be seen as follows. Using a single stage CES utility function to solve for C_F from (3) gives

$$(6) \quad C_F = \frac{a_{C_F}{}^{\sigma} I}{(\frac{P_s P_{C_F}}{P_K \gamma})^{\sigma} (\sum_j a_j{}^{\sigma} P_j{}^{1-\sigma} + a_{C_F}{}^{\sigma} (\frac{P_s P_{C_F}}{P_K \gamma})^{1-\sigma})}$$

where a_{C_F} is the distribution parameter on C_F in the CES function, the a_j and p_j are the distribution parameters and prices associated with the vector of current consumption goods, C_0, and I is current period income. Rewriting (6) as a savings function gives

$$(7) \quad P_s S = \frac{a_{C_F}{}^{\sigma} I}{(\frac{P_s P_{C_F}}{P_K \gamma})^{\sigma-1} (\sum_j a_j{}^{\sigma} P_j{}^{1-\sigma} + a_{C_F}{}^{\sigma} (\frac{P_s P_{C_F}}{P_K \gamma})^{1-\sigma})}$$

If a_{C_F} is relatively small the elasticity of $P_s S$ with respect to $(P_K \gamma / {}^{P_s P_{C_F}})$, the rate of return on capital, can be shown to be approximately $\sigma - 1$. As noted in Chapter 6, this is a similar argument to that appearing in Feldstein [1978b].

In a recent piece Summers (1981) has argued that the short-run savings elasticity is larger than 0.4 and suggests that in a life-cycle model the revision of lifetime plans as a result of changes in the real net of tax rate of return yields a substantially larger elasticity. Summers' analysis recognizes the difference between the compensated and uncompensated elasticity of savings with respect to the real net of tax rate of return. Summers calibrates to a Boskin-type estimate in terms of the pure substitution effect but argues that there is a capitalization effect in terms of human

wealth which sharply increases the uncompensated elasticity,
suggesting a short-run savings elasticity in the region of
two. We have chosen a value of 1.4 for our elasticity of
substitution, but have also performed analyses in which this
elasticity is increased to two.

As noted earlier the choice of elasticities in this analysis is of some importance because it can significantly
change the measured effect of tax distortions of savings.
Summers, for instance, calculates that tax distortions of
savings costs the US an amount approximately equivalent to
10% of GNP on an annualized equivalent basis. His result is
partly accounted for by the choice of a low discount rate
even though a significantly higher marginal productivity of
capital prevails. While this large loss estimate is dependent upon this assumption, the elasticity value chosen is
also of some significance.

Having chosen the elasticity value for our calculations,
we then incorporate the anticipated taxes which will prevail
in the future as part of our benchmark equilibrium. These
taxes are brought forward into the current period and are
collected by the government and then returned in lump sum
form to those who paid the taxes. We use our replication
procedure in the benchmark as before and generate parameters
for all the preference and production functions including
the preference function parameters affecting anticipated
future consumption. We then proceed to our tax replacement
analysis where we are able to abolish the tax distortion of
savings along with all other distortions or the tax distortion of savings alone.

Because of the role played by expectations in the endogenous savings variant of the model, it is necessary to qualify
the interpretation of the Hicksian compensating and equivalent variation calculations stressed in earlier chapters.
Because current period utility from savings depends on the
expected future consumption stream which in turn depends on
the expected rate of return on capital, changes in expectations can affect current period utility.

In a more complete treatment analyzing a sequence of
single period equilibria, increases in savings induced

through tax changes produce capital deepening, and the rate of return falls as the economy moves through the sequence of equilibria. Myopic expectations based on initial rates of return are excessively optimistic, and ex post utility to savers is lower than ex ante utility based on inaccurate expectations. Thus, in the savings variant of our model, when P_K rises, an apparent utility gain is created due to the increased rate of return on capital, and when P_K falls an apparent utility loss arises. In most of the cases we consider this effect appears to be relatively insignificant, but in one case it is pronounced and clearly affects the interpretation of results. This qualification should thus be kept in mind in evaluating the results which follow in this and the next section.

In Tables 9.2, 9.3 and 9.4 we report results from the savings variant of the model. In Table 9.2 we consider the removal of tax distortions of savings, along with all other distortions in the tax system. These cases are not directly comparable to the central case which we have reported in Table 7.1 because of the different values of elasticities involved, and we have recalculated our central cases with elasticity values which correspond to those used in the savings variant. As can be seen from the calculations, there is only a small additional welfare impact from incorporating the savings distortions into the calculation of the combined distorting costs of the tax system. Additional welfare losses from the tax distortion of savings are in the region of £0.5 billion even with an elasticity of two. In all cases there is a 25-30% increase in savings. These results contrast with Summers' [1981] finding that welfare losses from tax distortions of savings are large (in his results annually exceeding the collections from the whole income tax). Additional distributional impacts of incorporating tax distortions of savings are small.

In Table 9.3 we report cases which remove the distortion of savings that operates through the capital factor tax system. In this case the additional welfare losses involved are again small.

TABLE 9.2

Analysis of Model Extension Incorporating Endogenous
Household Savings Behaviour (no inflation)
(1973 prices)

	'Basic Variant' Central Case with top level elasticity of 1.0	Equal Yield Abolition of all distorting taxes and subsidies with endogenous savings and top level elasticity of 1.0	'Basic Variant' Central Case with top level elasticity of 1.4	Equal Yield Abolition of all distorting taxes and subsidies with endogenous savings and top level elasticity of 1.4	'Basic Variant' Central Case with top level elasticity of 2.0	Equal Yield Abolition of all distorting taxes and subsidies with endogenous savings and top level elasticity of 2.0
A. Aggregate Welfare Impacts						
Sum of CVs	£6.2 billion	£6.8 billion	£6.9 billion	£7.3 billion	£7.5 billion	£8.0 billion
Sum of EVs	£5.8 billion	£6.6 billion	£6.5 billion	£7.2 billion	£7.1 billion	£7.8 billion
B. Percentage Change in Savings	--	27.6	--	26.9	--	28.3
C. Percentage Change in Rate of Return on Capital	--	-6.6	--	-12.0	--	-17.2
D. Distributional Impacts						
Gini coefficient of size distribution of net of tax/gross of transfer incomes	Benchmark .299 New .330	Benchmark .304 New .335	Benchmark .299 New .330	Benchmark .304 New .336	Benchmark .299 New .330	Benchmark .304 New .336
CV of top 10% of households	£3.2 billion	£3.6 billion	£3.3 billion	£3.6 billion	£3.3 billion	£3.7 billion
CV of top 50% of households	£6.4 billion	£7.5 billion	£6.9 billion	£7.9 billion	£7.3 billion	£8.5 billion
CV of bottom 10% of households	-£0.2 billion	-£0.2 billion	-£0.2 billion	-£0.2 billion	-£0.2 billion	-£0.2 billion

TABLE 9.3

Further Welfare Analysis of Savings Distortions
(1973 prices)

	Equal Yield Abolition of Savings Distortions Alone (top level elasticity = 1.4)	Equal Yield Abolition of Capital Factor Taxes with Endogenous Savings (top level elasticity = 1.4)	Equal Yield Abolition of Capital Factor Taxes with Fixed Savings (as in Chapter 8)(top level elasticity = 1.4)
A. Aggregate Welfare Impacts			
Sum of CVs	£0.8 billion	£2.5 billion	£2.3 billion
Sum of EVs	£0.8 billion	£2.5 billion	£2.2 billion
B. Percentage Change in Savings	19.2	37.7	--
C. Percentage Change in Rate of Return to Capital	-3.2	31.0	--
D. Distributional Impacts			
Gini coefficient of size distribution of net of tax/gross of transfer incomes	Benchmark .304 New .305	Benchmark .304 New .302	Benchmark .299 New .295
CV of top 10% of households	£0.3 billion	£6.6 billion	£0.8 billion
CV of top 50% of households	£0.8 billion	£1.1 billion	£1.7 billion
CV of bottom 10% of households	-£0.003 billion	£0.02 billion	£0.03 billion

TABLE 9.4

Analysis of Changes in Existing Income Tax   (1973 prices)

	Equal Yield Change to Pure Income Tax (Assuming zero inflation)
A. Aggregate Welfare Impacts	
Sum of CVs	-£0.1 billion
Sum of EVs	-£0.1 billion
B. Distributional Impacts	
Gini coefficient of size of distribution of net of tax/gross of transfer incomes	Benchmark .304 New .304
CV of top 10% of households	-£0.1 billion
CV of top 50% of households	£0.05 billion
CV of bottom 10% of households	£0.04 billion
C. Percentage Change in Savings	-22.3
D. Percentage Change in Consumption of Owner Occupied Housing Services	-16.1

$\dot{\pi}$ is the expected inflation rate, r is the real net of tax rate of return on capital. The significance of these assumptions is discussed in Section 9.4.

Equal Yield Change to Pure Consumption Tax (Assuming zero inflation)	Equal Yield Change to Pure Consumption Tax (π = 10%, r = .04)
£1.2 billion £1.4 billion	£2.0 billion £2.3 billion
Benchmark .304 New .304	Benchmark .300 New .301
£0.4 billion	£0.5 billion
£1.4 billion	£1.8 billion
£0.02 billion	£0.02 billion
12.1	27.7
-14.3	-30.5

In Table 9.4 we examine the effects of moving to either a pure consumption tax or a pure income tax from the existing income tax. We partially anticipate some of the discussion from the next section by including a case where the inflation rate is assumed non-zero. Because of the lack of indexation in the income tax this has significant real effects.

As can be seen from the results, the difference between the consumption tax and the pure income tax reflected in the intertemporal distortion through the income tax turned out to be significant, especially in the presence of inflation. The move to a pure income tax involves extension of the savings distortion to all savings, since pension fund and homeowner preferences are withdrawn. This produces a welfare loss which is partially offset by the static welfare gain from removal of homeowner preferences in the income tax. With a move to a pure consumption tax two sources of gain from distortion removal occur which compound to a £1.2 billion gain. We comment on the significance of inflation in these calculations more fully in the next section, but we note in passing that these calculations add support to the recommendation of the Meade Committee for a consumption tax in the UK.

9.4   Inflation and Distortion of the Tax System

Since the tax system in the UK (like all other tax systems) is not completely indexed, tax-inflation interactions can generate additional distortions. In this section we examine these and estimate their quantitative impact.

The distorting effects of inflation through the tax system can be broken down into a number of different components. In the income tax the effects through non-indexed rate brackets and personal allowances are well known. In our calculations we assume that the political system approximately adjusts these for inflation in the sequence of annual budgets. Although this is not an exact form of indexing, over a period of 10 years in the UK this has been approximately the case. This is the most widely analyzed issue with inflation and the tax system, but is not the one which we stress here.

We focus instead on the intertemporal distortions which

occur with taxation of nominal asset returns with perfectly
anticipated inflation. Inflation revalues assets and liabilities in the economy with the nominal revaluation taxable
(at capital gains rates for equity assets and income tax
rates for debt financed real asset purchases). In terms of
assets and liabilities, we assume all interest transactions
outside of house mortgages are associated with business
investment activities of various kinds. As an approximation
the tax system will tax all nominal interest received and
allow as a deduction all nominal interest paid. Thus if we
assume a constant single marginal income tax rate, all
financial intermediation would be symmetrically treated
under the tax system since the inflation portion of the
nominal asset return would be taxed in the hands of the
recipient but would be deductible by the payer, and the
government would generate no revenue from inflation. We thus
ignore financial intermediation in our treatment.

Since the economy has real wealth along with claimants on
the income stream from that wealth, a uniform inflationary
process would revalue the wealth stock of the economy every
year and that would show up as taxable income in various
forms. Owners of corporate stocks would find that they receive a nominal capital gain which, if realized, would be
taxable under the capital gains tax (although only taxable
at one half of the marginal income tax rate). We assume that
the capital gains treatment results in one half of the inflation return being taxed.

Other components of the wealth stock of the economy generate income streams which are paid out to bondholders. If we
think of a single corporation generating all the profits in
the economy, then the financial structure of that corporation can be changed through its debt-equity ratio. Recipients of interest paid on debt will receive a payment for
inflation in the form of a fully taxable coupon on their
bond. Thus outside of the financial intermediation between
households, the revaluation of capital assets through uniform inflation generates a stream of nominal return to capital which is taxable. The inflation on the real wealth stock
is taxable either in the form of capital gains to stock-

holders or in terms of a nominal interest coupon to bondholders.

There are further difficulties which inflation creates
with the tax system. Because there are certain kinds of
capital gains which accrue tax free, further asymmetries are
created which are accentuated by the deductibility of nominal interest. The most dramatic of these occurs in the housing market where all nominal capital gains on houses accrue
tax free, while nominal interest paid on mortgage debt is
fully deductible. The UK tax system gives mortgage interest
deductibility on top of personal allowances, and is even
more generous than the US. This system has a large asymmetry
built in with respect to the inflation rate since the inflation accruing in the form of a capital gain on a house comes
entirely tax free while inflation on other assets is taxable. It is therefore hardly surprising that UK house prices
rise dramatically with changes in inflationary expectations
and loans for acquisition of houses are frequently allocated
by queue. This interaction of inflation and the housing
market is a sharp distorting feature of the tax system which
we stress heavily in our calculations.

In addition to these features in the income tax there are
characteristics of the corporate tax which produce asymmetries with respect to inflation. One of the better known
of these is the tax treatment of depreciation. With depreciation calculated on an historical cost basis, depreciation
allowances over the asset life (calculated as a fraction of
real asset value) fall as inflation rises. This is not as
major an issue in the UK as in many other countries because
of the extensive use of 100% first-year depreciation allowances on many assets. A further feature in the corporate
tax, relevant to the model since it uses 1973 data, is the
treatment of stock appreciation. Under a tax treatment of
capital gains on inventories based on FIFO accounting, a
nominal capital gain which accrues to a firm as a result of
holding of inventories is fully taxable, and this introduces
a further asymmetry with respect to inflation. As we have
noted earlier, this tax feature was substantially changed in
the 1974 budget, although we still consider it here since
our data relate to 1973.

We have not been able to fully incorporate all of these
non-neutralities towards inflation in our calculations of
welfare costs. We capture the portion of the inflation tax
implicit in the capital gains tax. However, because we are
unable to estimate the value of interest income received by
households which represent claims on income from real assets
rather than simply financial intermediation, we are unable
to fully incorporate taxation of nominal rather than real
interest. The aggregate debt to equity ratio of the economy
is relatively small, and therefore we feel we have captured
the most important elements of the inflation tax through our
treatment of capital gains. We consider the one half of the
capital gains taxable under the 1973 system to represent a
pure inflation tax. In addition, the tax discriminant on
future consumption is sharply affected by inflation in our
endogenous savings variant, and we stress the interaction
between savings and inflation. All capital income is taxable
on nominal returns at capital gains rates, but we introduce
a separate discriminant in the form of an inflation dependent subsidy to residential construction to allow for the
capital gains feature stressed above.

In the case of the corporate tax we consider the treatment
of stock appreciation to reflect a tax on a pure inflationary capital gain and we treat this as part of the inflation
non-neutrality in the tax system. We do not consider the
non-neutrality with respect to depreciation because of the
sharp acceleration in UK depreciation allowances.

We are thus able to capture a significant portion of the
distorting effects of inflation on the tax system and make
calculations of the costs of these distortions.

In Tables 9.5 and 9.6 we present our calculations of the
effects of removal of these inflation distortions. In Table
9.5 we analyze the removal of inflation non-neutralities in
our basic model variant ignoring savings endogeneity. We
consider cases with and without the inflation subsidy to
residential construction. Welfare losses from the inflation
distortion are in the region of £1.0 billion with most of
this accounted for by the treatment of stock appreciation in

TABLE 9.5

Removal of Inflation Induced Commodity and Industry

Distortions in the Tax/Subsidy System

	Removal of inflation non-neutralities in central case ($\dot{\pi}$ = 10%, r = 0.04)	Removal of inflation non-neutralities in central case plus housing distortion ($\dot{\pi}$ = 10%, r = 0.04)[1]
A. Aggregate Welfare Effects		
Sum of CVs	£0.9 billion	£1.3 billion
Sum of EVs	£0.9 billion	£1.4 billion
B. Percentage change in consumption of housing services	-1.7	-12.7
C. Percentage change in output of manufacturing industry	2.2	3.4
D. Distributional Impacts		
Gini coefficient of size distribution of net of tax/gross of subsidy incomes	Benchmark .299 New .300	Benchmark .299 New .297
CV of top 10% of households	£0.4 billion	£0.4 billion
CV of top 50% of households	£0.7 billion	£0.9 billion
CV of bottom 10% of households	£0.01 billion	£0.03 billion

[1] $\dot{\pi}$ refers to the assumed inflation rate in the benchmark equilibrium and r to the assumed value for the real net of tax rate of return to capital.

TABLE 9.6

Removal of Inflation Induced Intertemporal Distortions

in Tax/Subsidy System[1]

(1973 prices)

	$r = .04$ $\dot{\pi} = 10\%$	$r = .06$ $\dot{\pi} = 5\%$
A. Aggregate Welfare Effects		
Sum of CVs	£1.6 billion	£2.3 billion
Sum of EVs	£1.7 billion	£2.4 billion
B. Percentage change in residential construction	-23.5	-11.2
C. Percentage change in savings	3.6	5.7
D. Percentage change in return on capital	-9.2	1.0
E. Distributional Impacts		
Gini coefficient of size distri- bution of net of tax/gross of subsidy incomes	Benchmark .300 New .301	Benchmark .298 New .301
CV of top 10% of households	£0.5 billion	£0.8 billion
CV of top 50% of households	£1.2 billion	£2.0 billion
CV of bottom 10% of households	£0.02 billion	£0.008 billion

1.
π refers to the assumed inflation rate in the benchmark
equilibrium and r to the assumed value for the real net of
tax rate of return to capital.

the corporate tax. As we have already noted this feature appears due to our use of 1973 data and has been substantially modified following the 1974 budget.

Table 9.6 reports cases which include our savings endogenous variant and here more significant effects occur. Some care is needed in interpreting the reported welfare effects since in this case they are heavily affected by changes in the expected rate of return on capital. This feature explains the inverse ranking of welfare effects and inflation rates. In the case of an assumed inflation rate of 10% and a net of tax real rate of return of 4% the return to capital falls by 9% because of the removal of the housing inflation subsidy. With a moderate inflation rate of 5% and real return of 6% a welfare gain of £2.3 billion occurs suggesting inflation significantly compounds distorting losses occurring elsewhere with the tax system. We interpret the large changes in housing as indicating that housing interacts sharply with inflation.

9.5 Transfers and Welfare Reform

In order to give an indication of the dependence of the central case results reported in Chapters 7 and 8 on the large income transfers which appear on the expenditure side of public sector activity, we have made some further calculations where we change the transfer system as well as the tax/subsidy system. Results from the abolition of all transfers along with the removal of distortions are reported in Table 9.7. Although we abolish all transfers, the size of real activity in the public sector remains unchanged.

As can be seen from Table 9.7, the impact of this on our aggregate welfare measure of the costs of the tax system is not pronounced. Our central case estimates of £5-5.3 billion increase to around £6 billion. There is however a pronounced change in the Gini coefficient. The Gini coefficient of the size distribution of net of tax, gross of transfer household incomes rises from 0.3 in the benchmark equilibrium to 0.41. These calculations confirm that the major redistributive mechanism in public sector activity is not the tax system, but the transfer mechanism (as suggested in the calculations by Musgrave, Case and Leonard [1974], Gillespie [1980], and others for economies outside the UK). We also report a case in which we abolish all transfers. In this case there is a relatively small measured welfare effect since no distortions are changed, but the redistributive impact is very large.

In Table 9.8 we attempt to incorporate some possible distortions which operate on the expenditure side as a result of the transfer mechanism. One of the complaints frequently heard about transfers is that they produce high implicit marginal tax rates for low income households because of the withdrawal effect for welfare payments which are income related. Indeed, many economists argue that it is easy for households in low income ranges to be confronted by a high marginal tax rate as a result of features such as income ceilings in several different components of a welfare system operating simultaneously. We have therefore recalculated one of our labour-leisure cases from Section 9.1 in which we incorporate high marginal tax rates for low income households. These tax rates are set at 70% for the bottom 30% of the income distribution. When we abolish all distortions of the tax system, including the tax distortion to leisure, then the cost of the distortions in the economy is seen to increase slightly to £5.6-£5.8 billion. This suggests that further investigation of welfare costs of the expenditure side of public sector activity, although not undertaken in this monograph, may be valuable but is unlikely to produce welfare loss estimates which are comparable to some of the distorting losses which we have identified for other areas of the tax/subsidy system.

9.6 Public Provision: Equilibria with Public Goods and Distorting Taxes and Subsidies

The primary purpose for which we have used our model is the analysis of taxes. The modelling of government expenditures has thus remained highly stylized. The combined UK public authorities are treated in the basic variant model as making both real expenditures and transfers. Real expenditures reflect provision of particular goods and services such as

TABLE 9.7

Estimates of Welfare and Distributional Effects in Treatment of
Transfers   (1973 prices)

	Results from Table 7.1	Abolition of all transfers along with removal of distortions (as in central case, Table 7.1)
A. Welfare Gains		
Sum of Compensating Variations	£5.0 billion	£5.9 billion
Sum of Equivalent Variations	£5.3 billion	£5.9 billion
B. Distributional Impacts		
Gini coefficient of size distribution of net of tax/gross of subsidy incomes	0.328 0.299 in Benchmark	0.409 0.299 in Benchmark
CV of top 10% of households	£3.2 billion	£4.2 billion
CV of top 50% of households	£5.7 billion	£8.5 billion
CV of bottom 10% of households	-£0.2 billion	-£0.4 billion
C. Proportion of Gainers	68%	64%
Gains of Gainers (EVs)	£6.0 billion	£9.7 billion
Losses of Losers (EVs)	-£1.0 billion	-£3.8 billion

	Abolition of all Transfers	Abolition of all tax distortions with maintenance of transfers indexed to consumer prices
	£1.2 billion	£5.03 billion
	£1.5 billion	£5.35 billion
	0.391 0.299 in Benchmark	0.328 0.299 in Benchmark
	£1.2 billion	£3.2 billion
	£3.4 billion	£5.9 billion
	-£0.2 billion	-£0.2 billion
	65%	68%
	£5.0 billion	£5.8 billion
	-£3.8 billion	-£0.8 billion

TABLE 9.8

Re-examination of Central Case with Labour Supply Distortions for Income Related Transfers

	Central Case all tax/subsidy replacement; goods-leisure substitution elasticity = 0.5 (from Table 9.1)	Same Central Case but with 70% marginal tax rate for low income groups
A. Aggregate Welfare Effects		
Sum of CVs	£5.6 billion	£5.8 billion
Sum of EVs	£5.4 billion	£5.6 billion
B. Distributional Impacts		
Gini coefficient of size distribution of net of tax/ gross of subsidy incomes (benchmark = .319)	.340	.341
CV of top 10% of households	£3.4 billion	£3.4 billion
CV of top 50% of households	£5.9 billion	£6.0 billion
CV of bottom 10% of households	-£0.2 billion	-£0.2 billion

national defence, education, health and social services, maintenance of highways, police and fire protection, and judicial services and capital expenditures, such as highway construction.

These activities are incorporated through public sector expenditures on commodities acquired to provide goods and services. Primary factor services (capital and labour services) are bought by the public sector, and along with commodity purchases are treated as inputs into the production of a single public good for which there is no direct articulation of demands. The composition of these inputs is determined from a public sector utility function which is maximized subject to a budget constraint given by tax receipts not transferred to persons, income from publicly owned assets and borrowed funds. Public goods do not appear as arguments of individual utility functions, and there is no process through which private demands for public goods can be determined. As a further extension to our model we also consider cases where decisions on provision of public goods are based on household preference functions which include public goods. The Samuelson (1954) condition for Pareto optimality in the presence of public goods is that the sum of the marginal rates of substitution between public and private goods over households equals the marginal rate of transformation between these two goods. For an economy with K households, a vector of private goods $C [C = C_1, \ldots, C_i, \ldots, C_N]$ and a single public good, G, with an implicit production possibilities set in terms of C and G given by $F(C,G) = 0$, and household utility functions for the kth household given by $U^k = U^k(C^k,G)$, the Samuelson rule can be written as

$$\sum_k \frac{\partial U^k/\partial G}{\partial U^k/\partial C_i} = \frac{F_G}{F_i} \, , \quad \text{for all } i.$$

We consider public goods equilibria where the Samuelson rule guides public good provision (even if distortionary taxes on private goods are present), and households pay taxes which cover costs of production for the public good. Like general equilibrium with taxation, these public goods equilibria can also be explored in a general equilibrium computational framework.

We include a single public good in the utility function of all UK households. We define equilibrium as a situation where the sum of the marginal rates of substitution between the public good and private goods across all households equals the marginal rate of transformation between the public good and all private goods, and taxes cover public good production costs.

A feature which this model extension explores is the extent to which distortionary taxes are associated with an oversupply of public goods relative to a Pareto optimal (no distortion) situation. This notion of oversupply (or undersupply) can be given a number of alternative interpretations. As Atkinson and Stern (1974) point out, it can mean that the equilibrium where public goods are financed by distortionary taxation but where the non-optimal provision rule $\Sigma MRS = MRT$ is followed leads to output levels which are larger (or smaller) than output levels associated with a provision rule modified for the presence of taxes, where the distorting taxes remain in place. It can also mean that the optimum output level where public goods are financed by distortionary taxation is larger (or smaller) than the level of provision in the full optimum. The interpretation of oversupply in our model contains elements of both these concepts. We address the question of whether the solution to the problem where public goods are financed by distortionary taxation, but where the non-optimal $\Sigma MRS = MRT$ provision rule is followed, leads to a public good output level which is larger or smaller than the output level which would prevail in the full optimum with lump sum taxes (where $\Sigma MRS = MRT$ will hold as a necessary condition for Pareto optimality).

Using this model extension, we consider our central case of removal of all distorting taxes for the public goods equilibrium variant. We assume a benchmark equilibrium where the sum of the marginal rates of substitution across households equals the ratio of producer prices of private and public goods in the presence of the 1973 distortionary

tax/subsidy system which, in turn, finances public good
provision. Household preferences for the public good are
inferred by imputing an expenditure of an equal per capita
portion of the cost of the public good to each of the 100
household types. Transfers are eliminated, so that household
benefits from revenues are directly related to pure public
good provision, although this is not a necessary feature of
the model.[2] When the model is calibrated (similarly to that
described in Chapter 4), the parameter values for household
utility functions satisfy the condition that the sum of the
marginal rates of substitution between the public good and a
composite of private goods is equal to the corresponding
ratio of producer good prices. The level of provision of the
public good will however not be optimal, since distortionary
taxes are present.

We then consider the replacement of all existing taxes and
subsidies with the lump sum taxes needed to finance optimal
provision of the public good. We thus compute a new equilibrium in which there is a level of provision of the public
good associated with the situation where the sum of the
marginal rates of substitution once again equals the marginal rate of transformation, but financed by lump sum taxes.
Unlike the case of differential incidence, government revenues in real terms are not held constant and the level of
provision of the public good changes. The quantity of the
public good, rather than revenues or a tax rate, is the
additional element on the simplex. The Samuelson rule provides the equilibrium condition, with $\Sigma MRS = MRT$ being
treated as the condition to be satisfied through the computational procedure. The public good equilibrium thus calculated is based on the assumption that all households pay the
same lump sum tax, and the level of public good provision
associated with $\Sigma MRS = MRT$ is solved for.

As can be seen from Table 9.9 our results indicate that
there is a significant impact on the aggregate measure of
the distorting costs of the tax system through this model
modification. We have no simple intuition as to why these
costs are calculated to be significantly lower in the case
of an equilibrium with public goods. The expectation had

TABLE 9.9

Re-Examination of Central Case Analysis Using
Public Good Equilibrium as Replacement
(1973 prices)

	Central Case (Table 7.1)	Public Good equilibrium in replacement after abolition of all tax/ subsidy distortions
A. Aggregate Welfare Effects		
Sum of CVs	£5.3 billion	£4.7 billion
Sum of EVs	£5.0 billion	£3.7 billion
B. Percentage change in output of public good	1.2	-9.3
C. Distributional Impacts		
Gini coefficient of size distribution of net of tax/gross of subsidy incomes	.328 (Benchmark .299)	.408 (Benchmark .299)
CV of top 10% of households	£3.2 billion	£3.4 billion
CV of top 50% of households	£5.9 billion	£7.2 billion
CV of bottom 10% of households	-£0.2 billion	-£0.01 billion

been that welfare cost estimates would increase with the
introduction of the additional distortion on the choice
between public and private goods. However, it must be remembered that the incorporation of public goods has led to
changes in the parameters of the model, so that comparisons
between the two model variants must be treated with caution.

These results also suggest that there is a significant
impact on the level of provision of the public good resulting from the removal of tax distortions. Table 9.9 indicates that under the assumptions used to characterize a
public good equilibrium, the tax system in taxing private
goods produces an oversupply of public goods of around 9%.

While it is somewhat fanciful to assume that the political
process achieves this public goods equilibrium, this extension to existing applied general equilibrium tax models
highlights the sensitivity of model findings to the formulation of the expenditure side of government intervention
used. No doubt, further sensitivity would be found to other
formulations such as use of voting equilibria and median
voter preference determination of public good provision.

9.7 A Reverse Analysis of the 1973 Tax Reform

In the final section of this chapter we report some results
which demonstrate the applicability of our model to more
practical situations of evaluation of tax reform proposals.
We have retroactively examined the tax changes which came
into operation in the UK in 1973. We have removed the new
taxes introduced at that time and restored the old taxes
which were abolished.

This is a larger scale variant of the same tax reform
process analyzed by Whalley (1975) but in reverse. In the
the earlier piece, some ex ante calculations were reported
on the effects of the introduction of the 1973 tax reforms.
In this case we run the process in reverse, and remove the
tax changes introduced in 1973.

The characteristic of this particular reform was that a
number of changes in taxes occurred at a single point in
time. The corporate tax was changed from the previous classical system to an imputation system involving a dividend

TABLE 9.10

Analysis of the Effects of the 1973 Tax Reforms: Effects of
Reverting to Pre-1973 Tax Regime
(1973 prices)

	With Terms of Trade Neutralizing Tax; No Equal Yield Replacement	High Export Elasticities; No Terms of Trade Neutralizing Tax; Equal Yield Replacement
A. Aggregate Welfare Effects		
Sum of EVs	-£0.1 billion	-£0.01 billion
Sum of CVs	-£0.1 billion	-£0.01 billion
B. Distributional Impacts		
Gini coefficient of size distribution of net of tax/gross of transfer household incomes	Benchmark .299 New .291	Benchmark .299 New .298
CV of top 10% of households	-£0.04 billion	£0.02 billion
CV of top 50% of households	-£0.3 billion	-£0.06 billion
CV of bottom 10% of households	£0.04 billion	£0.0007 billion
C. Proportion of Gainers		
Gains of Gainers	£0.3 billion	£0.2 billion
losses of losers	-£0.4 billion	-£0.2 billion

tax credit; the selective employment tax, a differential tax on labour according to industry of use, was abolished; the purchase tax system was abolished and a value added tax introduced and a number of changes made to the income tax. At the time it was argued that this new regime improved allocative efficiency. One of the features stressed in the earlier study by Whalley was the inability of other methods to analyze the simultaneous interaction of the distorting taxes which were involved in this change.

In analyzing this issue, we use the basic model variant and central case specification, restore the pre-1973 tax regime, and compute the welfare gain or loss for the economy. This involves modifying the corporate and labour income taxes, removing the value added tax, reinstituting a purchase tax, and incorporating a slight modification in the income tax. As suggested in the earlier study, the net effect of all these changes is very small in quantitative terms. We report our results in Table 9.10. The welfare and other effects are negligible, suggesting that tax reform, in practice, tends to be concerned with relatively minor changes in policy.

9.8 Summary

This chapter considers a number of extensions to the basic model variant reported on in Chapters 7 and 8. The main findings are as follows:

1. Incorporating the tax distortions of labour supply into the model produces additional welfare loss estimates which are quite small (perhaps £0.3 billion per year) relative to welfare cost estimates of other tax/subsidy distortions.

2. Ignoring for the moment the interaction of tax distortions with inflation, distortions of savings in the tax system also produce modest incremental welfare costs.

3. Moving from the existing income tax to a 'pure' income tax appears to be a welfare losing proposition; distortions in housing are removed but distortions of savings worsened. A move to a pure consumption tax is a significant gaining proposition.

4. Inflation non-neutralities potentially produce significant welfare impacts, although our model results face some difficulties of interpretation due to our expectations assumption.

5. We find significant effects from the interlinkage between housing distortions and inflation since inflationary capital gains on houses are tax free.

6. Transfers produce marked income distribution effects, but changing the transfer system simultaneously with an abolition of all tax/subsidy distortions does not substantially change welfare loss estimates.

7. A crude modelling of a 'welfare trap' case for low income households does not significantly affect estimates of the combined welfare costs of all tax/subsidy distortions.

8. An alternative solution concept for the model on the
    expenditure side involving public good equilibria does
    change welfare loss estimates. Under particular assump-
    tions on the rule followed in setting the level of
    public good provision, results suggest that the tax
    system may lead to an approximate 10% oversupply of
    public goods.

9. We also analyze a more concrete tax reform change to
    demonstrate the applicability of the model to practical
    tax reform proposals. We examine the same 1973 tax
    reform as in Whalley (1975) and find small effects to
    be involved.

Notes

1. This is an important omission since a gain from comparison between steady states can be offset by a loss during the transition. This is in fact what frequently occurs since a tax change which encourages savings will result in a balanced growth path with a higher capital stock and higher income. If consumption has increased in the new steady state it will have been acquired at the expense of reduced consumption during the transition.

2. In order to maintain the budget balance in the benchmark, transfers are replaced by a non-distortionary subsidy on all goods and services.

SUMMARY AND CONCLUSIONS

In this study we report on a model of the UK economy and tax
system which we have used to provide a numerical appraisal
of the main impacts of the UK tax/subsidy system. With the
basic variant of the model, we concentrate on the distorting
effects of taxes and subsidies within a static full employment neo-classical general equilibrium framework, and calculate the resource allocation and distributional effects of
alternative tax policy packages. We then consider a sequence
of model extensions incorporating intertemporal and labour
supply distortions due to taxes, and public good equilibria.
In Part I of the study we outline the methods that we used.
Both general and particular features are described, along
with the functions and parameter values we use. We also
summarize the data which give us estimates of tax and subsidy parameters for the model.

The main method of analysis we employ is counterfactual
equilibrium analysis. We adopt an assumption that the UK
economy achieves an equilibrium in the presence of existing
tax/subsidy policies. We use data for a single year drawn
from national accounts and other sources which we extend and
transform into a form which is consistent with the equilibrium conditions of the model; this we term our benchmark
equilibrium. We generate parameter values for the functions
in the model such that we can replicate the benchmark equilibrium observation as a model equilibrium solution. The
counterfactual analysis then involves the introduction of
alternative policy regimes into the model. This is in the
tradition of comparative static theoretical work, but our
analysis is conducted within an empirically based numerical
general equilibrium model. Importantly, we do not attempt
any forecasting with our model as is conventional with
numerical macro models.

We place most stress on the welfare calculations which we
have made of the effects of the tax/subsidy policies in
place in our data. We use Hicksian compensating and equivalent variations as the monetary measure of the change in

welfare involved between equilibria under existing and
alternative policy regimes for each household, and take the
arithmetic sum for each of these two measures across households. This gives an aggregate welfare measure in monetary
terms associated with changes in tax policies. We emphasize
differential incidence in the Musgrave sense of replacing
existing taxes and subsidies by yield preserving broadly
based alternative taxes such that the size of the public
sector is unchanged.

In Part II of the study we present a detailed report on
our results which are contained in a number of tables. At
the end of each chapter we summarize the main findings. We
stress an overall calculation of the tax/subsidy system as
yielding distorting losses to the economy in the region of
6-9% of NNP (at factor cost) per year. This is a recurring
annual flow loss which, when calculated as a fraction of the
total annual tax revenues, produces a loss estimate in the
region of 30% of tax collections. The picture we portray is
that in collecting something in the region of 25% of NNP in
taxes (net of subsidies paid), the tax system 'destroys'
approximately $\frac{1}{4}$ of that revenue through distorting losses of
various kinds. We calculate this welfare loss to be equivalent to £250 per household using 1973 data and in current
1980 prices we project this figure to be approximately £650
per household.

We have also analyzed the various components of the tax
system and we stress the importance of subsidies to local
authority housing as a large and significant source of welfare loss. We downplay the significance of tax distortions
of labour supply and savings. In the case of savings we do
however emphasize the importance of distortions accentuated
through inflation given the non-indexed character of the tax
system. We also analyze the distributional impacts of the
tax/subsidy system. In contrast to the conventional view
from incidence calculations using shifting assumptions that
the tax system in total does little to redistribute income,
we find significant annual redistribution to be involved.
This is particularly the case with welfare impacts which
capture redistributive effects of changes in relative consumer prices induced through the tax/subsidy system.

Our purposes in constructing this model and presenting our results are multifold. Narrowly the study can be viewed as a contribution to the UK policy debate in evaluating the effects of the tax/subsidy system within the framework which we have laid out. We also emphasize the wider objective of demonstration of the applicability of numerical general equilibrium analysis for policy appraisal. We would, however, stress that this type of analysis involves a significant amount of subjective judgement and in our opinion is not particularly useful if used mechanically as a rigid forecasting or appraisal tool.

Future extensions of this kind of approach would seem to be worth pursuing. We feel there is substantial value in analyzing the distorting effects of the expenditure policies by government and indeed the wider set of distorting policies which governments pursue. Policies which intervene in the labour market through minimum wage and other legislation along with the regulatory activity of government seem to us to be a substantial and potentially significant source of welfare loss. A further question remaining unanswered by our analysis is whether the tax system represents the major source of distorting loss in the economy or whether it is only one of several interacting areas of distorting policy which need to be jointly analyzed.

STRUCTURE OF THE BASIC VARIANT MODEL

1. Outline of Model Structure
   Dimensions –
   33 commodities and industries in UK.
   27 of 33 commodities internationally traded.
   2 Primary Factors (Capital and Labour) mobile across
       industries, immobile across countries.
   100 Households classified by income, occupation,
       family status.
   Production –
   CES value added functions for each industry.
   Fixed input-output coefficient intermediate production
       ('comparable' domestic and imported products
       treated as qualitatively different).
   Fixed Coefficient joint production.
   Demand –
   3 Level Nested CES preference functions.
   Separate demand functions for government, investment,
       and exports.
   Taxes –
   Capital taxes – corporate and rates.
   Labour taxes – National Insurance and Related
       Contributions.
   Consumer taxes – Value Added taxes, Excises, tariffs,
       Motor Vehicle Licences.
   Intermediate Production taxes – Tariffs, Excises,
       Motor Vehicle Licenses.
   Income tax system – Income, capital gains, and estate
       taxes.
   Subsidies –
   Consumer subsidies – Local authority housing.
   Industry subsidies – Nationalized industry,
       Agriculture, Regional subsidies.
   Equilibrium –
   Set of Equilibrium Prices such that

(i)   Demands equal supplies for all goods and factors.

(ii) Zero profits prevail in each industry (net of taxes).

(iii) External sector balance holds.

(iv) Revenue collections equal revenue disbursements.

2. Production

(i)   Value Added Functions(CES)

$$Y_j = \gamma_j [\delta_j K_j^{-\rho_j} + (1 - \delta_j) L_j^{-\rho_j}]^{-\frac{1}{\rho_j}}$$

(ii) Intermediate   Production   Requirements   (Fixed Coefficient)

$$H_{ij} = a_{ij} Y_j$$

(iii) Joint Production of Commodities (Fixed Coefficient)

$$J_{ij} = m_{ij} Y_j$$

$$\sum_i m_{ij} =- 1.0$$

3. Consumer Demands and Incomes

(i)   Preferences (3 level nested CES)
      Each level involves subutility function for each household

$$\left[\sum_i b_i X_i^{\frac{(\sigma-1)}{\sigma}} \right]^{\frac{\sigma}{(\sigma-1)}}$$

Hierarchy	Top level	8 categories
	Middle level	33 nests
	Bottom level	2 goods ('Comparable' Domestic and Imported Products; only 1 good for non-traded products)

(ii)   Disposable Incomes (Budget constraints).

Each household (q=1....100):

$$I^q = \underset{\substack{(\text{capital} \\ \text{income})}}{P^K \bar{K}^q} + \underset{\substack{(\text{labour} \\ \text{income})}}{P^L \bar{L}^q} + \underset{(\text{transfers})}{\alpha^q R} - \underset{\substack{(\text{income} \\ \text{taxes})}}{IT^q}$$

Government:

$$I^{101} = \underset{\substack{(\text{capital} \\ \text{income})}}{P^K \bar{K}^G} + \underset{\substack{(\text{tax collections} \\ \text{returned by} \\ \text{government})}}{\alpha^G R}$$

Investment:

$$I^{102} = \underset{\substack{(\text{capital} \\ \text{income})}}{P^K \bar{K}^I} + (\text{income from abroad})$$

Rest of world:

$$I^{103} = (\text{foreign source income}) + \underset{\substack{(\text{capital income} \\ \text{from the UK})}}{P_K \bar{K}^{ROW}}$$

(iii)   Demands

A single level CES utility function yields the demands

$$X_i = \frac{b_i{}^\sigma I}{P_i{}^\sigma \sum_{j=1}^{N} b_j{}^\sigma P_j{}^{(1-\sigma)}} \qquad i=1....N$$

To solve for demands in the multi-nest case, the top level is solved first to determine demands for top level composites of middle level products. The middle level is then solved to generate demands for middle level composites of bottom level products. Finally the lower level is solved to generate commodity demands.

At each stage price indices for composite products are required ('true' cost of living indices). For the single stage CES function above, the price index for the corresponding composite product is

$$\bar{P} = \sum_{i=1}^{N} b_i^{\sigma} P_i^{1-\sigma}$$

We denote total final demands for all products by the vector X (P).

4. Industry and Factor Demands

(i)   Industry production levels which meet commodity demands.

$$G(P) = [M - A]^{-1} X(P)$$

(ii)   Derived industry demands for factors.

$$K_j(P) = \delta_j \left[\left[\frac{(1-\delta_j) \cdot P^L (1+t_j^L)}{\delta_j P^K (1+t_j^K)} \right]^{\frac{\rho_j}{(\rho_j+1)}} + [1-\delta_j] \right]^{\frac{1}{\rho_j}} \cdot \gamma_j^{-1} \cdot G_j$$

$$L_j(P) = (1-\delta_j) \left[\left[\frac{\delta_j P^K (1+t_j^K)}{(1-\delta_j) P^L (1+t_j^L)} \right]^{\frac{\rho_j}{(\rho_j+1)}} + \delta_j \right]^{\frac{1}{\rho_j}} \cdot \gamma_j^{-1} \cdot G_j$$

5. Equilibrium Conditions

(i) Demand-supply equalities for factors.

$$\sum_{j=1}^{33^{UK}} K_j(P) = \bar{K}$$

$$\sum_{j=1}^{33^{UK}} L_j(P) = \bar{L}$$

(ii) Zero profit conditions for industries.

$$\sum_{i=1}^{33} m_{ij} P_i = (1+t_j^P) \ [P^K \cdot (1+t_j^K) \frac{K_j(P)}{G_j}$$

$$+ \ P^L \cdot (1+t_j^L) \frac{L_j(P)}{G_j} + \sum_{i=1}^{60} a_{ij} P_i (1+t_i^I)]$$

(iii) Government budget balance.

$$\sum_{q=1}^{100} \alpha^q R \qquad + \qquad \alpha^G R$$

(transfers   (Real expenditures
to persons)   on goods and services)

$$= \sum_{j=1}^{33} t_i^K K_j(P) + \sum_{j=1}^{33} t_i^L L_j(P) \qquad \text{[factor taxes]}$$

$$+ \sum_{i=1}^{60} \sum_{j=1}^{33} a_{ij} P_i G_i(P) t_j^I \qquad \text{[intermediate purchase taxes]}$$

$$+ \sum_{j=1}^{33} \sum_{i=1}^{33} P_i m_{ij} G_j(P) t_j^P \qquad \text{[producer output taxes]}$$

$$+ \sum_{q=1}^{100} IT^q \qquad \text{[income taxes]}$$

APPENDIX B

NOTES TO THE TABLES APPEARING IN CHAPTER 5

This appendix gives notes on the derivation of the data
tables reported in Chapter 5. The notes are not meant to be
comprehensive in reporting all the details involved but do
aim to provide readers with the main sources used along with
a brief outline of major adjustments.

Table 5.1
Summary Production and Demand Transactions, UK, 1973

1. Definition of Terms
   Profit Type Return: This includes the net of tax, gross
   of subsidy, and net of depreciation, returns on capital
   use. Major differences between the concept employed here
   and that used in the National Accounts include:
   (i)   the allocation of some self-employment income as a
          return to capital;
   (ii)   the subtraction of a portion of interest payments
          attributed to a charge for financial services;
   (iii) the addition of hire and rental expenses;
   (iv)   the subtraction of corporation tax payments;
   (v)   the addition of capital type subsidy payments;
   (vi)   the subtraction of stock appreciation.

   Labour Costs: These are the net of tax, gross of subsidy,
   returns to labour. Major differences between the concept
   employed here and that used in the National Accounts
   include:
   (i)   the allocation of some self-employment income as a
          return to labour;
   (ii)   the subtraction of National Insurance payments;
   (iii) the addition of labour subsidies.

Net Capital Tax Payments: These estimates represent corporation tax payments and rates, less capital type subsidy payments.

Net Labour Tax Payments: These estimates represent National Insurance payments, less regional employment premiums.

Total Primary Costs: These are calculated by summing the above items. Total Primary Costs, or total value added, is the model consistent concept which corresponds to GDP at factor cost. (See Table 5.2 for a reconciliation.)

Value of Intermediate Use: This is the value of commodities purchased for intermediate use. The estimates include any taxes payable on intermediate purchases, and include the value of imported as well as domestic intermediate inputs.

Net Production Taxes: These are taxes and subsidies which are assumed to be based upon the total value of industry sales.

Total Costs: These are the sum of Primary costs, intermediate costs, and net production tax payments.

Value of Total Output: These estimates represent the value of total commodity output at producer prices.

Value of Intermediate Output: These estimates represent that portion of total commodity output which is used in the production of other commodities. An estimate of the value of imported inputs is included. They are at producer purchase prices.

Intermediate Purchase Taxes: These are taxes paid on the purchase of produced commodities for intermediate use.

Final Output Taxes: These are taxes paid or subsidies received on the purchase of goods and services by any non-producing agent. These include consumption, investment, external and government sectors.

Value of Personal Sector Demands: These represent all personal sector consumption and net capital expenditures, and unincorporated business expenditures. They are valued at consumer prices.

Value of Net Corporate Investment Expenditures: These estimates include all corporate investment expenditures (net of depreciation), valued at consumer prices.

Value of Government Expenditures: These estimates include government expenditures on real goods and services, and expenditure on "Public Services", (of which it is the only consumer).

Value of Exports: These are estimates of exports, valued at producer prices.

2. Sources

This summary has been constructed from the more detailed tables to follow. Sources will be found in the notes to these tables.

3. Notes

The £205 million model commodity trade imbalance must be taken into account to derive the income-expenditure accounts in Table 5.13. Taxes further complicate this calculation. Total incomes are given by adding to Total Primary Cost, the value of net Production Tax Payments, Intermediate Purchase Tax Payments, and Final Output Tax Payments. This sum is equal to the sum of the values of domestic final expenditures, less £205 million, which is the excess of commodity imports over commodity exports in the model. The resulting total of £71085 million is the model magnitude corresponding to NDP at market prices.

Table 5.2

Reconciliation of Model Value Added with GDP at Factor Cost

Major Sources: NIBB 1963-73, Tables 18, 45 and 61.
                Unpublished CSO and IRS worksheets.
                Authors' calculations.

Notes: The estimate of GDP at factor cost is taken from NIBB, Table 18. The value of rates is taken from Table 45, and the value of capital consumption from Table 61. It should be noted that "Transfer Costs of

Land and Buildings" valued at £565 million are
included in the CSO capital consumption series, but
are excluded from our estimate, and that the capital
consumption of Mining and Quarrying has been reduced
by about £120 million. See notes to Table 5.3 for
further comment.

Other figures have been taken from the authors'
calculations, and are explained further in the notes
to Tables 5.3 and 5.4.

Table 5.3
Profit-type Return by Industry: UK, 1973

Major Sources: NIBB 1963-1973, and 1964-1974.
                  IRS. Inland Revenue Statistics, 1974.
                  New Earnings Survey, 1973.
                  1968 Census.
                  Unpublished CSO and Inland Revenue
                  Worksheets.

Notes:
1.   Trading Profits and Surpluses: Estimates of the gross
      operating surpluses by industry and type, reported in
      columns 1, 3, and 4, are from unpublished CSO
      worksheets. Some further disaggregation uses NIBB
      1964-74 estimates of GDP in Manufacturing Industries,
      reported in Table 19.

2.   Self-employment Income: This is split between a
      return to labour and a return to capital by using the
      New Earnings Survey Tables 29-32 and Inland Revenue
      estimates of numbers of self-employed by industry to
      calculate a return to labour by industry, and
      treating the return to capital as a residual.

3.   Imputed Returns to Private and Local Authority
      Housing and Public Service Capital: These are esti-
      mated by assuming a rate of return on net capital
      stock estimating a replacement cost by industry. The

rate of return used in the imputation is calculated
from the estimated profit-type return for non-housing
private sector industry expressed as a percentage of
the corresponding net capital stock estimate, taken
from Table 65 of NIBB, 1963-73. This gives a 5.3 per
cent rate or return.

(i)   Value of Private Housing Stock. The 5.3 per cent rate
of return is applied to the average price of all
dwellings mortgaged with building societies.
(£9942 for 1973 - Housing and Construction Statistics
No.11, Table 38). Depreciation is assumed to be £100
per year and this figure is subtracted. The difference is multiplied by 10.2 million, the number of
owner-occupied dwellings in 1973 (Housing and
Construction Stats. No.5 and 9, Table 11). Finally,
income from "Rented Properties" (£503 million) and
capital consumption (£583 million) are added in.

(ii)   Value of Local Authority Housing Stock. It is assumed
that the ratio of the estimated private net housing
stock to that reported in NIBB, Table 65, also
applied in the case of houses owned by Local
Authorities.

(iii)   Value of Public Service Capital Stock. This is
assumed to be the NIBB net capital stock estimate for
non-dwelling public sector assets, plus an estimate
for military equipment of £12 billion.

4.   Financial Charges: Unpublished CSO data estimates
give the value of interest receipts by Financial
Companies from Industrial and Commercial Companies
- £1810 million in 1973. It is assumed that 25 per
cent of this represents a charge for Financial Services, and this is subtracted from the NIBB surplus
estimates, which are gross of interest payments.
Disaggregation by industry uses unpublished Inland
Revenue data.

5.   <u>Hire of Plant and Machinery</u>: Estimates from 1968
        Census, Table 4, column 4 are used to give an
        allocation by industry.

6.   <u>Rental Expenses</u>: Rental payments by the Public
        sector and Agriculture were provided in unpublished
        form by the CSO. In addition, £522 million of rental
        incomes from "Land and Buildings Rented to Trading
        Concerns" is allocated among industries. Retail
        trade is allocated half this total; the remainder is
        split according to industry income.

7.   <u>Capital Consumption</u>: "Transfer Costs of Land and
        Buildings", valued at £565 million, are included in
        the CSO capital consumption series, but excluded
        here. In addition, the capital consumption of Mining
        and Quarrying has been reduced by about
        £120 million, to remove a negative capital return in
        these industries from our data.

8.   <u>Corporation Tax</u>: The treatment of this item is
        complex and important, and is therefore discussed in
        detail. Figures represent an accrual of corporation
        tax liability on domestic source corporate income
        under a (hypothetical) full-year operation of the
        imputation system (actually introduced in April
        1973). The model treatment of the "imputation"
        corporate tax system corresponds (roughly) to the
        legal arrangements, i.e., corporation tax paid by
        companies at the full rate and credits given to
        dividend recipients as offset of personal tax
        liability at basic rate on (dividend plus credit).
        Figures provided by CSO (e.g., Table 28, NIBB, 1963-
        73, p.34; Table 32, NIBB, 1964-74, p.37) give the
        "accruals" figure for all UK resident companies on
        all income of "total UK taxes on the total income of
        companies, including tax on distributions made by
        companies". This is assumed to represent three
        months' accruals from operation of the "classical"

system and nine months from operation of the "imputation" system. The NIBB, 1963-73 (p.34) gives a 1973 accruals figure of £3641 million. This is reduced by £206 million (the overstatement in the published figure) giving £3435 million. This compares with a 1974 NIBB (p.37) published figure of £3375 million.

It is assumed that £3435 million represents accruals from:

(i)   Three months classical system, i.e., 40% corporation tax + 30% basic rate income tax on the balance = 58% in total;

(ii)   Nine months operation of the imputation system, i.e., 50% corporation tax. 50% was the rate used by the Inland Revenue in their calculations communicated to the CSO for the year, 52% was the rate announced (retrospectively) in the 1974 budget. Under the imputation system, Advanced Corporation Tax is solely an advanced payment of corporation tax (although there are some complications with the treatment of foreign source income in the UK) and as this is an accruals basis being corrected no addition is made to the figure, i.e., a total rate of 50% is used.

Had an imputation system operated for a full year rather than nine months, this would give an accruals figure of £3303 (i.e., gross trading profits net of capital allowances of £6606 in 1973 which compares to a published £3710 million(NIBB, 1964-74, p.43). This accruals figure contains some tax due on income from abroad not fully covered by double tax relief. This figure is impossible to determine precisely, but a defensible procedure is to guess a minimum bound by taking 5/2 of the amount of "overspill relief" given in 1973 (see Inland Revenue pamphlet 18, "Corporation Tax", pp.71-73). 5/2 x £21 million (NIBB 1963-73, p.44) gives £53 million. We believe it is defensible to increase this by 50% to get £79 million.

This gives a total accruals figure on domestic source income from a full year's operation of the imputation system in 1973 (had that happened) of £3224 million.

9.   Capital Type Subsidies: These include Investment grants, Regional Development grants, and Nationalized Industry subsidies, which include the authors' calculations of the subsidies implicit in the writing-off of debt and cheap credit policies.

10.   Stock Appreciation: These estimates are derived from unpublished CSO worksheets, from NIBB, 1963-73, Tables 68, 69 and 71; and NIBB, 1964-74, Tables 76 and 77.

Table 5.4.
Return to Labour by Industry

Major Sources: Unpublished CSO Worksheets.
                  Unpublished IRS data on graduated contri-
                  butions.
                  DHSS National Insurance Pamphlets.
                  NIBB 1964-74, Table 20.

Notes:
1.   Income from Employment: This is derived from CSO worksheets. Disaggregation is achieved mainly by recourse to "Wages and Salaries in Manufacturing Industries", NIBB 1964-74, Table 20.
2.   Self-Employment Income: This is calculated as indicated in Note 2 to Table 5.3.
3.   National Insurance Contributions: This is calculated from DHSS pamphlets, from unpublished IRS data, and from NIBB 1963-73, Table 49.

Table 5.5.   Production Taxes and Subsidies on Return to
               Labour and Profit-type Return

Major Sources: Unpublished CSO Worksheets.
                NIBB 1963-73, Tables 39 and 45.

Notes:

1.   Labour Subsidies: These are Regional Employment
        Premiums, which total £114 million in 1973 (NIBB,
        Table 39). They are disaggregated according to
        Selective Employment Tax payments in 1968.

2.   Rates: These total £2617 million in 1973 (NIBB,
        Table 45). They are disaggregated according to
        unpublished Input-Output data for 1968, provided by
        the CSO.

3.   All other payments columns here have been reported
        in previous tables. Effective tax rates are simply
        the tax payment expressed as a percentage of the net
        of tax factor return, by industry.

4.   In the model, a tax on capital employed in the pro-
        duction of public services has been imputed to take
        account of the difference between gross and net
        returns in the private and public sectors. The tax
        rate used is 33%, and is calculated to be equal to
        the average rate of capital tax on private sector
        capital income. This rate is reported in the final
        column of Table 5.5, but the imputed payment has not
        been included in any of the tables or charts.

Table 5.6.

Costs of Production by Industry

Major Sources: Unpublished CSO Worksheets.

NIBB 1963-73.

Input-Output Tables, 1971 (updated to 1973 in our calculations).

Notes:

1.   Net Taxes on Production: Most of these are subsidies to Nationalized Industries, and Agriculture. The "Banking Insurance and Finance" entry represents Stamp Duties. Estimates of subsidies to Nationalized Industries are discussed in the text.

2.   Cost of Intermediate Usage: This is calculated by subtracting from Input-Output estimates of total costs of production, the total primary costs. The difference is assumed to be the value of intermediate usage.

3.   All other data have been discussed in previous tables.

Table 5.7.

Values of Final Demands for Commodities

Major Sources: Business Monitor - Input-Output Tables for the United Kingdom 1971, Tables B and C (updated to 1973 in our calculations).

NIBB 1963-73 and 1964-74.

Economic Trends, May 1975. CSO.

Notes:

The final demand vectors, reported in the Input-Output Tables separately for domestically produced commodities and imports, are scaled so that after allowance is made for final output tax liabilities, expenditures by sector are equal to the budget constraints (the derivation of these constraints is reported in Table 5.13). Special treatment is given to large purchases such as "residential construction", public service output and housing services.

Table 5.8.
Consumer Taxes and Subsidies

Sources: NIBB 1963-73.
                 Unpublished CSO Worksheets

Notes:

Excise, Tariff, and "Other" tax payments are allocated by commodity. Where necessary, they are split between domestic and imported commodities using final demand values as weights.

VAT payments are calculated using the authors' own calculations. Capital goods are assumed to be exempt in these calculations. The calculation of subsidies to local authority housing is discussed in the text.

Table 5.9.
Consumer Incomes

Source: Unpublished FES data.

Notes:

Total income by source assigned to the private sector is split between household groups using unpublished FES data on household income by source as weights. Self-employment income is split between capital and labour income in proportions given by the industrial allocation of self-employment income. Savings are also computed using FES data.

Table 5.10

Major Categories of Expenditures by Household

Source: Unpublished FES data.

Notes:

>FES data provide an initial guess on household expenditures by commodity. This matrix is then subjected to an RAS procedure to equalize incomes and expenditure along with a supply-demand equality by expenditure category.

Table 5.11

Public Expendiures and Receipts

Major Sources: NIBB 1963-1973, various tables.
Authors' calculations of imputed income (see especially Table 5.3).
Balance of Payments Statistics.

Notes:

Receipts:

1. Tax Receipts are taken from NIBB 1963-1973, Tables 39, 41, 43, and 49. VAT and Corporate tax liabilities have been separately estimated, since neither tax was in force for the whole of 1973.
2. Imputed income calculations are explained in the notes to Table 5.3.
3. "Net Receipts from Changes in Financial Assets and Liabilities" are taken from NIBB, 1963-1973, Tables 45 and 46.
4. "Income from Public Corporations" is estimated for the profit type return to Nationalized Industries reported in Table 5.3. Except for "Metals" and "Transportation", the government was assumed to be the only owner of capital in model industries corresponding to Nationalized industries.

5.   "Other Business Income". This is an approximate
        allocation designed to capture trading activity in
        non-nationalized industries.

Expenditures:

1.   Subsidies. The calculations of these have been
        reported in the notes to Tables 5.3, 5.5, and 5.8.
        The most important is the £3136 million subsidy to
        Local Authority Housing.

2.   "Transfers to Persons". See NIBB, 1963-1973, Table
        21.

3.   "Expenditures on Public Services". This is assumed
        to be equal to the cost of Public Services'
        production.

4.   "Expenditure on Market Commodities". This estimate
        is calculated by residual.

5.   "Debt Interest". See NIBB, 1963-1973, Table 45.

Table 5.12

Income Sources by Sector and Adjustments Accommodating
Financial Transactions (£ million, 1973).

Major Sources: NIBB 1963-73, and 1964-74
                  UK Balance of Payments 1963-73 (BOP)
                  Authors' calculations

Notes:

1.   Personal sector capital income is calculated as a
        residual, after deducting from total domestic
        capital income UK capital income accruing to the
        external and public sectors. For the derivation of
        total capital and labour income, see Tables 5.3 and
        5.4, and associated notes.

2.   External sector transactions are taken from BOP,
        Tables 11, 18, and 20.

3.   Interest on Public Sector Debt is taken from NIBB
        1963-73, Table 45. It is treated as a transfer from
        the Public to the Personal sector.

4.   Inward foreign investment is treated as a transfer
        to the corporate sector from the external sector.
        The figure is derived from BOP, Tables 2 and 18.

5. Personal Sector Net Savings is the sum of debt and
    equity issued by government and corporations. It is
    treated as a transfer from the personal sector to
    the government and corporate sectors. Government
    debt issue is taken from Table 5.12. Personal
    savings to the Business sector is calculated by
    subtracting from gross domestic fixed capital
    formation of companies and public corporations,
    capital consumption for these types of business
    organization. See NIBB 1963-73, Tables 29, 36 and
    59.

APPENDIX C

NOTES ON PROGRAMMING AND COMPUTATION

1. Computational Experience with the Model

A substantial amount of computational experience has been acquired with the UK model.

The majority of execution time in solution is spent in function evaluation, particularly in evaluating the market demands for commodities at candidate price vectors. This suggests that execution times are sensitive to the functional forms which are used to describe demand patterns and this seems to be borne out by experience.[1] If steps taken across a simplex have associated with them a fixed number of function evaluations per step,[2] even if the number of steps remain constant for higher dimensional problems (which typically does not happen) the increased time spent in function evaluation per step will cause execution times to rise considerably.

The amount of execution time needed to numerically determine a competitive equilibrium can therefore be directly related to 'dimensionality'. In its crudest terms, this can be thought of as the overall size of the model, but in practice there are specific dimensions which can be identified as critical.

Two dimensions in the model are especially important.

(i) The Dimensionality of Function Evaluation:

This is the dimension in which calculations underlying market demand and supply functions must be made. On the demand side of the economy the critical features are the twin dimensions of the number of consumers and the number of commodities. In the model of the UK this is a dimension of 103 by 64. On the supply side the dimensions involved are those of the number of industries and the number of inputs. As intermediate production enters the model this is a dimension of 60 by 64, although the treatment of the four primary factors is more complex than the other products. Most execution time is spent evaluating household demand functions because the fixed coefficient intermediate production struc-

ture makes the calculation of cost covering product prices
relatively simple. Although the dimensionality of function
evaluation is critical (especially in demand), the complexity of the functions involved must also be evaluated and
this is a matter returned to below.

(ii) The Dimensionality of Search:

The dimensionality within which function evaluation takes
place is larger than that involved for the search procedure
over a unit simplex.[3] The dimensionality of this simplex is
important in determining the number of steps which must be
made in the search for an equilibrium and thus the number of
times function evaluation is required. In the case of the
model used here, simplifying devices reduce the dimension of
search to 6 from the full price-revenue simplex of 66. From
a computational point of view, solution of the model would
be impractical without this reduced dimension. A model with
the same number of households and commodities could be computationally much more expensive to solve than the present
one if because of a difference in model structure the dimensionality of search is larger than 6.[4]

The dimensionality of the model also has computational
implicatons beyond execution time; additional difficulties
are encountered with space requirements. Although these
usually represent constraints on the ease with which calculations can be made rather than irreconcilable limitations,
space difficulties can usually be overcome only at a cost of
increased execution times and complexity of coding.

A programme structure comprising some four subprogrammes
with communications via permanent file has been used to fit
within space limitations. The most complex of these programmes comprises some eight separate subroutines and the
total length of code over the four programmes is around
10,000 statements. In extensions of the model, space difficulties have forced use of a further facility of mass storage which, while yielding an enhanced capability, is expensive. Current estimates indicate that a single execution of
programmes may involve 2 million accesses of the extended
core facility imposing an execution time overhead of some
10%. Were these accesses to go through mass storage, over-

head would be some 40%. Through reprogramming it would be possible to eliminate these overheads but these modifications would require a significant input of time.

Our production run use of the model has on occasions involved some 10-12 execution runs per week with all output from these runs stored for later comparative exercises. This rate can yield more than half a million characters in store within a month. This quickly exhausts any file space allocation conventionally available to machine users and such output stored on tapes would continue to increase at the rate of one every two months. Selectivity is therefore needed in deciding which runs to store and considerable time is involved in classifying and recording the outputs from solutions.

2.   Programme Design and Checking Procedures

The programme design used comprises four separate programmes, with communication between these programmes by a system of permanent files. The overall design of these programmes is outlined in Figure C-1. FESFOR deals with the detailed aggregation of basic household expenditure data; ACCOUNT modifies and transforms the basic data into a model admissible data set; COMPUT calculates alternative equilibria for the various tax replacements considered; and RESULT analyzes the final equilibrium data produced for each run.

Both ACCOUNT and COMPUT are lengthy programmes in terms of code; programme COMPUT is the more complex in terms of programme structure and interlinking function calls. Programme COMPUT is also the portion of the overall programme where most execution time is spent.

One of the more difficult problems of numerical work using computational methods is designing systems in which the accuracy of arithmetic calculatons can be checked. In the construction of our model a considerable amount of time and attention has been devoted to this issue. As explained in Chapter 4, the procedures through which parameter values are

330

FIGURE C-1

Structure of Overall Computational Procedure

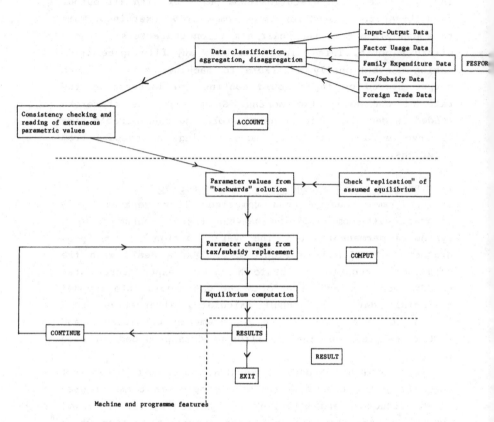

Machine and programme features

Machines Used:	CDC 7600/Cyber 73
Programme length in number of statements:	(approx.) equilibrium computation 1,500; parameter generation (approx.) 1,000, data classification 1000, print format (approx.) 2000.
Execution time:	depending on parameter values complete run with replication and one tax replacement in the range of 250-400 seconds of execution time on a CDC 7600.
Compilation time:	Approximately 10-12 seconds for each of the three main blocks.
Core requirement:	Jobs are run using LCM of 7600 and overlay structure. On the Cyber-73 mainframe a full extended core facility is used. Maximum available core storage is currently close to the combined size of working arrays and considerable adaptation is needed for larger dimensional work.
Data requirement:	"Crude" data usage 80,000 numbers; "model" data requirement 20,000 parametric values.
Behavioural functional evaluations:	To calculate excess demand and correspondence for any given price vector requires evaluation of over 4,000 derived demand functions (from joint production and intermediate usage). On the run described above excess demand correspondences would be evaluated approximately 120 times.

chosen for the model rely on the construction of a benchmark equilibrium data set. Use of these data can, however, be alternatively viewed as the construction of a general equilibrium problem for which the solution is already known. The ability of the computational procedures to reproduce this solution serves as a check on accuracy of programming and the extent of error propagation in solution can also be analyzed. Our experience suggests that error propagation is very small.[5]

The ability to reproduce a benchmark equilibrium data set, while an integral and vital part of the computational procedures, is by no means a sufficient set of checking procedures. It is only a test for the internal consistency of computations and to check for particular errors is more difficult. Errors are possible in misreading basic data, in extracting data from worksheets and publications, in incorrectly carrying out specific procedures on individual numbers which do not reveal themselves in subsequent more general checking procedures. For all of these problems resort must be made to purely mechanical checking and errors have been revealed at various stages of the work with the model. Experience suggests that the errors revealed tend to be of less importance as work proceeds, but the possibility of significant error always remains.

A problem which is endemic to computational and indeed all numerical analysis is that a finding which accords with intuition will tend to be accepted whereas one which offends intuition tends to be ascribed to arithmetic error or some unrealistic behaviour assumption of the model. Checking against intuition in this way is a vital and necessary part of sensible use of large-scale modelling and is a procedure we have extensively used to detect errors. In spite of this, the fundamental difficulty remains that the complexity and number of calculations performed by a computer along with the volume of raw data required imply that findings cannot be checked in any simple manner. Thus, even if one accepts a particular finding as reasonable, there must be a willingness to dismiss the findings at some later date if numerical errors are subsequently revealed. A number of errors have

332

been uncovered during checking of computations and while we believe that errors remaining are likely to be of limited quantitative significance, the possibility of remaining inaccuracies cannot be excluded.

Notes

1. For instance, our initial experience with changing utility functions to a three level nesting structure in place of a two level structure gave execution time increases of about 25%.

2. A typical solution for the model requires between 120 and 150 evaluations of market demand functions. For the six dimensional unit simplex used, Hansen [1975] reports approximate estimates for a six dimensional equilibrium problem of 144 iterations using the Eaves/-Merrill simplicial subdivision refinement (no restart) methods. This supports the suggestion made earlier that little difference would be experienced in execution times through use of a Newton method or Merrill's algorithm.

3. This type of procedure is called 'reduced format' computation by Ginsburgh and Waelbroeck [1976], and indirect computation by Dixon [1975].

4. For instance, incorporating full substitutability between all intermediate products into the model would mean that the reduced dimensionality of search might not be able to be used. It is because of the computational problems of the amount of execution time required rather than the formal problems of model specification that full substitutability between intermediate products has not been considered. More limited substitutability enters the international trade general equilibrium model assembled by Whalley [1980].

5. To some extent this might be due to the word length on the CDC machine used. Solution in single precision on alternative machines may encounter difficulties, particularly where exponentiation with large magnitudes is involved.

BIBLIOGRAPHY

BOOKS AND JOURNALS/ARTICLES

(Entries marked with an asterisk [*] were used in the
construction of Table 6.4)

Aaron, H.J. (1975), Who Pays the Property Tax? A New View,
Washington, D.C.: The Brookings Institution.

Allingham, M. (1973), Equilibrium and Disequilibrium: A
Quantitative Analysis of Economic Interaction, Cambridge,
Massachusetts: Ballinger Publishing Company.

Anderson, R. and J.G. Ballentine (1976), "The Incidence and
Excess Burden of a Profits Tax Under Imperfect
Competition", Public Finance, 31, (2) 159-176.

Archibald, G.C. and R.G. Lipsey (1958), "Monetary and Value
Theory: a Critique of Lange and Patinkin", Review of
Economic Studies, Vol 26, No. 69, October, 1-22.

Armington, P.S. (1969), "A Theory of Demand for Products
Distinguished by Place of Production", International
Monetary Fund Staff Papers, 16, March, 159-176.

Arrow, K.J., H.B. Chenery, B.C. Minhas, and R.M. Solow
(1961), "Capital-Labour Substitution and Economic
Efficiency", Review of Economics and Statistics, 43,
August, 225-250.

Arrow, K.J. and F.H. Hahn (1971), General Competitive
Analysis, San Francisco: Holden Day.

Atkinson, A.B. and N.H. Stern (1974), "Pigou, Taxation and
Public Goods", Review of Economic Studies, 41, 119-128.

Atkinson, A.B. and A.J. Harrison (1978), Distribution of
Personal Wealth in Britain, Cambridge: Cambridge
University Press.

*Ayanian, Robert (1969), "A Comparison of Barten's Estimated
Demand Elasticities With Those Obtained Using Frishch's
Method", Econometrica, 37, January, 79-94.

Bacharach, M. (1970), Bi-Proportional Matrices and Input-
Output Change, Cambridge: Cambridge University Press.

Bailey, M.J. (1962), National Income and the Price Level,
McGraw-Hill, New York.

334

Bailey, M.J. (1976), "Inflationary Distortions and Taxes", in Aaron, H.J., ed., Inflation and the Income Tax, Washington, D.C.: The Brookings Institution.

Balassa, B. and M.E. Kreinin (1967), "Trade Liberalization Under the 'Kennedy Round': The Static Effects", The Review of Economics and Statistics, 49, May, 125-137.

Barro, R.J., (1974), "Are Government Bonds Net Wealth", Journal of Political Economy, 82, November, 1095-1117.

*Barten, A.P. (1964), "Consumer Demand Functions Under Conditions of Almost Additive Preferences", Econometrica, 32, January, 1-38.

*Barten, A.P. and Richard W. Parks, "Effects of Various Factors on Consumption Patterns", Economic Journal, March 1973.

Bergstrom, T.C. and R.P. Goodman, (1973), "Private Demands for Public Goods , American Economic Review, 63, 280-296.

Berndt, E.R. (1976), "Reconciling Alternative Estimates of the Elasticity of Substitution", The Review of Economics and Statistics, 58, February, 59-68.

Blinder, A.S. (1974), Toward an Economic Theory of Income Distribution, MIT Press, Cambridge, Massachusetts.

Boadway, R.W. (1974), "The Welfare Foundations of Cost-Benefit Analysis", Economic Journal, 84, December, 026-929.

Boadway, R. and J.M. Treddenick (1978), "A General Equilibrium Computation of the Effects of the Canadian Tariff Structure", Canadian Journal of Economics, 11, August, 424-466.

Boskin, M.J. (1978), "Taxation, Saving, and the Rate of Interest", Journal of Political Economy, 86, April, S3-S28.

Brittain, J.A. (1973), The Payroll Tax for Social Security, Washington, D.C.: Brookings Institution.

Brown, M. and D. Heien, (1972), "The S-Branch Utility Tree: A Generalization of the Linear Expenditure System", Econometrica, 40, July, 737-747.

*Byron, R.P. (1969), "Methods for Estimating Demand Equations Using Prior Information: A Series of Experiments with Australian Data", Australian Economic Papers.

*Byron, R.P. (1970), "The Restricted Aitken Estimation of Sets of Demand Relations", Econometrica, 38, November, 816-830.

Caddy, V. (1976), "Empirical Estimation of the Elasticity of Substitution: A Review", Mimeo - Industries Assistance Commission, Melbourne, Australia.

*Court, Robin H. (1967), "Utility Maximization and the Demand for New Zealand Meats, Econometrica, 35, July, 424-446.

Deaton, A. (1974a), "A Reconsideration of the Empirical Implications of Additive Preferences", The Economic Journal, 84, June, 338-348.

*Deaton, Angus S. (1974b), "The Analysis of Consumer Demand in the United Kingdom 1900-1970, Econometrica, 42, March, 341-367.

*Deaton, Angus S. (1975), "The Measurement of Income and Price Elasticities", European Economic Review, 6, 261-273.

Debreu, G. (1959), Theory of Value, New Haven: Yale University Press.

Dixon, P.B. (1975), The Theory of Joint Maximization, Amsterdam: North Holland.

Douglas, P. (1934), The Theory of Wages, Macmillan, New York.

Eaves, B.C. (1972), "On the Basic Theorem of Complementarity", Mathematical Programming, 1, 68-75.

Feldstein, M.S. (1974), "Social Security, Induced Retirement, and Aggregate Capital Accumulation", Journal of Political Economy, 82, September/October, 905-926.

Feldstein, M.S. (1978a), "The Welfare Cost of Capital Income Taxation", Journal of Political Economy, 86, April, S29-S52.

Feldstein, M.S. (1978b), "The Rate of Return, Taxation, and Personal Savings", Economic Journal, 88, September, 482-487.

Feldstein, M.S. (1979), "The Welfare Cost of Permanent Inflation and Optimal Short-Run Economic Policy", Journal of Political Economy, Vol. 87, No. 4, August, 749-768.

Flemming, J.S. (1976), "Reappraisal of Corporation Income Tax", Journal of Public Economics, 6, July-August, 163-169.

336

Fullerton, D., J.B. Shoven and J. Whalley (1978), "General Equilibrium Analysis of U.S. Taxation Policy", in 1978 Compendium on Tax Research, Washington, D.C.; Office of Tax Analysis, U.S. Treasury.

Fullerton, D., J.B. Shoven and J. Whalley (1979), "General Equilibrium Impacts of Replacing the U.S. Income Tax with a Progressive Expenditure Tax". [A conference paper presented at NBER Conference on Taxation of Capital, November 16-17].

Fullerton, D., J.B. Shoven and J. Whalley (1983), "Replacing the U.S. Income Tax with a Progressive Consumption Tax: A Sequenced General Equilibrium Approach", Journal of Public Economics, Vol. 20, No. 1, pp. 3-23.

Gillespie, W.I., (1976), "On the Redistribution of Income in Canada", Canadian Tax Journal, 24, July/August, 419-450.

Gillespie, W.I., (1980), The Redistribution of Income in Canada, Gage Publishing Ltd., Ottawa.

Ginsburgh, V. and J. Waelbroeck (1976), "Computational Experience with a Large General Equilibrium Model", in Los, J. and M., eds., Computing Equilibria: How and Why, Amsterdam: North Holland, 257-269.

*Goldberger, Arthur S. and Theordore Gamaletsos, (1970), "A Cross-Country Comparison to Consumer Expenditure Patterns", European Economic Review, 1, 357-

Hansen, T. (1975), "Description of Fixed Point Algorithms", in H.R. Grumms (ed.) Analysis and Computation of Equilibria and Regions of Stability, IIASA Conference Proceedings.

Harberger, A.C. (1959), "The Corporation Income Tax: An Empirical Appraisal", Tax Revision Compendium, 1, in U.S. Congress, House Committee on Ways and Means, Washington, D.C.: Government Printing Office, 231-250.

Harberger, A.C. (1962), "The Incidence of the Corporation Tax", Journal of Political Economy, 70, June, 215-240.

Hargerger, A.C. (1964), "Taxation, Resource Allocation and Welfare", in The Role of Direct and Indirect Taxes in the Federal Reserve System, Princeton: Princeton University Press for the National Bureau of Economic Research and the Brookings Institution.

Harberger, A.C. (1966), "Efficiency Effects of Taxes on Income from Capital", in Krzyzaniak, M., ed., Effects of Corporation Income Tax. Symposium on Business Taxation, Wayne State University, Detroit: Wayne State University Press.

Harberger, A.C. (1974), Taxation and Welfare, Boston, Massachusetts: Little, Brown and Company.

*Hirsch, W.Z., (1951-52), "A Survey of Price Elasticities", Review of Economic Studies, 19, 50-60.

*Hoa, Tran Van, (1968), "Interregional Elasticities and Aggregation Bias: A Study of Consumer Demand in Australia", Australian Economic Papers, 7, December, 206-226.

Hotelling, H. (1938), "The General Welfare in Relation to Problems of Taxation and of Railway and Utility Rates", Econometrica, 6, July, 242-269.

*Houthakker, H.S. (1965), "New Evidence on Demand Elasticities", Econometrica, 33, 277-288.

*Houthakker, H.S. and L. Taylor (1970), Consumer Demand in the United States: Analysis and Projection, Harvard University Press, Cambridge, Massachusetts.

Johnson, H.G. and M. Krauss (1970), "Border Taxes, Border Tax Adjustments, Comparative Advantage, and Balance of Payments", Canadian Journal of Economics, Vol. 3, November, 595-602.

Johnson, H.G. (1971), The Two-Sector Model of General Equilibrium, London: Allen and Unwin.

Kakwani, N.C., (1972) "On the Bias in Estimates of Import Demand Parameters", International Economic Review, 13, 2, 239-244.

Kay, J.A. and M.A. King, (1978), The British Tax System, Oxford: Oxford University Press.

Kay, J.A. (1980), "The Deadweight Loss from a Tax System", Journal of Public Economics, 13, 1, 111-120, February.

Kehoe, T.J. and J. Whalley (forthcoming), "Uniqueness of Equilibrium in a Large Dimensional Numerical General Equilibrium Tax Model", Journal of Public Economics.

Keller, W.J. (1976), "A Nested CES type Utility Function and its Demand and Price-index Functions", European Economic Review, 7, February, 174-186.

338

Kemp, M.C. (1962), "Errors of Measurement and Bias in Estimates of Import Demand Parameters", The Economic Record, 38, September, 369-372.

King, M.A. (1974), "Taxation and Cost of Capital", The Review of Economic Studies, 41, January, 21-35.

*Kohn, Robert E. (1972), "Price Elasticities of Demand and Air Pollution Control", Review of Economics and Statistics, LIV, November, 392-400.

Krauss, M.B. and H.G. Johnson (1974), General Equilibrium Analysis: A Micro-Economic Text, London: Allen and Unwin.

Lewis, H.G. (1975), "Economics of Time and Labour Supply", American Economic Review, 65, May, 27-34.

Liviatin, N. (1966), "Multiperiod Future Consumption as an Aggregate", American Economic Review, Vol. 57, No. 4, Part 1, September, 828-840.

McLure, C.E., Jr. (1969), "The Inter-Regional Incidence of General Regional Taxes", Public Finance, 457-484.

McLure, C.E. Jr. (1971) "The Theory of Tax Incidence with Imperfect Factor Mobility", Finanzarchiv, 30.

McLure, C.E., Jr. (1975), "General Equilibrium Incidence Analysis: The Harberger Model after Ten Years", Journal of Public Economics, 4, February, 125-161.

*Mattei, Aurelio (1971), "A Complete System of Dynamic Demand Equations", European Economic Review, 2, 1971, 251-

Meade, J.E. (1978), The Structure and Reform of Direct Taxation, G. Allen and Unwin, London.

Merrill, O.H. (1971), "Applications and Extensions of an Algorithm that computes fixed points of certain non-empty convex upper semi-continuous point to set mappings", Technical Report, No. 71-7, Department of Industrial Engineering, University of Michigan.

Mieszkowski, P.M. (1969), "Tax Incidence Theory: The Effects of Taxes on the Distribution of Income", Journal of Economic Literature, 7, December 1103-1124

Mieszkowski, P.M. (1972), "The Property Tax: An Excise or a Profits Tax?" Journal of Public Economics, 1, April, 73-96.

Miller, M.H. and J.E. Spencer (1977), "The Static Economic Effects of the U.K. Joining the E.E.C.: A General Equilibrium Approach", The Review of Economic Studies, 44, February, 71-94.

Musgrave, R.A. (1959), The Theory of Public Finance, New York, New York: McGraw-Hill.

Musgrave, R.A. and P.B. Musgrave (1973), Public Finance in Theory and Practice, New York, New York: McGraw-Hill.

Musgrave, R.A., K. Case and H. Leonard, (1974), "The Distribution of Fiscal Burdens and Benefits", Public Finance Quarterly, Vol. 2, No. 3, July 259-311.

Musgrave, R.A. and P.B. Musgrave (1976), Public Finance in Theory and Practice, 2nd ed., New York, New York: McGraw-Hill.

Nerlove, M. (1967), "A survey of Recent Evidence of C.E.S. and Related Production Functions", in Brown, M., ed., The Theory and Empirical Analysis of Production, (Conference on Research in Income and Wealth. Studies in Income and Wealth, 31), New York: Columbia University Press for National Bureau of Economic Research.

Neumark Report (1963), Report of the Fiscal and Financial Committee, in The E.E.C. reports on tax harmonization (International Bureau of Fiscal Documentation).

Orcutt, G.H. (1950), "Measurement of Price Elasticities in International Trade", The Review of Economics and Statistics, 32, May, 117-132.

Patinkin, D. (1965), Money, Interest and Prices, 2nd Edition, Harper and Row, New York.

*Parks, Richard W. (1969), "Systems of Demand Equations: An Empirical Comparison of Alternative Functional Forms", Econometrica, 37, October, 629-650.

*Pearce, I.E. (1961), "A Method of Consumer Demand Analysis Illustrated", Economica, XXXVIII, November, 371-394.

Pechman, J.A. and B.A. Okner (1974), Who Bears the Tax Burden?, Washington, D.C.: The Brookings Institution.

Piggott, J.R. and J. Whalley (1977), "The Numerical Specification of Large Scale Walrasian Policy Models", paper prepared for the Summer Meetings of the Econometric Society, Ottawa, Canada, June 22 1977.

Piggott, J.R. and J. Whalley (1981), "A Summary of Some Findings from a General Equilibrium Tax Model for the United Kingdom", in Carnegie-Rochester Conference Series on Public Policy, Vol. 14, Spring 1981.

Piggott, J.R. and J. Whalley (eds.), New Developments in Applied General Equilibrium, forthcoming.

Pommerehne, W.W. and F. Schneider (1978), "Fiscal Illusion, Political Institutions and Local Public Spending", KYKLOS, 31, 381-408.

Prest, A.R. (1955), "The Statistical Calculation of Tax Burdens", Economica, 22, August, 234-245.

Prest, A.R. (1974), How Much Subsidy?, Institute for Economic Affairs, London.

Prest, A.R. (1975), Public Finance in Theory and Practice, 5th ed., London: Weidenfeld and Nicolson.

Revell, J. (1967), The Wealth of the Nation: The National Balance Sheet of the United Kingdom, 1957-1961, Cambridge: Cambridge University Press.

Revell, J. and A. Roe, (1971), "National Balance Sheets and National Accounting - A Progress Report", Economic Trends, 211, May, viii-xix.

Rolph, E.R. (1952), "A Proposed Revision of Excise-Tax Theory", Journal of Political Economy, 60, April, 102-117.

Rosenberg, L.G. (1969), "Taxation of Income from Capital, by Industry Group", in Harberger, A.C. and M.J. Bailey, eds., The Taxation of Income from Capital, Washington, D.C.: The Brookings Institution.

Ruggles, R. and Ruggles, N. (1970), The Design of Economic Accounts, General Series 89, New York: Columbia University Press for National Bureau of Economic Research.

Samuelson, P.A. (1954), "The Pure Theory of Public Expenditure", Review of Economics and Statistics, 36, 387-389.

Sato, K. (1967), "A Two Level Constant Elasticity of Substitution Production Function", 34, April, The Review of Economic Studies, 201-218.

Scarf, H.E. (1967a), "The Core of an n person game", Econometrica, 35, January, 50-69.

Scarf, H.E. (1967b), "The Approximation of Fixed Points of a Continuous Mapping", SIAM Journal of Applied Mathematics, 15, September, 1328-1343.

Scarf, H.E. (1967c), "On the Computation of Equilibrium Prices", in W.M. Fellner, et. al., eds., Ten Essays in Honour of Irving Fisher, New York: Wiley, 207-230.

Scarf, H.E. (1973), with the collaboration of T. Hansen, The Computation of Economic Equilibrium, New Haven: Yale University Press.

Scarf, H.E. (1977), The Computation of Equilibrium Prices: An Exposition, Cowles Foundation Discussion Paper No. 473, November.

Scarf, H.E. and J.B. Shoven (eds.) (1984), Applied General Equilibrium Analysis, Cambridge University Press, New York.

Scitovsky, T. (1958), Economic Theory and Western European Integration, London: Allen and Unwin.

Shoven, J.B. and J. Whalley (1972), "A General Equilibrium Calculation of the Effects of Differential Taxation of Income from Capital in the U.S.", Journal of Public Economics, 1, November, 281-321.

Shoven, J.B. and J. Whalley, (1973), "General Equilibrium with Taxes: A Computational Procedure and an Existence Proof", The Review of Economic Studies, 40, October, 475-489.

Shoven, J.B. and J. Whalley, (1974), "On the Computation of Competitive Equilibrium on International Markets with Tariffs", Journal of International Economics, 4, November, 341-354.

Shoven, J.B. and J. Whalley, (1977), "Equal Yield Tax Alternatives: General Equilibrium Computational Techniques", Journal of Public Economics, 8, October, 211-224.

Shoven, J.B. and J. Whalley (1984), "Applied General Equilibrium Models of Taxation and International Trade", Journal of Economic Literature, , September, .

Stern, R.M., J. Francis and B. Schumacher, (1976), Price Elasticities in International Trade: An annotated Bibliography, London: MacMillan, for the Trade Policy Centre.

Stern, N. (1976), "Taxation and Labour Supply – A Partial Survey", in Institute for Fiscal Studies", Taxation and Incentives, pp. 4-10.

Stiglitz, J.E. (1973), "Taxation, Corporate Financial Policy, and the Cost of Capital", Journal of Public Economics, 2, February, 1-34.

Stiglitz, J.E. (1976), "The Corporation Income Tax", Journal of Public Economics, 5, April-May, 303-312.

*Stone, R. and D.A. Rowe (1960), "The Durability of Consumers' Durable Goods", Econometrica, 28, April, 407-416.

Stone, R. (1962), "Multiple Classifications in Social Accounting", Bulletin of the International Statistics Institute, 29, Bk. 3, 215-233.

Summers, L.H. (1980), "Tax Policy in a Life Cycle Model", a conference paper presented at NBER Conference on Taxtion of Capital, November 16 and 17, 1979, Cambridge, Massachusetts.

Summers, L.H. (1981), "Capital Taxation and Accumulation in a Life Cycle Growth Model", American Economic Review, Vol. 71, No. 4, September, 533-544.

Surrey, S.S. (1973), Pathways to Tax Reform: The Concept of Tax Expenditures, Cambridge: Harvard University Press.

Theil, H. (1967), Economics and Information Theory, North Holland, Amsterdam.

Thirsk, W. (1972), "The Economics of Farm Mechanization in Columbia", unpublished doctoral dissertation, New Haven: Yale University.

Van der Laan, G. and A.J.J. Talman, (1979), "A Restart Algorithm for Computing Fixed Points Without an Extra Dimension", Mathematical Programming, 17, 74-84.

Vandendorpe, A.L. and A.F. Firedlaender (1976), "Differential Incidence in the Presence of Initital Distorting Taxes", Journal of Public Economics, 6, October, 205-229.

Whalley, J. (1973), A Numerical Assessment of the April 1973 U.K. Tax Reforms, unpublished Ph.D. Thesis, Yale.

Whalley, J. (1975), "A General Equilibrium Assessment of the 1973 United Kingdom Tax Reform", Economica, 42, May, 139-161.

Whalley, J. (1977), "The United Kingdom Tax System 1968–
1970: Some Fixed Point Indications of its Economic
Impact", Econometrica, 45, November, 1837–1858.

Whalley, J. (1978), "Discriminatory Features of Domestic
Factor Tax Systems and their Impact on World Trade: A
General Equilibrium Approach", mimeo.

Whalley, J. (1980), "Discriminatory Features of Domestic
Factor Tax Systems in a Goods Mobile-Factors Immobile
Trade Model: An Empirical General Equilibrium Approach",
Journal of Political Economy, Vol. 88, No. 6, 1177–1202.

Wright, C. (1969), "Saving and the Rate of Interest", in
Harberger, A.C. and M.J. Bailey, eds., The Taxation of
Income from Capital, Washington, D.C.: The Brookings
Institution.

GOVERNMENT PUBLICATIONS

Bank of England Quarterly Bulletin, (1973), Bank of England, December.

Bureau of Census, U.S. Government (February 1974), Survey of Current Business Trends, 1967 U.S. Input-Output Tables.

C.S.O. (1968), Standard Industrial Classification, 1968, 3rd edition, London, H.M.S.O.

C.S.O. (1971), "Commodity Analysis of Central Government Current Expenditure on Goods and Services", Economic Trends, August.

C.S.O. (1973), Economic Trends, "A Quarterly Series on Production Indices by Industry in Statistical Series", November. Also, 1975 May.

C.S.O. (1973), Housing and Construction Statistics, No. 11.

C.S.O. (1973), Studies in Official Statistics No. 22, Input-Output Tables for the United Kingdom 1968, London, H.M.S.O.

C.S.O. (1974), Annual Abstract of Statistics 1974, London: H.M.S.O.

C.S.O. (1974), Balance of Payments Statistics, United Kingdom Balance of Payments -1963-73, H.M.S.O.

C.S.O. (1974), Input-Output Tables for the United Kingdom 1971, London: H.M.S.O.

C.S.O. (1974), National Income and Expenditure 1963-73, London, H.M.S.O.

C.S.O. (1975), National Income and Expenditure 1964-74, London: H.M.S.O.

C.S.O. (1975), "Summary Input-Output Tables for 1971", Economic Trends, April, Government Statistics Office, H.M.S.O.

C.S.O. (1975), Economic Trends, May.

Department of Economics and Social Affairs (1968), A System of National Accounts: Studies in Methods, Series F, No. 2, Rev. 3, Statistical Office, United Nations, New York.

Department of Employment (1974), Family Expenditure Survey, 1973, London: H.M.S.O.

Department of Employment (1974), New Earnings Survey, 1973, London: H.M.S.O.

Department of Employment (1975), British Labour Statistics Yearbook 1973, London: H.M.S.O.

Department of Employment Gazette, (1974), August and October, London: H.M.S.O.

Department of Health and Social Security (1974), National Insurance Contribution Tables.

Department of Industry [1974], Business Monitor - Input-Output Tables for the U.K. 1971, London: H.M.S.O.

Hansard, (1975), August 4, Vol. 897, No. 173, Col. 13-14.

Inland Revenue Statistics (1974), London: H.M.S.O.

Inland Revenue Statistics 1975 (1976), London: H.M.S.O.

Maurice, Rita, ed., (1967), National Accounts: Sources and Methods, H.M.S.O.

1968 Census of Production (197), H.M.S.O.

Report of the Royal Commission on the Taxation of Profits and Incomes, Command 9474, H.M.S.O., 1955.

Report of Royal Commission on Taxation, (1955), Carter Commission, Ottawa: Queen's Printer.

Royal Commission on the Distribution of Income and Wealth, 1975, Report No. 1, initial report on the Standing Reference Command 6171, H.M.S.O.

64th Report of the Commissioners of Her Majesty's Customs and Excise for the year ended 31 March 1973, London: H.M.S.O.

Standard International Trade Classification.

U.S. Department of Treasury (1977), Blueprints for Basic Tax Reform, Washington: Government Printing Office.